Surviving
on the Gold Mountain

Surviving on the Gold Mountain

A History of Chinese American Women and Their Lives

HUPING LING

STATE UNIVERSITY OF NEW YORK PRESS

Published by
State University of New York Press, Albany

For information, address State University of New York Press,
State University Plaza, Albany, N.Y., 12246

Production by Diane Ganeles
Marketing by Anne Valentine

Library of Congress Cataloging-in-Publication Data

Ling, Huping, 1956–
    Surviving on the gold mountain: a history of Chinese American
women and their lives / Huping Ling.
        p.   cm.
    Includes bibliographical references and index.
    ISBN 0-7914-3863-5 (alk. paper). — ISBN 0-7914-3864-3 (pbk. : alk.
paper)
    1. Chinese American Women—History.   2. Chinese American women-
-Social conditions.   3. United States—Emigration and immigration-
-History—19th century.   4. United States—Emigration and
immigration—History—20th century.   I. Title.
    E184.C5L6   1998
    305.48′895′1073—dc21   97-50217
                                                                           CIP

10 9 8 7 6 5 4 3 2 1

To My Parents
Linghu Pu and Ma Huiyuan

Contents

Part One
Early Chinese Immigrant Women, 1840s–1943

Tables

Illustrations

Photographs

Figure

Acknowledgments

Being an Asian and a woman, I naturally became interested in the experiences of Asian American women. My professional training in American social history, especially immigration and ethnicity, enabled me to cast my personal interest into scholarship. In completing this work, I have had the good fortune to get assistance from a number of individuals and institutions.

First, Allan Winkler deserves my many thanks. His continuous support, encouragement, and firm confidence in me, as well as numerous valuable suggestions were essential at various stages of the work. Roger Daniels' enthusiastic support, guidance, and knowledge in the field warranted the successful completion of the manuscript. Mary Frederickson was indispensable throughout with her enthusiasm, encouragement, patience, and critical comments that helped shape the work. Haiming Liu, Gary Okihiro, Louis C. Wade, and Stacey G. H. Yap generously offered their constructive comments on the earlier draft that greatly improved the work. Many of my colleagues and friends also read various drafts of this work and gave me critical and valuable suggestions. I am grateful to all the above individuals.

Without my interviewees this work wouldn't have been possible. They generously contributed their precious time and valuable life experiences to this project. I have learned a great deal from their individual histories and made personal friends with many of them. I am especially thankful to Isabelle C. Chang, Sze-Kew Dun, Liyan Liao, Pai-Yen Lin Lu, Alice C. Phillips, and Bella Shao for their generosity and kindness.

Many librarians, archivists, and other staff members at the following institutions greatly assisted with my research: Pickler

Memorial Library at Truman State University, King Library at Miami University, the Special Collection at the University of Oregon, the New York City Public Library, the East Asian Library at Columbia University, the Ethnic Studies Library at the University of California at Berkeley, the Special Collection at the University of Hawaii at Manoa, the National Archives in Washington, D.C., Pacific Sierra Regional Archives in San Bruno, California, Central Plain Regional Archives in Kansas City, and the San Francisco District Court. I wish to express sincere appreciation to Jenny Presnell, my friend and librarian at Miami University, who wholeheartedly and enthusiastically helped with my search for materials. Sheila Swafford, assistant in the Department of Interlibrary Loan at Pickler Memorial Library, processed numerous interlibrary loan requests for me, and has my thanks. I was most impressed by the dedication, enthusiasm, and patience of Neil L. Thomsen, archivist at Pacific Sierra Regional Archives, and Michael J. Brodhead, archivist at Central Plain Regional Archives.

I am also grateful to Miami University, Truman State University, and the American Association of University Women Educational Foundation for their generous financial support of my research.

This work involves over a decade of research and writing. During this long process my family stood firmly behind me. My husband, Sami, contributed countless ideas and all possible help. My sons, William and Isaac, accommodated me with my busy schedules and compromised their vacations with my research trips. Without their loving support, I would not have been able to complete this work.

Author's Note

There have been two Chinese spelling systems—Wade-Giles and Pinyin—prevalent in scholarly writings. In order to avoid confusion, I have used Pinyin system when the Chinese names are encountered, unless a preferred transliteration of certain proper nouns, such as "Chiang Kai-shek" (Wade-Giles) for "Jiang Jieshi" (Pinyin), and "Yangtze" (Wade-Giles) for "Changjiang" (Pinyin), has been widely used.

Introduction

In 1834, Afong Moy, the first recorded Chinese woman to come to America, arrived in New York City. She was used by the American Museum as a showpiece to display how different a Celestial lady looked from the Western women. Between 1834 and 1835, according to the *Commercial Advertiser*, Afong Moy, in Chinese costume, was placed at the American Museum to show the American audience Chinese costumes, manners, and life styles.[1] Following Afong Moy, more women came to America. Four decades after Afong Moy's arrival, the number of Chinese women in America reached 4,574, mainly distributed throughout California, Nevada, Hawaii, and Idaho.[2]

During the California Gold Rush era, prostitution thrived in the predominantly male society. At first, the majority of prostitutes were of Mexican, Spanish, or French descent from Mexico, Brazil, or Peru. Later, they were white prostitutes from the East Coast.[3] Chinese women, most under coercion, also joined this trade. In 1870, among the 3,536 adult Chinese women in California, there were approximately 2,157 listed as prostitutes.[4] The rapid development of prostitution disturbed many middle-class American women. Since the 1870s, Protestant middle-class American women initiated an organized campaign against prostitution on the West Coast. Pressured by the anti-prostitution crusade, several western states' legislatures and the federal government passed laws to bar prostitution. An exemplary measure was the Page Law of 1875, which prohibited the interstate importation and entry of women for the purpose of prostitution. It also imposed fines and punishment on those convicted for such an act. Although written in general terms, the act was executed with the Chinese in mind. The evils of Chinese

1

prostitution were also used as one of the arguments for passing the Chinese Exclusion Act of 1882. This act prohibited the entry of Chinese laborers until it was repealed in 1943.

White workers, particularly those in California who had succeeded in gaining approval of the 1882 Exclusion Act, were dissatisfied with its effectiveness. To tighten the law further, on October 1, 1888, Congress passed the Scott Act. It declared all return certificates "void and of no effect,"[5] and thus prevented the re-entry of some 20,000 Chinese who had return certificates.[6] Since the wives of laborers had been able to enter as former residents, the Scott Act also effectively barred the return of these women. Wives and daughters of merchants who had been former residents, however, were allowed to join their husbands and fathers. These exclusion acts restricted the coming of Chinese immigrant women to the United States. As a result, beginning in 1870, the number of Chinese immigrant women remained steady at about 4,000 a year for five decades.[7] Most of them were married to Chinese merchants, farmers, and laborers.

In the nineteenth and early twentieth centuries, as wives of laundrymen, restauranteurs, grocers, farmers, cooks, and laborers, these early Chinese immigrant women faced hardship, hostility, and a frightening and alienating environment. They cooked, cleaned, and raised their children. In addition to domestic chores, many rural wives gardened, cut and dried fruit, and tended livestock. Meanwhile, urban immigrant women helped their husbands manage laundries, restaurants, or grocery stores. They were confined to their quarters within Chinatown boundaries, being afraid of racial prejudice and violence.

During World War II and the brief period after the war, a more sympathetic attitude in America toward China and Chinese Americans appeared. The Chinese benefitted from Chiang Kai-shek's close relationship with Franklin D. Roosevelt. One by one, anti-Chinese laws were revoked, and favorable laws were passed. These allowed more Chinese women to enter the United States as war brides, G.I. fiancées, displaced persons, refugees, and wives of American citizens.[8] By the 1950s, the number of Chinese American women had increased to 40,415.[9]

During this period, more Chinese American women than ever before entered the American work force. Most of the immigrant women were confined to menial jobs while the American-born were concentrated in clerical work. Meanwhile, more American-born Chinese women received a higher education. Among them, Jade

Snow Wong (author of *Fifth Chinese Daughter* and a ceramicist), Emma P. Lum (San Francisco attorney), and Dr. Rose Hum Lee (historian and chair of the Sociology Department at Roosevelt University, Chicago) distinguished themselves in new fields of endeavor. Some prominent Chinese American women like Dr. Jianxiong Wu [Chien-shiung Wu] even entered advanced scientific fields and earned world fame.

After the 1960s, Chinese American women benefitted from the civil rights movement, broke discrimination barriers in many fields, and attained national prominence. Connie Chung was hired by the Columbia Broadcasting System in 1971, due to the pressure from the Federal Communication Committee demanding the hiring of minorities and women. She became one of the most famous and successful female news anchors in the national television industry. Maya Lin, while an undergraduate at Yale at the age of twenty-one, became the most influential female architect in America. Her design for the Vietnam Veteran Memorial in Washington, D.C. was selected in 1981. Michelle Kwan, with her mature and flawless skating, won the world ladies figure-skating championship in 1996 when she was fifteen years old.

A number of other Chinese American women were politically active and were appointed to prominent government posts. Elaine Chao [Xiaolan Zhao], a first generation immigrant, was named the Assistant Secretary of Transportation in 1989. Julia Chang Bloch, also a first generation immigrant, was appointed as the U.S. ambassador to Nepal in the same year.

Although Chinese American women have made remarkable progress in past decades, they remain misrepresented in American popular culture and rarely visible in historical works. Since the first arrival of Chinese women in America, they have been stereotyped by the American public as exotic and seductive dolls. According to the *Commercial Advertiser*, Afong Moy, the first reported Chinese woman to be in America, was exhibited in New York City in 1834 as "a Chinese lady in native costume," and was used to show "New York belles how different ladies look in widely separated regions."[10] P.T. Barnum's Chinese Museum, a traveling show, also described Chinese women as "strange" and "wonderful": "Miss Pwan-Yekoo, the Chinese belle, with her Chinese suite of attendants, is drawing all Broadway to the Chinese collection. She is so pretty, so arch, so lively, and so graceful, while her minute feet are wondrous!"[11] According to an article in *Harper's Weekly* of January 30, 1858, these "celestial" ladies' exotic look even fanned the author's imagination that they might taste "like that for mangoes."[12] These early public images of Chinese women still plague some current magazines. In one contemporary advertisement, publicizing a stocking sale in the feminist magazine *Ms.*, Chinese American women today "continue to be stereotyped and exploited for their exoticism."[13]

In motion pictures, Chinese American women have often been portrayed as seductive creatures. Even in recent movies, film makers are still affected by this stereotype. In Michael Cimino's 1984 movie *Year of the Dragon*, Stanley White, a Vietnam veteran and a member of the New York City Police Department, appears to be a saint, trying to stem an eruption of youth-gang violence. Meanwhile, Tracy Tze, a celebrity Chinese American newscaster, is pictured as both an assertive career woman and a sexy doll.[14] *China Girl*, produced in 1986, is a new version of Romeo and Juliet set in Canal Street of New York with the indisputable borderline separating the opposing worlds of Little Italy and Chinatown. Tyan, a lovely Chinese girl, falls in love with Tony, a second-generation Italian. This film, like others in the past, is plagued by stereotyped images: exoticism, seduction, and feebleness.

Contrary to the above movies, Wayne Wang's *Dim Sum* depicts Chinese American women in a more realistic and positive light. Geraldine Lum, a second-generation Chinese woman, inherits many Chinese traditional virtues and exposes her beautiful intrinsic human value.[15] This contrasts with a seductive mysterious world that has appeared in many other motion pictures.

Along the same lines, a new multicultural arts organization brings a different outlook on Asian American women. Founded in 1980, the National Asian American Telecommunications Association (NAATA) has the primary goals of educating the public about the Asian Pacific American experience and replacing stereotyped images of Asians with accurate, realistic portrayals. The NAATA also promotes the artistic quality and merit of Asian Pacific American media productions.

Liru, produced and directed by Henry Chow in 1991, is one of the products distributed by the NAATA. An Academy Award-nominated drama, it portrays a Chinese American woman's search for ethnic and personal identity. Liru has been torn between the relations she has with her mother and her boyfriend. She has to decide whether to stay in San Francisco to look after her mother, or move to Yale to be with her Korean-Japanese boyfriend. Eventually, the memory of the closeness she had with her mother during her childhood makes her comfortable with the idea of displaying affection instead of aggression toward her mother.[16]

Some documentaries distributed by the NAATA also shatter the stereotypes of Asian American women. Based on Wayne Wang's feature film *Dim Sum, Dim Sum Take-Out* tells a fast-paced story with the feel of a music video. In this film, five Chinese American women explore personal issues of ethnicity, independence, and sexuality by comparing their individual methods of dealing with their cultural and class legacies.[17] Produced and directed by Deborah Gee in 1990, *Slaying the Dragon* chronicles Hollywood's recycling of inaccurate images of Asian American women over the past sixty years. Through film clips and interviews with media critics and Asian American actresses, it shows how today's media stereotypes have changed little from those of bygone days.

With Silk Wings, Asian American Women at Work, produced in 1990, portrays Asian American women's various experiences, by combining four short documentaries. *Four Women*, produced and directed by Loni Ding, sketches the lives of four Asian American career women: Heidi, a community social worker; Sara, a tenured professor and practicing architect; Shirley, a physician who directs a community health clinic; and Pat, a union business agent. Their courage and uncompromised idealism are exemplary of many Asian professional women. Loni Ding's *On New Ground*, shows how ten Asian American women broke the barriers of such traditional male jobs as stockbroker, police officer, and welder. They discuss what they have learned about confronting the conflicts between traditional expectations and personal aspirations. In Loni Ding's third documentary *Frankly Speaking*, high school students, teachers, employers, and counselors discuss the challenge faced by young Asian women as they move from adolescence to adulthood. *Talking History*, produced and directed by Spencer Nakasako, tells the stories of five outspoken women and their journey to America. Japanese, Chinese, Korean, Filipino, and Laotian women thoughtfully reveal a mosaic of feminist, ethnic, and immigrant "herstories" through personal interviews and poignant historical footage.[18]

Among the newly-produced films by and about Asian Americans, Arthur Dong's *Forbidden City, U.S.A.* has drawn wide attention in media circles. Gold Award and Special Jury Award winner, *Forbidden City, U.S.A.*, is a provocative, exuberant documentary. Through historical footage and interviews with witnesses, it leads the audience to the fabled all-Chinese Forbidden City nightclub on San Francisco's Sutter Street, which became an international hot spot in the 1930s and 1940s. It reveals how cultural barriers and racism had been challenged by the younger generation of Asian Americans in the 1930s and 1940s. Dong has explained his motivation for making this movie: "We Chinese Americans are not just hard workers; we are not just concerned about the critical issues of Asian Americans; we also have leisure time, have fun."[19] This fact was evidenced by the film's showing that Chinese Americans ventured out to nightclubs for their entertainment in the 1930s and 1940s, and some of them even became professional performers.[20]

Sewing Woman is another excellent production by Arthur Dong in 1982. This film documents a woman's experience of immigration and her determination to survive—from war-torn China to a new life in America.[21] Its sensitive treatment of confusion and fear is very much a part of the immigrant experiences of most immigrant women. It provides firsthand materials for a discussion of issues involving family, cultural differences, and the role of women.

While Chinese American women have remained exotic and seductive creatures in American popular culture, they have been virtually ignored by historians until recent decades. The historiography of Chinese American women has gone through three periods. In the first, from the late-nineteenth century to the 1960s, Chinese American women's experiences were totally neglected. During the second period, from the 1960s to 1970s, historians began to consider Chinese American women's experiences as part of Chinese American history. In the 1980s and the 1990s, historians have started to develop independent works on Chinese American women.

Due to anti-Chinese sentiment in America and restrictive Chinese immigration laws since the 1870s, most historians of the first period tackled the "Chinese problem" by studying the various facets of anti-Chinese movement and Chinese exclusion laws.[22] Mary Coolidge attributed causes and formation of the Chinese exclusion laws to the anti-foreign feelings in California in her *Chinese Immigration*, the first influential scholarship in the field.[23] Stuart Creighton Miller has reinforced Coolidge's view over a half century later, arguing that the unfavorable image of Chinese in America was the major reason for the Chinese exclusion.[24] Whereas, Gunther Barth has suggested that the "sojourner" nature of Chinese immigration made Chinese incapable of involving themselves in the mainstream culture.[25]

Meanwhile, scholars have also begun to write books on Chinese immigrants from a positive point of view. S. W. Kung, for instance, has collected a wealth of materials about so-called old immigrants and considered their lives heroic because they sacrificed themselves in true Chinese tradition for the benefit of the next generation. He has also pointed out that in the 1950s and 1960s Chinese scholars in America made numerous contributions to the sciences and the humanities. He has shown how engineers, scientists, teachers, doctors, and nurses, as well as laundrymen and restauranteurs, rendered valuable services in meeting community demands. They in turn received many benefits from the country they adopted. He has finally argued that Americans had much to learn from the Chinese civilization, especially in moral and spiritual values.[26]

The repeal of the Chinese exclusion acts in 1943 and the reform of American immigration laws in 1965 dramatically changed the make-up of Chinese communities in America. The Chinese "bachelor society" was gradually replaced by family-oriented communities. Moreover, the revival of feminism led to the women's movement in the late-1960s and 1970s. American women rose to challenge every aspect of the still male-dominated society. Reflecting on the historical and social changes, sociologists and historians have begun to incorporate issues related to family and women into their scholarship. Rose Hum Lee first studied Chinese family organization and social institutions in Chinese communities of the Rocky Mountain region.[27] Stanford M. Lyman has continued to examine the family and marriage, and the community organizations among the Chinese Americans.[28] Similarly, Loren W. Fessler has devoted a chapter of his book to issues concerning marriage and family.[29] Shih-shan Henry Tsai discussed Chinese women's experiences in urban Chinese communities since 1965 in a section of a chapter.[30]

The independent work on Chinese women in America did not appear until the late-1970s. Since the late-1970s and the 1980s, some scholars have published articles on Chinese women's experiences in America. Most of these articles, however, have focused primarily on either investigating the lives of Chinese prostitutes in nineteenth-century America or examining the effect of Chinese exclusion laws to Chinese women from 1870s to 1943. Lucie Cheng Hirata has discussed three major methods of procurement of Chinese prostitutes in her article entitled "Free, Indentured, Enslaved: Chinese Prostitutes in Nineteenth-Century America." She has argued that because Chinese society was patriarchal, patrilineal, and patrilocal, women were expected to bear children and serve their husbands' families. As a result, only girls from impoverished families

worked elsewhere as prostitutes or as servants to support themselves and send remittances home to help sustain their families.[31]
George Anthony Peffer has stated that the 1875 Page Law was the
first major legal restriction that denied Chinese women's entry to
America.[32] Sucheng Chan has further argued that the restrictive
immigration laws and enforcement of these laws were responsible
for the shortage of women in Chinese communities in America
prior to World War II.[33] The latest and probably the only book-
length study on Chinese prostitutes in nineteenth-century America
has been Benson Tong's, *Unsubmissive Women, Chinese Prostitutes
in Nineteenth-Century San Francisco.*[34] Inspired by Lucie Cheng
Hirata's works on Chinese prostitutes, Tong has asserted that
Chinese prostitutes were not merely victims of oppression, but also
unsubmissive individuals who struggled to change their fate. The
above studies have greatly contributed to our knowledge of Chinese immigrant women in the early time, but their limitations on
topics (mainly prostitute) and scope (Chinese exclusion period)
prevented them from providing a complete picture of Chinese
women in America.

In the 1980s, works reflecting other dimensions of Chinese
women's experiences in America have also appeared. Stacey G. H.
Yap's *Gather Your Strength, Sisters: The Emerging Role of Chinese Women Community Workers* has revealed an unknown fact in
Chinese women's history in America: Chinese women were politically involved in their communities since the 1940s.[35] Xiaolan
Bao's doctoral dissertation "'Holding Up More Than Half the Sky':
A History of Women Garment Workers in New York's Chinatown,
1948–1991" has represented the history of a large group of Chinese immigrant women in the postwar time.[36] Although these works
have filled some of the gaps in Chinese American women's history,
a comprehensive history of Chinese women in America is still
missing.

Judy Yung's *Chinese Women of America: A Pictorial History*
was the first published effort to construct a history of Chinese
women in America.[37] Rich in visual photographs and terse in text,
it offered a good sketch of Chinese women's history in the past one
hundred-fifty years. After the completion of the previous versions
of this book, Judy Yung has also published *Unbound Feet, A Social
History of Chinese Women in San Francisco.*[38] Combining manu-
scripts and oral history interviews, this work has portrayed the
changing social lives of Chinese women in San Francisco. However,
it has limited its scope to Chinese women in San Francisco prima-

rily during the first half of the century. Clearly, a comprehensive work on the history of Chinese American women is needed.

⚘

This study seeks to contribute to the existing knowledge about Chinese women in America. First, it bridges the gap between scholarship on Chinese American women and the life experiences of these women. Although much work on Chinese immigration has been done, few writers have addressed the issues that have shaped Chinese American women's lives and affected their daily experiences completely from the women's perspective.

Second, the scope of this study is broader than the existing literature dealing with Chinese American women. Chronologically, this work reconstructs the history of Chinese women in the United States from the early nineteenth century to the present, whereas Benson Tong's *Unsubmissive Women: Chinese Prostitute in San Francisco, 1849–1882* focuses on the Chinese prostitutes in San Francisco before the Chinese Exclusion Act in 1882 and Judy Yung's *Unbound Feet: A Social History of Chinese Women in San Francisco* primarily concentrates on Chinese women in San Francisco during the first half of the century. Geographically, this study not only includes Chinese women in larger urban Chinese communities in Honolulu, San Francisco, New York City, and other major cities in the United States, but also Chinese women in rural areas of different regions of the country and other places where Chinese are sparsely populated. Tong and Yung's works, in contrast, limit their scope to San Francisco. Socially, this book examines various groups of Chinese women, including servant girls and prostitutes, wives of merchants, laborers, and farmers, and students and intellectuals. The existing works on Chinese women have mostly dealt with Chinese prostitutes, while the lives of Chinese merchant wives, farmers' wives, and especially female students, which are the primary interests of this work, have seriously remained understudied.

Third, this study exploits a comparative approach in the spirit of multiculturalism. The literature, dealing with Chinese immigrant women, has mostly narrowed its focus merely to Chinese. This study, however, compares Chinese women's lives with other immigrant women's experiences, including those of other Asian immigrant women, other ethnic minority women, and European immigrant women in the United States. Therefore, it presents the history of Chinese American women from a multiethnic and multicultural perspective that better reflects and explains the social interactions of a multiracial and multicultural society.

This study outlines the immigration patterns of Chinese American women, beginning in the mid-nineteenth century with the first arrival of Chinese women. It also defines the ways in which these women adapted to life in the United States. Following the "new ethnicity" approach,[39] it depicts Chinese women in America not only as victims of discrimination and prejudice but also as survivors of hardships and obstacles. Chinese women drew strength and energy from the preservation of their tradition as well as the adaptation to the new environment.

This study also compares the life histories of Chinese American women to the lives of women in other nineteenth and twentieth century immigrant groups. It compares and contrasts the adaptation patterns of Chinese women who settled in urban areas and rural communities. It answers the questions about how and why Chinese immigrant women's experiences resembled or differed from those of other immigrant groups.

Like other immigrant women, Chinese immigrant women sailed across the Pacific Ocean to the New World for a better life. Distinct physical and cultural differences, however, made their settlement experiences different from, and often more difficult than, those of other immigrant groups. In urban settings, confined in ethnic ghettoes—Chinatowns—Chinese immigrant women's employment opportunities were limited to menial jobs in laundries, restaurants, grocery stores, and garment factories. In rural areas, where Chinese immigrant women were better assimilated into local communities, they engaged in housekeeping and farming. Confronting hardship and alienation, these women managed to survive and succeed on their own terms.

Like other immigrant women, Chinese women's lives were affected by the new environment. Immigrant experiences in a new country changed the family structure of many immigrant households. To survive, Chinese immigrant women were not only responsible for housekeeping and childbearing, but also found themselves involved in farming, family businesses, and other wage-earning jobs. Participation in profitable or wage-earning work reinforced a Chinese wife's position in her family, and it enabled her to share family decision-making with her husband. Influenced by a strong traditional ideology, however, Chinese men were still dominant figures in many Chinese immigrant families. Like their immigrant parents, American-born daughters of Chinese immigrants were also affected by the immigrant experiences. Following the cultural tradition at home, but adapting to western ways in public, they gradually felt that they became "marginal women," neither Chinese nor American.

Chinese immigrant women shared concerns and problems that confronted other immigrant women. Many Chinese immigrant women were primarily concerned about family prosperity; they saw the well-being of the family as more important than their own personal fulfillment. Some Chinese immigrant women came to America with high expectations and struggled to realize the dreams they had before immigration; but like their counterparts from other groups, they experienced cultural alienation from both American society and their own native-born children.

Different from other ethnic women, Chinese American women were less active and less visible in social activities and politics than women of other groups. This was especially true when compared to Jewish and Irish women in trade union activities. This lack of participation has gradually changed since the 1960s and 1970s. More Chinese American women than ever began to take part in political movements, and some Chinese American women have even become national figures.

Conventionally, historians of Chinese American studies have tended to divide Chinese American history into three periods: the period of unrestricted immigration (1848–1882), the period of exclusion (1882–1943), and the postwar period (1943–present time). This periodization, however, has not reflected the history of Chinese American women accurately. For example, during the period of so-called unrestricted immigration, Chinese immigrant women had been discouraged from coming. When prostitution prospered in the western cities after the 1850s, the middle-class Protestant women began to appeal for the elimination of this "social evil" and the restriction of the entry of Chinese immigrant women, many of whom, Protestant missionary women believed, were prostitutes. The Page Act of 1875 was designed for this purpose. Though the law limited its restrictions to prostitutes, the prevailing anti-Chinese stereotypes led American officials to enforce this legislation as a Chinese female exclusion law.[40] Therefore, the conventional division fails to explain Chinese American women's history adequately during this period.

Similarly, treating Chinese American women since World War II in one single period cannot completely interpret the dramatic economic, social, cultural, political, and psychological changes among

Chinese American women since the 1960s. In the history of Chinese American women, two historical events have had far-reaching
impacts on the lives of these women—World War II and the 1965
Immigration Act. The former not only resulted in the repeal of
Chinese exclusion laws but also the introduction and enforcement
of bills that specially favored the entry of Chinese women such as
the War Bride Act of 1945 and the G.I. Fiancées Act of 1946. The
later, with its focus on family reunification, brought large waves of
new immigrants who mostly came as families. Considering World
War II and the 1965 Immigration Act as two turning points in
Chinese American women's history, this study takes them as
watersheds and divides Chinese American women's history into
three periods accordingly. The first period deals with early Chinese
immigrant women from the middle nineteenth century to 1943; the
second, postwar Chinese American women, from 1943 to 1965; and
the third, contemporary Chinese American women, from 1965 to
the present time.

Within this framework, the source materials and analysis are
organized topically. Following the introduction, chapters 1, 2, and
3 explore early Chinese immigrant women's motivation for immigration and modes of entry, their work, their home, and their community lives. In these three chapters, two groups of early Chinese
immigrant women—the merchant wives and prostitutes—are treated
with special attention, for they formed the main body of early
Chinese immigrant women, and complete scholarly treatment of
these two groups of women has been limited. In addition, Chinese
female students are also examined closely. Chapter 4 discusses the
motivation of postwar Chinese immigrant women, the upward social and economic mobility for Chinese Americans, and Chinese
American family lives and social activities. Chapter 5 examines the
economic, social, cultural, political, and psychological changes among
contemporary Chinese American women since 1965. Chapter 6
addresses some of the current issues and concerns of Chinese
American women. Finally, a conclusion highlights the significance
of Chinese American women's century and a half-long history.

The information included in this study has been primarily
derived from archival documents, oral history interviews and surveys, census data, contemporary newspapers in both English and
Chinese, and existing secondary literature. The primary sources
were mostly collected from Immigration and Naturalization Service Records in the National Archives and Records Service in
Washington, D.C., the National Archives-Pacific Sierra Region in

San Bruno, California, and the National Archives-Central Plain Region in Kansas City, Missouri.

In the National Archives at Washington, D.C., I examined cases of Chinese immigrant women, mainly wives of merchants or daughters of American citizens. These cases were from large volumes of documents such as Passenger Arrival Records (1834–1954), Register of Chinese Letters Received (1898–1903), Chinese General Correspondence (1898–1908), Chinese Letters Sent (June 9, 1900–August 19, 1908), Customs Case File Related to Chinese Immigration (1877–1891), Chinese Smuggling File (1914–1921), Chinese Division File (1924–1925), Applications for Duplicate Certificates of Residence (1893–1920), and Record of Chinese Deportation (1902–1903).

In the Pacific Sierra Regional Archives at San Bruno, I collected several hundred cases related to Chinese prostitutes and wives of Chinese merchants in San Francisco and Hawaii, and information on the structure and operation of Chinese business in San Francisco and Hawaii from Chinese Exclusion Act Cases, Chinese Merchant Partnership List Records, and Maps and Directories of Chinese Firms in San Francisco Chinatown. I also found Chinese Mortuary Records in San Francisco and California (1870–1933). The listings of death causes and occupations of individuals provided valuable information on the early Chinese immigrant women.

I also discovered more than one hundred cases involving Chinese Exclusion laws in Iowa, Missouri, Kansas, Nebraska, Minnesota, North Dakota, and South Dakota from the Records of the United States District Court in the Central Plain Regional Archives in Kansas City. In addition, more than one hundred cases were also gathered from interviews with and autobiographies of Chinese immigrants and first-generation Chinese Americans in California and Hawaii in the William Carlson Smith Documents at the University of Oregon's special collection. The documents contained information on various aspects of Chinese immigrant lives.

Oral history interviews are also part of primary sources used in the study. I have interviewed over two hundred Chinese women residing in the northern, eastern, midwestern, and western regions of the United States. Their ages range from twelve to ninety, and their occupations include professors, teachers, researchers, librarians, counselors, technicians, students, grocery owners, motel owners, restauranteurs, garment workers, farmers, and homemakers. The questionnaire for these interviews was designed to gather information regarding interviewee's immigration background, education, employment, marriage, family, social and political activities.

I interviewed many of the women several times. When these vivid individual accounts are combined with archival documents, they are not only credible but also give life to the latter. In addition, I have also conducted several surveys of Chinese female students in the United States since 1979 and included the results of the surveys into the study.

Census and statistical information used in this work was collected from national and regional archives as well as Annual Reports produced by Immigration and Naturalization Services, and occasionally from secondary sources. Many contemporary newspapers in Chinese published in major Chinese urban communities between the 1880s and 1990s also served as significant sources on the many facets of Chinese American women's lives.

All available existing literature related to the subject has been consulted. It has provided me with background knowledge, sharpened my thinking, and prepared me for this work. Even though I am not able to discuss all materials in the text, I am grateful for all contributions.

Now a few words about terminology in this book. I use the terms *emigrants* and *emigration* when discussing the social and economic conditions for Chinese women in China, and *immigrants* and *immigration* when in America. I also use terms *Chinese American women* or *Japanese American women* without placing hyphens between *Chinese* or *Japanese* and *American* to indicate these women's dual identities. I use the term *Chinese immigrant women* in discussions of prewar foreign-born Chinese women since Chinese immigrants had been denied citizenship before 1943 and of postwar foreign-born Chinese women during their initial years of being in America. Whereas, I use the term *Chinese American women* to describe American-born Chinese women and postwar foreign-born Chinese women who have obtained citizenship or intended to do so. However, in general discussions where time frame or status of citizenship is not specified, I tend to use the term *Chinese American women,* as indicated in the title of the book, to emphasize the theme of this study—Chinese women as an integral part of multiethnic America.

To protect the interviewees' privacy, I quote only the first letters of the interviewees' last names and cite each interview by a number assigned to it.

Part One

❀

Early Chinese Immigrant Women, 1840s–1943

Chapter 1

Nineteenth Century Immigration: Chinese Women Came to the Gold Mountain

When I came to America as a bride, I never knew I would be coming to a prison.

—A Chinese women in Butte, Montana

American history tells of the odyssey of one group of newcomers after another who came from different shores. The nineteenth and twentieth century women who migrated to the United States came from diverse backgrounds, with different motivations for migration. Irish and German women grew to adulthood in agrarian settings. Eastern European Jewish women's lives revolved around centuries-old legal and moral religious institutions. Southern Italian women gave their energies and loyalties to the close, virtually self-sufficient extended family. Despite the differences among them, these immigrant women had one thing in common: all were driven by economic forces.[1]

Why did Chinese immigrant women come to America? Were their motives for immigration similar to or different from non-Chinese immigrant women? Historians have completed a great deal of research on the immigrant motivations for Chinese men. Shih-shan Henry Tsai has pointed out that internal problems in China such as the rapid increase in population since the late seventeenth century and the land concentration had caused Chinese immigration to overseas. However, Ronald Takaki has stressed that Chinese immigrants called *Gam Saan Haak* (or "gold mountain guest") came to America "searching for gold mountain."[2] Roger Daniels has concluded that Chinese immigrants were pushed by such forces in China as political persecution and the lack of economic opportunity, and

17

were pulled by the discovery of gold in California.[3] Yet, few have addressed the above questions about Chinese women. To find out the particular reasons for the immigration of Chinese women, it is important to first look at the social conditions for women in nineteenth-century China.

Social Conditions for Women
in Nineteenth-Century China

The position of women may have been high in prehistoric China as reflected in Chinese mythology.[4] However, Chinese women lost their power as the society became patriarchal before 2,000 B.C. The predominance of Confucianism in the Han dynasty and its reinforcement in the Song dynasty contributed to the rapid deterioration of women's position.[5] Nineteenth-century China was still a feudal society dominated by Confucianism. In this society women were generally subjected to at least three types of restrictions: ideological, socioeconomical, and physical.

First, the traditional Chinese philosophy provided an ideological system in which women were believed to be inferior and therefore they had to subject to male dominance. According to the Naturalists, one of the ancient Chinese philosophic schools, the universe was formed by two basic elements: *yin* and *yang*. The *yin* elements included female, earth, moon, darkness, weakness, and passivity; the *yang* elements were male, heaven, sun, light, strength, and activity.[6] Although *yin* and *yang* elements are naturally complementary and balancing, female and male were not considered equal, as indicated in Confucian teachings, which adopted and developed the Naturalist belief.[7] Throughout history, Confucian ideas served as social norms and legal codes to regulate women's behavior and conduct.[8] According to these Confucian norms and codes, a woman should possess "four virtues" of obedience, timidity, reticence, and adaptability. She should subject her entire life to the dominance of men; "an unmarried girl should obey her father and elder brother, a married woman—her husband, a widow—her son."[9]

The above ideological theory justified and perpetuated women's lower socioeconomic status. Women were excluded from civil service, a main source of income for the ruling class in China. Women were not employed outside the home except for occupations related to reproduction or providing amusement and sexual pleasure for men: matchmakers, midwives, entertainers, prostitutes, and procuresses.[10] Although peasant women largely participated in household handicraft such as spinning and weaving in North China, and in farmwork in South China to help support their families, the income they earned from such activities went to the family, and only the male head of the family could dispose of it.[11]

Physical restrictions such as footbinding were also social practices that reinforced the concept of women as weaker, and inferior creatures. The exact origins of footbinding are obscure. It may have begun with dancers at the imperial court during the Tang dynasty. By the Song dynasty, the custom was introduced among upper class women.[12] During the Qing dynasty, the custom had become a practice throughout Chinese society at large.[13] At quite a young age, girls had their feet tightly wrapped and gradually bent until the arch was broken and toes turned under. The "lily foot," produced by such practice, crippled women to the extent that they could barely walk without support.

Scholars have argued that footbinding had strong erotic appeal to the Chinese male, and this sexual psychopathology made it a common practice in China and lasted until the twentieth century.[14] The more serious concern behind footbinding probably was the control of women in a male-dominated society. This was indicated explicitly in *Nu Er Jing* [Doctrines for Women], one of the classical books about virtuous women. "Feet are bound, not to make them beautiful as a curved bow, but to restrain the women when they go outdoors."[15]

Chinese women were not the only subordinate women of this time. Similar cases were also found among women of other cultures. The women of the Yi dynasty (1392-1910) in Korea led very comparable lives. They, too, were subjected to the male control of their fathers, husbands, and sons. Their roles primarily consisted of reproduction, nurturing, caretaking, and homemaking.[16] Likewise, the women of Meiji Japan were also subordinate in the male-dominated society. They were denied property ownership, legal representation of the family, public education, and voting rights.[17] A recent study of German immigrant women by Linda Schelbitzki Pickle has shown that German women in the nineteenth century were stripped of rights for owning property and attaining education.[18] Similarly, a work on Irish immigrant women by Hasia R. Diner has also pointed out that in nineteenth-century Ireland, girls had no chance to inherit family land, and women were ruled by their husbands and usually lived with their parents-in-law.[19] Compared to women of other cultures, Chinese women not only endured ideological and socioeconomic constraints of the society, a trait common among women of most traditional cultures, but also suffered the physical abuse of footbinding imposed by the male authorities. Therefore Chinese women had more obstacles to overcome than did their counterparts in other cultures when they decided to come to America.

Motives for Immigration

Similar to their counterparts from other countries, early Chinese immigrant women were "pushed" by forces in China and "pulled" by attractions in the United States. The "push" mainly came from natural disaster and internal upheavals in China in the 1840s and 1850s. The "pull" resulted from a strong desire for family reunion, economic pursuit, and the will for personal fulfillment.

The decades of the 1840s and the 1850s in China were full of natural calamities. The major ones were the severe draught in Henan in 1847, the flooding of the Yangtze River in the four provinces of Hubei, Anhui, Jiangsu, and Zhejiang, and the famine in Guangxi in 1849. Flood and famine in Guangdong gave way to the catastrophic Taiping Revolution (1850-1864), which devastated the land, uprooted the peasantry, and dislocated the economy and polity.

Moreover, the importation of opium deepened the social and economic crisis. As a result of the Opium War, opium traffic practically became unrestrained. The volume of import rose from 33,000 chests in 1842 to 46,000 chests in 1848, and to 52,929 chests in 1850. The year 1848 alone witnessed the outflow of more than ten million taels of silver, which exacerbated the already grave economic dislocation and copper-silver exchange rate. The disruptive economic consequence of opium importation was further compounded by the general influx of foreign goods in the open ports. Canton was particularly hit due to its longest history of foreign trade and the widest foreign contact. Local household industries collapsed and the self-sufficient agrarian economy suffered. Those who were adversely affected became potential emigrants.

Guangdong and Guangxi were the regions where *Hakka* (or "guest people") lived in compact communities. The *Hakka* were originally residents of central China who migrated to Guangdong and Guangxi during the Southern Song (A.D. 1127–1278) period when the dynasty moved south under the Mongol threat. Their different dialects, habits, and mode of life made them social outcaste, and it certainly was difficult for them to mix or assimilate with the natives. Collision between the two groups was bound to occur. As people without deep social roots, the *Hakka* were more independent, daring, and prone to action than were the natives. The *Hakka*

Figure 1.1. Young Ng She and Young Sum Wood, wife and child of Chinese merchant Young Kwong Hoy of Hawaii, 1918. Courtesy National Archives-Pacific Sierra Region, San Bruno, California. Note Young Ng She's bound feet.

provided a large proportion of Chinese immigrants in the nineteenth century, especially to Hawaii. It is important to notice the fact that *Hakka* women had more physical mobility with their natural feet than did other contemporary Chinese women, which enabled them to better endure the hardship of immigration.

According to Ronald Takaki, of the 25,767 Chinese in 1900 in Hawaii, 3,471 (or 13.5 percent) were females, but of the 89,863 Chinese on the United States mainland, only 4,522 (or five percent) were females. Takaki has claimed that ethnic differences helped explain the reason why more Chinese women came to Hawaii: most inese immigrants to Hawaii were *Hakka*, whereas the Chinese immigrants to the continental United States were *Punti* (or "local people"). The *Hakka* did not practice footbinding, and hence these women had a greater mobility to travel and work abroad. He has also noted the encouragement from the Hawaiian government and the plantation owners for women to come, and the favorable attitude toward the Chinese from whites in Hawaii.[20]

Among the pulling factors, the desire for family reunion played an important role from the beginning of Chinese women's immigration. The ancient Chinese philosopher Confucius firmly believed that the family was the basic and fundamental unit of social organization and that family integrity and harmony was essential for a functioning society. Only if family bonds and socialization were developed properly throughout China could social harmony reign. A passage from the *Great Learning*, one of the "Four Books" that formed the core of Confucian learning, conveys this set of assumptions:

> By enquiring into all things, understanding is made complete; with complete understanding, thought is made sincere; when thought is sincere, the mind is as it should be; when the mind is as it should be, the individual is morally cultivated; when the individual is morally cultivated, the family is well regulated; when the family is well regulated, the state is properly governed, the world is at peace.[21]

This Confucian ideology affected most Chinese families. Thus maintaining family solidarity seemed to be a vital cause for Chinese women entering the United States. According to immigration records, among the thousands of women who were admitted to enter the United States between 1898 and 1908, more than ninety percent were joining their husbands or fathers in America.[22]

In 1886, Kwong Long, a Chinese merchant residing in New York, went to China and brought his wife and daughter back with him.[23] In the same year, Lai Lee Shee came to San Francisco from Canton to meet her merchant husband, Lai Moow.[24]

Many Chinese daughters also came to America to unite with their fathers who were American citizens or to marry Chinese merchants in the United States. Most Chinese immigrants during the late-nineteenth and early-twentieth century believed that it was safer and less expensive to raise their daughters in China, due to the anti-Chinese sentiment on the West Coast and their financial difficulties.[25] As soon as these daughters came of age, they would be brought to America for a prospective marriage. An article in an unidentified newspaper on July 12, 1888 in "Customs Case File Related to Chi-

Figure 1.2. Chinese bride, San Francisco, 1900. Courtesy Ethnic Studies Library at the University of California, Berkeley.

nese Immigration, 1877–1891" reported a story in which four Chinese girls came to America to join their fathers and to marry Chinese merchants. Lum Pink Hee and Lum Pink On, daughters of Lum Dock Fune, a Chinese merchant of San Francisco, and Ng Ah Hoe and Ng Ah Ying, daughters of Ng Hog Hoy, also a Chinese merchant from San Francisco, arrived in San Francisco on the steamer George W. Elder in July 1888. Their entry to America, however, was denied because they failed to provide certificates. They sued with a writ of habeas corpus in the United States circuit court and were granted the right to land. Ng Ah Hoe, who was twenty-one years old and had bound feet, and Lum Pink Hee were going to marry Chinese merchants respectively.[26]

In addition to the desire for a family reunion, Chinese immigrant women were also driven by economic conditions to enter the United States. Ah Toy, one of the first Chinese immigrant women, arrived alone in San Francisco in 1849 from Hong Kong to "better her condition." She soon became the earliest and most successful Chinese courtesan in San Francisco. Men were known to line up for a block and pay an ounce of gold (sixteen dollars) just "to gaze upon the countenance of the charming Ah Toy."[27] She also became a well-known figure in the courtroom. Unlike most Chinese prostitutes who were taught to fear the police and avoid the courts at all costs, Ah Toy "was tremendously impressed with the American judiciary system and took many of her personal problems there for settlement."[28] She appeared in court a number of times to defend her profession and to sue those clients who paid her with brass fillings instead of gold.[29] To Ah Toy, America was really a "mountain of gold."

The lure of gold also led other Chinese women to become slaves or prostitutes. Wong Ah So, one of the early Chinese prostitutes in California, described her tragic experience. "I was nineteen when this man came to my mother and said that in America there was a great deal of gold. . . . He was a laundryman, but said he earned plenty of money. He was very nice to me, and my mother liked him, so my mother was glad to have me go with him as his wife. I thought I was his wife, and was very grateful that he was taking me to such a grand, free country, where everyone was rich and happy." But two weeks after Wong Ah So arrived in San Francisco, she was shocked to learn that her companion had taken her to America as a "slave" and that she would be forced to work as a prostitute.[30]

Many merchant wives were also attracted by the economic opportunities in the United States. Mrs. C, a second generation Chinese American woman, recalled her family history in which her mother's marriage exemplified the common belief that America was a place full of gold.

> My father spent many years to save enough money for his marriage. So when he had enough money to support a family, he was already a middle-aged man. He went to Guangdong, China to marry my mother when she was sixteen (my father was twenty-seven years older than my mother). . . . My mother was eager to

come to America. Influenced by her parents and (
believed that America was a great place.[31]

Some Chinese women came to the United States neitner out or
a desire for family union nor for economic pursuit. They sailed the
Pacific Ocean for their own personal fulfillment. A few Chinese
female students arrived in the United States as early as 1881.[32]
According to a survey conducted by the China Institute in America
in 1954, the number of these students continued to increase after
the turn of the century. Between 1910 and 1930, their population
increased sixfold in direct proportion to the overall increase in
Chinese student population as a whole (see table 1.1). Since the
survey probably did not include all Chinese students in the United
States, the actual number of Chinese female students in America
was likely even greater than the number indicated in table 1.1.

Restrictions on the Entry of Chinese Women

Initially, very few women followed their men to the "Gold
Mountain," and the Chinese communities in America were characterized as "bachelor societies" for a long time.[33] There are three
main factors contributing to the shortage of women in Chinese
immigration: (1) lack of financial capability of Chinese immigrant
men, (2) restrictions from Chinese society, and (3) restrictive American immigration policies and their enforcement.

Many of the first Chinese male immigrants came to the United
States as indentured, contract laborers, and coolies.[34] They relied
on the credit-ticket system, under which they obtained their passage from Chinese merchants who were reimbursed by relatives of
the travelers or by future employers. In turn, the newcomers worked
for whomever extended the credit until the debt was paid. Given
this situation, the early Chinese male immigrants had to leave
their women behind.

Even after they paid the debt, their meager earnings did not
permit them to support families in the United States. A laundryman, the typical Chinese immigrant in the late-nineteenth and
early-twentieth century, for example, made $100 a month at most
in the 1910s, which was not sufficient to support a family.[35]

Some interviews of Chinese immigrants in the mid-1920s along
the Pacific Coast conducted by researchers from the Survey of Race
Relations project also revealed that financial constraint was a major
reason for Chinese men not to bring their wives. As one wrote:

Table 1.1
Chinese Students in American Colleges
and Universities, 1900–1930
(Number of Students by Year of Entry)

Year of Entry	Male	Female	Sex not Indicated	Total
1900	3			3
1901	12		2	14
1902	7	1		8
1903	4	1		5
1904	18	2	1	21
1905	24		1	25
1906	55	4	1	60
1907	69	1	1	71
1908	64	6	7	77
1909	58	3	8	69
1910	90	6	11	107
1911	77	7	6	90
1912	69	4	6	79
1913	109	14	15	138
1914	155	16	19	190
1915	172	17	24	213
1916	143	19	19	181
1917	136	21	16	173
1918	183	26	20	229
1919	219	20	22	261
1920	322	26	47	395
1921	304	40	43	387
1922	307	49	47	403
1923	351	32	43	426
1924	322	32	29	383
1925	279	37	33	349
1926	266	42	33	341
1927	233	50	19	302
1928	237	43	26	306
1929	286	34	20	340
1930	248	40	28	316

Source: China Institute in America, *A Survey of Chinese Students in American Colleges and Universities in the Past Hundred Years* (New York, 1954), 26–27.

Not enough money to bring her over here. I would bring her here if I had enough money. She wants to come very bad.[36]

In addition to the limited financial resources, restrictions in Chinese society also prevented Chinese women from coming to America. As discussed earlier, the ideological, socioeconomical, and physical constraints imposed on women in feudal China crippled women and restricted all aspects of their lives. As a daughter-in-law, a woman was supposed to bear children and serve her husband and parents-in-law. Since Confucian ideas placed filial piety above all other virtues, a daughter-in-law should consider staying in China to serve her parents-in-law a greater moral responsibility than joining her husband in America. In addition to preservation of moral values, it also made economic sense for many parents of emigrant sons to keep their daughters-in-law in China. Some parents deliberately kept their daughters-in-law with them in order to secure the remittances from their sons abroad.[37] Immigration records also revealed that some Chinese women who came to America to join their husbands did so after their parents-in-law passed away.[38]

The financial incapability of the early Chinese immigrants and the restrictions of Chinese society discouraged Chinese women from emigrating. Yet, a more important reason for the gross disproportion between males and females in Chinese immigrant communities was anti-Chinese sentiment among the American public which led to American exclusion acts. Scholars in Asian American studies have completed comprehensive research on the anti-Chinese movement in America in recent decades. Such scholars as Stuart C. Miller argued that hostilities toward the Chinese were a part of the general xenophobia of white Protestant Americans. Racists viewed these supposed fears, the belief that "Mongolia" blood was debased and the Chinese mind was politically retarded, and further Chinese immigration would threaten Aryan dominance in America. Other writers, like Elmer C. Sandmeyer, believed that economic considerations were most important in causing anti-immigrant feeling, particularly because Chinese laborers became unwitting pawns in American labor-management disputes during the series of economic recessions beginning in 1870. Cultural anthropologist Francis L. K. Hsu has seen the problem as a classic cultural misunderstanding: the majority of white Americans were ignorant of Chinese culture and their ignorance produced prejudice. On the other hand, because of the language barrier, different customs, syncretistic religion, and other traditions, the Chinese remained isolated from the whites. They tried to place a comfortable distance between themselves and the unfriendliness in the looks and acts of their co-workers or neighbors. Unfortunately, the voluntary Chinese separation stamped them with a badge of inferiority.[39]

More recently, some historians have argued that restrictive immigration laws and their enforcement were mainly responsible for the shortage of Chinese women in Chinese immigrant communities. Vincent Tang claimed that beginning in 1882 a series of immigration acts (1882, 1888, 1892, 1902, 1907, and 1924) success-fully restricted the immigration of Chinese women. Since the exclusion acts did not define explicitly how the policy of exclusion was to be carried out, Tang further argued, "deportation sentences were carried out under the auspices of the Immigration Department with the sanction of the courts."[40] George Anthony Peffer's study asserted that even before the passage of the Chinese Exclusion Act in 1882, the Page Law of 1875 had effectively kept Chinese women out.[41] The Page Law of 1875 forbade the entry of Chinese, Japanese, and "Mongolian" contract laborers, and women for the purpose of prostitution. Supporting Peffer's argument, Sucheng Chan's findings further revealed that in the decade before the passage of Page Law, the state of California passed several pieces of legislation to restrict Chinese women. "An Act for the Suppression of Chinese Houses of Ill Fame," passed on March 21, 1866, denounced Chinese prostitution and penalized landlords who allowed their properties to be used for immoral purposes. In addition, "An Act to Prevent the Kidnapping and Importation of Mongolia, Chinese, and Japanese Female, for Criminal or Demoralizing Purposes," passed on March 8, 1870, made it illegal "to bring, or land from any ship, boat or vessel, into this state."[42]

These exclusion laws effectively banned most Chinese women from joining their husbands. The records of the Immigration and Naturalization Service indicate that the majority of the Chinese women entering the United States between 1882 and 1943 were wives and daughters of Chinese merchants. They were exempted from the exclusion laws due to the nature of class prejudice in the American immigrant policy and the U.S. trade with China.[43]

Despite the exclusion laws, many Chinese women were anxious to reunite with their families and to have a chance for a better life. They attempted to enter the United States by impersonating family members of classes exempted from the Exclusion Act—merchants and United States citizens. Some Chinese laborers, in order to bring their families to America, changed their status from laborer to merchant by faking a partnership in a grocery store.[44] Others were smuggled by train or boat from Canada, Mexico, and the Caribbean.[45]

How Chun Pong's case vividly depicts how the smuggling was conducted. How Chun Pong landed in Vancouver, Canada, in 1899, where he worked as a laundryman for four years and then was smuggled to the United States by train. Later he moved to St. Louis to run a hand laundry until he was arrested in 1913 for smoking and dealing opium. In his testimony, he described his illegal entry to Harry C. Allen, the United States Immigration Inspector:

> I boarded the train with a white man at Montreal. It was quite
> dark, and when I got in the car there was no one there except the
> white man and myself, when the train run about several hours
> until daylight and then the train stopped I don't know the name of
> the station. I was put in a small room on the train first and then
> I was brought out in the car where there [were] other passengers.
> And I left the train at New York City. . . . [I paid] $130 to the
> Chinese smuggler [in Montreal] and he paid the white man.[46]

After 1923, however, Canada and Mexico passed their own
exclusion laws, which meant a double barrier for smugglers to
overcome. Therefore, smuggling was not a commonly used method
of illegal entry.[47]

Immigration authorities responded by assuming all Chinese
immigrants were guilty of fraudulent entry until proven otherwise
and singled them out for prolonged detention and interrogation at
entry points. During the period when the Angel Island Immigration Station was operating (1910–1940), immigration officials
climbed aboard and inspected the passengers' documents each time
a ship arrived in San Francisco. They allowed those with satisfactory papers to go ashore. "The remainder were transferred to a
small steamer and ferried to the immigration station on Angel
Island to await hearings on their application for entry. Although a
few whites and other Asians were held at the detention center, the
majority of the detainees were Chinese."[48]

Even though some historians have compared Angel Island with
Ellis Island and called it the "Ellis Island of the West," they were
very different. Located in the Hudson River, Ellis Island was a
symbol of America's immigrant heritage. In the late-nineteenth
century, millions of immigrants left their homeland in the hope of
making a fortune in the New World. In the forty years before the
Civil War, five million immigrants poured into the United States;
from 1860 to 1900 that volume almost tripled.[49] The "old immigrants," those who came from the British Isles, Germany, and
Scandinavia before 1880, were predominantly English-speaking with
some skills and wealth. The "new immigrants" from rural areas of
southern and eastern Europe were poor, unskilled, unable to speak
English, and mostly Italian Catholics and eastern European Jews.
Conservative Americans saw the influx of new immigrants as a
threat to American democracy and ways of life when the new immigrants crowded urban industrial cities. The American union leaders looked at the cheap immigrant laborers as strike-breakers. The
racist nativists were afraid that the new immigrants would dilute
the American Anglo-Saxon Protestant stock. Responding to the

anti-immigration cry, the federal government revised its immigration regulations. It opened the immigration station on Ellis Island on January 1, 1892 as more than seventy percent of all newcomers landed in New York, the country's largest port. Ellis Island ushered in a new era of immigration with each newcomer's eligibility to land now determined by federal law.

The screening first began on the steamships that reached New York Harbor. First- and second-class passengers were processed on boardship, but third- or steerage-class passengers were ferried to Ellis Island where they underwent medical and legal examinations in the Main Building. In this regard, both Ellis Island and Angel Island immigration stations were designed to handle more effectively the increasing volume of new immigrants. They discouraged the newcomers, especially the poor, through humiliating medical examinations, separate hospitalization, and intimidating interrogation.

The two immigration stations, however, differed in their respective functions. Ellis Island was merely a way station; for the vast majority of European immigrants, the processing took only between three and five hours. During peak periods at Ellis Island, as many as five thousand people each day would be checked, questioned, and sent on their way. First, the immigrants entered the Registry room inside the immigration building where they underwent a medical examination. Doctors, hired by the immigration station, removed their hats, peeled back their collars, and flipped up their eyelids with buttonhooks. Then, the immigrants were marked on their coats with chalk: Sc for scalp diseases, G for goiter, or CT for trachoma, a highly contagious eye disease. About twenty percent of the immigrants were chalk-marked and pulled out of line for further examination. The rest moved forward for questioning from immigration officials. The questions asked in this two-minute-long process included occupation, sex, marital status, place and date of birth, political orientation, destination, and job situation. Suddenly, about eighty percent of the new immigrants found they were free. Most of those detained for medical reasons were eventually released. Only two percent of immigrants were denied entry and deported to their home countries. These unfortunate people usually were unaccompanied women, children, the elderly, trachoma patients, and contract laborers.[50]

On the other hand, Angel Island was set up as a detention center for Asian, mainly Chinese immigrants. The immigration detention center on Angel Island was a two-story wooden structure, where men and women were held separately. The duration of imprisonment was often months. Immigrants were first taken to a hospital for medical examinations. Those afflicted with parasitic diseases such as trachoma, hookworm, and liver fluke were excluded and deported. The rest were sent back to their dormitories to await the hearing on their application.[51]

Regardless of the validity of the Chinese arrival's legal documents for entry, a Chinese woman had to go through an extensive

Figure 1.3. Plaque in front of the Immigration Station, Angel Island, erected in 1978. The engraved Chinese characters say "Leaving home behind and being detained in wooden shed, looking for new life by the Golden Gate." Huping Ling Collection.

cross-interrogation on family, home life, and native village. The questions asked in the case of Wong Shee were typical of the cross-interrogation. Wong Shee was wife of Mark Tau, a native-born Chinese laundryman in San Francisco. In September 1920, she and her two young sons, Mark Woon Koey and Mark Woon Hew, came to America to join her husband and her elder sons, Mark Woon Nging and Mark Woon Noon. As soon as the ship arrived in San Francisco on September 1, Wong Shee and her sons were detained in the immigration station on Angel Island. During her hearing on

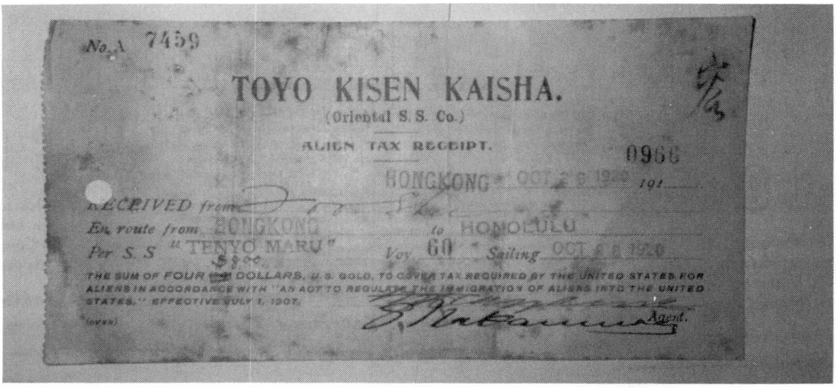
No. A 7459
TOYO KISEN KAISHA.
(Oriental S. S. Co.)
ALIEN TAX RECEIPT.
0966
HONGKONG OCT 26 1920 191
RECEIVED from
En route from HONGKONG to HONOLULU
Per S. S. "TENYO MARU" Voy. 60 Sailing OCT 26 1920
$4.00
THE SUM OF FOUR DOLLARS, U. S. GOLD, TO COVER TAX REQUIRED BY THE UNITED STATES FOR ALIENS IN ACCORDANCE WITH "AN ACT TO REGULATE THE IMMIGRATION OF ALIENS INTO THE UNITED STATES," EFFECTIVE JULY 1, 1907.
(over)
Agent.

Figure 1.4. Chinese merchant wife Foa Shee's steamship ticket, 1920. Courtesy National Archives-Pacific Sierra Region, San Bruno, California.

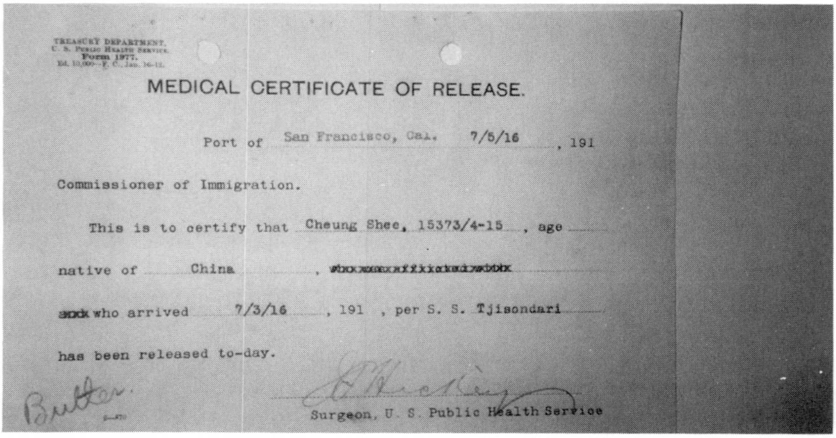
TREASURY DEPARTMENT,
U. S. Public Health Service.
Form 1977.

MEDICAL CERTIFICATE OF RELEASE.

Port of San Francisco, Cal. 7/5/16, 191

Commissioner of Immigration.

This is to certify that Cheung Shee, 15373/4-15, age

native of China,

who arrived 7/3/16, 191, per S. S. Tjisondari

has been released to-day.

Surgeon, U. S. Public Health Service

Figure 1.5. A Medical Certificate of Release issued to Chinese merchant wife Cheung Shee by the hospital on Angel Island Immigration Station, 1916. Courtesy National Archives-Pacific Sierra Region, San Bruno, California.

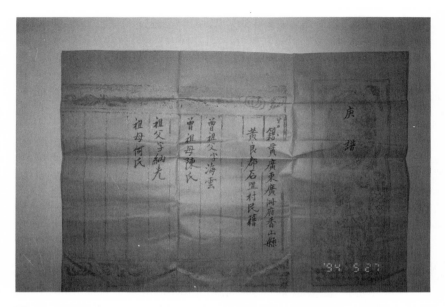

Figure 1.6. A family tree, served as marriage license brought by a Chinese immigrant woman, 1916. Courtesy National Archives-Pacific Sierra Region, San Bruno, California.

October 22, 1920, she was asked the following questions in an interrogation by immigrant inspector J. P. Butler:

Q: Which way does the village face?
A: It faces north.
Q: How are the houses arranged in the village?
A: Arranged in rows.
Q: How many in each row?
A: All in one row across the front of the village from head to tail.
Q: Which one is your house?
A: Counting from the east, mine is the second house.
Q: Have you ever lived in any other house in that village?
A: No.
Q: Is there a wall around your village or any side of it?
A: No.
Q: Any trees or bamboo on any side?
A: Trees and bamboo on both sides and a hill in the rear.
Q: Any trees or shrubs of any kind in the rear?
A: No.
Q: What is in front?
A: Nothing in front.
Q: Has your village a fish pond?

A: No.
Q: Was there ever a fish pond in the front of your village?
A: No.
Q: Is there any ditch of water in the front?
A: No.
Q: Is there any low land in the front of the village in which the water remains?
A: No.
Q: Is there a fish pond on any side of your village?
A: No.
Q: Do you know what a fish pond is?
A: Yes, it is a pond that holds fish but we have no pond in our village.
Q: Is there any pond near your village which might belong to some other village?
A: I don't know of any.
Q: What kind of country is your village located on?
A: It is farm land, level.
Q: State the name of the village in the immediate vicinity of yours, as well as direction and distance.
A: Gop Son village, two li east. Hock Bo to the west, two li. Lung Chee Hong, 21 li south. Lung Mee village to the north, two li.[52]

In Wong Shee's case, Butler repeatedly probed Wong Shee on the question of the fish pond because Mark Tau, Mark Woon Nging, and Mark Woon Noon had respectively testified that there was a fish pond in their native village. After comparing the testimony of Wong Shee, her husband, and her sons, Butler found that there were no other discrepancies except on the fish pond. On this issue, Butler considered Mark Tau's statement that the pond was dry for most part of the year. Therefore, he concluded that there was no discrepancy on this point. Consequently, Wong Shee and her two sons were granted the right to land after almost two months' detention.

In another case, the applicant's testimony disagreed with that of the witness, and her entry was denied. Wong Yee Gue was the wife of Yee Home Sue, a native-born Chinese in New York.[53] On April 19, 1915, Wong Yee Gue arrived in San Francisco and applied for admission as the wife of a native. Two days after she was detained in Angel Island, she went through her hearings. Immigrant inspector A. M. Long found Wong Yee Gue's testimony contradictory to that of other witnesses. The issues dealt mainly with the questions of natural feet and the status of the neighbor in Wong Yee Gue's village. Long therefore recommended Wong Yee Gue's admission be denied.

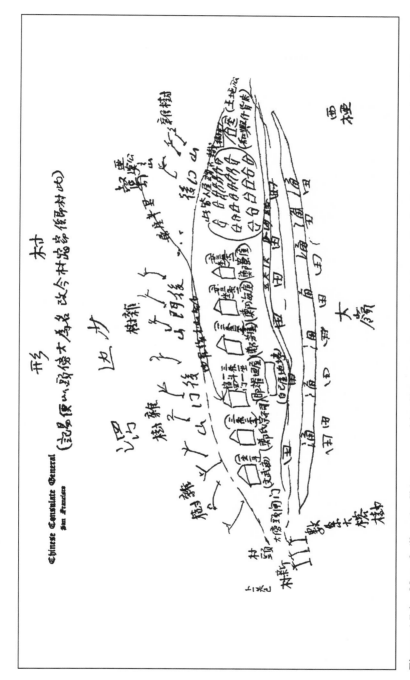

Figure 1.7.A. Map of village in China prepared by Chinese immigrants for interrogation by American immigration officials, 1927. Courtesy National Archives-Pacific Sierra Region, San Bruno, California.

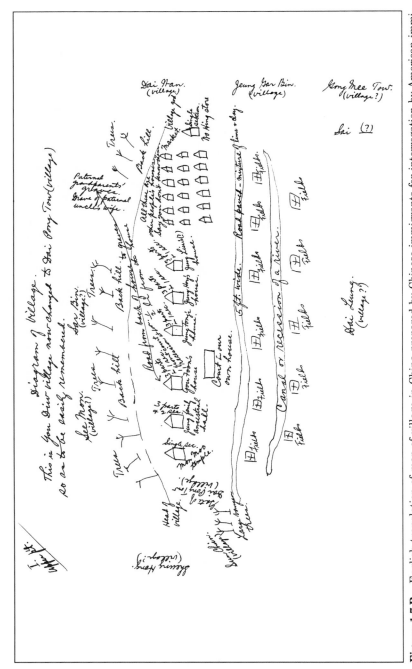

Figure 1.7.B. English translation of map of village in China prepared by Chinese immigrants for interrogation by American immigration officials, 1927. Courtesy National Archives–Pacific Sierra Region, San Bruno, California.

From the above two cases, an applicant's testimony could largely determine the result of her application. Under such practice, a felon could gain admission as long as she and her witnesses were prepared to produce the same testimony, while a bona fide applicant could be denied if she failed to provide expected testimony. Moreover, the different personalities and work styles of immigrant inspectors also played a role in the admission of an applicant. Some inspectors were meticulous but fair. Others were inclined to find discrepancies through tedious interrogation. Finally, the nature of the questions was also deceptive. Most of the questions were tedious, trivial, and had little relevance to the qualifications of the applicant. They often were difficult to answer. The immigration authorities, however, relied on these interrogations to determine an applicant's eligibility for entry.

While detained, Chinese immigrant women were separated from their husbands and sons (only children under twelve could stay with their mothers). Not knowing what would happen to them, many women became stressed and ill. Mai Shee, wife of Chinese merchant Lu Lian, arrived in San Francisco in May 1903. She was denied entry because the Customs office had questioned the mercantile status of Lu Lian. Detained in the Custom facility known as "the Shed" on the San Francisco waterfront, Mai Shee became deeply depressed and very ill. Lu Lian requested bail in order to have his wife treated by doctors. The Customs office denied his plea, which angered the Chinese community in San Francisco.[54]

Some Chinese women, unable to cope with the stress and desperation, committed suicide. The chopsticks slaying case was one such example. On October 24, 1941, Wong Shee, the wife of a New York businessman, arrived in San Francisco with her nine-year-old son, Hom Lee Min, to join her husband, Hom Hin Shew. Upon arrival, she and her son were held separately at the immigration station detention center on 801 Silver Avenue in San Francisco.[55] As days passed, Wong Shee's worry grew deeper. On November 18, 1941, Wong Shee became extremely upset when she heard the rumor about the denial of her application. In the early morning of November 19, she was found dead in the women's bathroom in the detention center. A chopstick had been thrust into her right auditory canal.[56]

Chinese women were, however, not always timid and passive victims. Some protested the brutal treatment of immigration authorities. One immigrant woman recalled her experience when she was interned on Angel Island. "While I was waiting in the immigration shed, Grandpa send a box of *dim sum*. I threw the box of *dim sum* out the window. I was still waiting to be released. I would have jumped

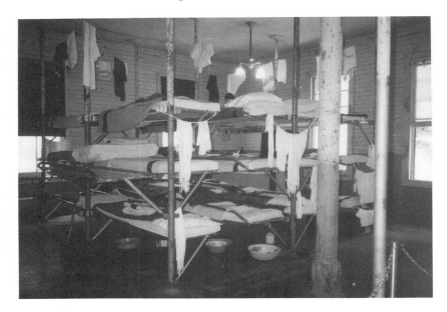

Figure 1.8. Room for detained immigrants before they were either admitted or denied to land, Immigration Station, Angel Island, 1910–1940. Huping Ling Collection.

Figure 1.9. Bathroom in the Immigration Station, Angel Island, 1910–1940. Huping Ling Collection.

in the ocean if they decided to deport me."[57] Though this wa
help in improving their situation, this form of resistance se
emotional outlet for these detained women. Their resistance reflected
the cruelty and inhumane nature of the Immigration Station on Angel
Island. To deal with the depressed and irritated detainees, the Immigration Station on Angel Island set up an isolation room, a nine square
foot room without windows. The offensive inmates were locked in this
room for hours until they managed to "calm down."[58]

Some strong and resourceful Chinese women fought for their
right of entry effectively by applying American immigration regulations to their cases. Gee Quock Shee was one of these courageous
and capable women. She went to China with her husband, a Chinese merchant at San Mateo, in 1907. Her husband remained in
China to do business. When she returned to the United States in
February 1910 with the status of the wife of a merchant, she was
denied entry because her husband was not presently in America.
Defiantly, she provided the evidence that she had one half share in
the business and she had been actively managing the family business, Yee Hing & Co. Therefore, she was qualified to be a merchant
herself. "If the law prevents me from being in this country at the
present time," she challenged J. B. McChesney, the immigration
inspector on Angel Island, "I therefore request that my application
be withdrawn and renew it, having a status of a merchant myself."
After investigation, the Immigration Service on Angel Island accepted her status as a merchant and admitted her entry.[59]

Immigration and Settlement Patterns

How did the early Chinese immigrant women come? Did they
follow immigrant and settlement patterns similar to those of non-
Chinese immigrant women? Groups of immigrant women followed
different patterns in the United States depending on when they
arrived and from where they came. While immigrant women from
European countries had a higher proportion of total immigrant
population and followed chain immigration patterns, Chinese immigrant women comprised a small percentage of the total Chinese
immigrant population and settled in isolated Chinese communities.

Beginning in the early nineteenth century, driven by the Po-
tato Famine, more and more Irish left their country. From 1821 to
1850, about one million of them came to America. About half of
these immigrants were women. Irish women emigrated to the United
States because of their disadvantageous position in the family land

arrangements of the Irish countryside—only one son per family could inherit land in Ireland.[60] Further migration continued along female lines: women brought over other women. Sisters brought sisters, aunts brought their nieces, and cousins assisted one another.[61]

Eastern European Jews resembled the Irish in that men and women came in roughly equal numbers. A sizeable proportion of the new Jewish arrivals were children, indicating that a large number of the immigrant women were married and brought their young with them.[62] Like Irish women, Italian women came to the United States as links in migration chains (the immigrants who had already settled in America brought their compatriots). Contemporary observers and historians have pointed to the important contributions of a few villages to Italian settlements in the United States, and argued that the most striking feature of the Italian migration was the dominance of large village chains.[63]

Japanese immigrant women resembled Irish and eastern European Jewish women in the sense that they came as members of family groups: wives, brides, and daughters. The majority of Japanese immigrant women before 1924 came as brides of Japanese male immigrants who had stayed in the United States for years. Some women were accompanied by their husbands who returned to Japan for the marriage. Many, however, were "picture brides." These women accepted the marriage proposals based on pictures of the prospective husbands, married in Japan without the presence of the grooms, and came to America to join them.[64]

Similarly, approximately seven thousand Korean immigrants came to America between 1910 and 1924. Of these, there were nearly two thousand women. Most Korean women were married and had families. With a sex ratio of 3:1 among Korean immigrants, Koreans were the most family-oriented group of immigrants from Asia at the time.[65]

Early Chinese immigrants shared features with Italian immigrants as they mainly came from one province, Guangdong, in China. Betty Lee Sung's research has shown that sixty percent of the Chinese immigrants in this country during the nineteenth and twentieth centuries came from Tai-shan, a small district of the Guangdong province in southern China. A large proportion of the remaining forty percent originated from the surrounding vicinity of that same district. These neighboring places included: Hsin-Hui, Hoi-ping, Yan-ping, Nan-hoi, Pan-yu, Hsun-tak, Canton, Hok-san, Tung-kwan, Chung-shan, Pao-an, Chin-hoi, Hakka, and Hong Kong.[66]

Immigration patterns for Chinese women were similar to those of other groups. The pattern of chain immigration was most noticeable among the Chinese immigrant women supported by their families or relatives. Like their counterparts from other countries, they tended to arrive near their families or relatives or at nearby places. The women who arrived through the slave trade in the nineteenth and early-twentieth centuries were more likely concentrated in California. Since exclusion laws only permitted the entry of Chinese merchants and their families to the United States, the Chinese immigrant women in the nineteenth and early-twentieth centuries were very likely a merchant's wife, a house servant of a merchant family, or a prostitute brought through illegal traffic.

In most cases, the Chinese man migrated to America first. He worked and saved until he had enough money to travel back to China to bring his wife and children. This was true in the cases of Kwong Long and Gue Lim. Kwong Long, a Chinese merchant in New York City, went back to China in 1886 and returned with his wife and daughter after he worked in the United States for several years.[67] Gue Lim, another Chinese merchant, petitioned the admission for his wife and children in 1900 and was granted the admission.[68]

Oral history interviews conducted by the author have underscored the above immigration pattern for Chinese women. A Chinese tea merchant from Guangdong, Mrs. C's father came to the United States around the turn of the twentieth century. He first arrived in San Francisco and later moved to Boston. There he worked as a bookkeeper. When he had enough money to support a family, he went to Guangdong to marry his bride and brought her to America. He then started his own business and bought a house in Boston.[69] Mrs. S's family history resembled that of Mrs. C:

> My father was a merchant when he came here [San Francisco] in early 1900s. My mother was in China and she came here a year after the earthquake in 1906. . .[70]

Usually, with sufficient funds, most Chinese merchants arranged for their families to join them.

Some Chinese women even entered this country to take over businesses run by their husbands. Gin Far, the wife of a Chinese merchant in San Francisco, went back to China with her husband and her son before 1900. When in China, her husband died. Since she wanted to take over his interest in the firm in America, a mercantile house, she applied to return to the United States with her six- or seven-year-old son. The Treasury Department authorized the Collector of Customs in San Francisco to admit her "as the surviving widow of a merchant with whom she formerly lived as his wife in this country."[71]

Most well-to-do merchants could either bring their families initially or send for them later. For Chinese laborers, however, the process of transplanting families proved long, painful, and sometimes even impossible. Fong, a first-generation Chinese immigrant in Lin Yutang's *Chinatown Family*, a novel about the acculturation and assimilation of Chinese immigrants, thought of his wife throughout his American experience. After a few years, "he took a boat back to his wife. Then after a while he came back. . . . He went back to his wife every five or six years. . . . He was smart [like] the eels that travel half across the Atlantic to . . . spawn."[72] This repetitious trans-Pacific odyssey to his Chinese Ithaca, where Fong fulfilled his duties of a man: making children and providing for his family, lasted until he established a hand laundry in the basement of 80th Street and Third Avenue in New York City. With a foothold on the Mountain of Gold, Fong began to transplant his family to American soil. To enter America, Fong's second son, Freddie, had to enlist as a seaman, jump ship, and slip in as an illegal alien.[73] Freddie worked hard and saved enough passage money for his mother and the two younger siblings to come to America, and they did after Fong faked a partnership in a grocery store. With the success of this ruse, the family was physically reunited on American soil.[74]

The variations of Lin Yutang's story were retold in the immigration records. Mark Tau, for instance, was a Chinese laundryman born in Stockton, California in 1881. Like many native-born Chinese men of his time, he sought his bride in his ancestor's land in 1905 when he was twenty-five years old. Unable to support a family in the United States as a laundryman, Mark Tau left his wife Wong Shee in China and visited her once every several years. He brought his two elder sons over in 1917 and 1919 respectively. With the help of his sons Mark Woon Nging (age sixteen) and Mark Woon Noon (age fourteen), he was finally able to arrange for his wife and two younger sons (ages eight and seven) to come to America in 1920. After the interrogations of Mark Tau, Wong Shee, and the two elder sons, Wong Shee and the two younger sons were granted entry.[75]

Unlike women entering America on their own or with family support, many Chinese immigrant women in the nineteenth century were smuggled to the United States through the slave trade.

Due to the shortage of women during the Gold Rush era, many young girls were sold to brokers by poor parents in China for $70 to $150, and resold in America by the brokers for $350 to $1,000 or more.[76] Lilac Chen vividly described her sale in China to authors Victor and Brett de Bary Nee:

> I was six when I came to this country in 1893. My worthless father gambled every cent away, and so, left us poor. . . . And the day my father took me, he fibbed and said he was taking me to see my grandmother, that I was very fond of, you know, and I got on the ferry boat with him, and Mother was crying, and I couldn't understand why she should cry if I go to see Grandma. She gave me a new toothbrush and a new washrag in a blue bag when I left her. When I saw her cry I said,"Don't cry, Mother, I'm just going to see Grandma and be right back." And that worthless father, my own father, imagine, had every inclination to sell me, and he sold me on the ferry boat. Locked me in a cabin while he was negotiating my sale. And I kicked and screamed and they wouldn't open the door till after some time, you see, I suppose he had made his bargain and had left the steamer. Then they opened the door and let me out and I went up and down, up and down, here and there, couldn't find him. And he left me, you see, with a strange woman.[77]

The story of Rose was typical among the Chinese women brought to the United States as prostitutes.

> Rose was born in interior China. . . , the sixth of eight children, five of whom are girls. There were many famines in her village and she was taken to Hong Kong at 14 to be near her working sister. . . . She was to be sent to America to be married to a man who owned a dry goods business. . . . On December 1920, while only 16, Rose came [to America]. The party arrived in San Francisco and landed in January 1921.
> Rose was bought for $500 in China. She was sold in San Francisco for $4500 to a first mistress and was later re-sold twice. For the very first owner she earned $7,000 in 22 months. A native daughter's certificate was provided for her and she was taught to say she was a native born.[78]

Chinese female students seemed to have followed immigration patterns different from those of their counterparts. While most Chinese immigrant women came to America either through family support or illegal slave trade, the majority of early Chinese female students arrived in the United States with the sponsorship of

Christian missionary organizations. Since the Opium War opened China's door to the Western powers, American missionary workers had been preaching along coastal areas and port cities. There they established schools, hospitals, and other charitable facilities. At a time when public education was not accessible to women in China, schools run by missions provided opportunities for women to obtain a western education.[79] In 1844, the first Christian school for girls in China was founded in Ningpo.[80] In 1846, a young couple, Dr. and Mrs. Dyer Ball, sent by the American Board of Commissioners for Foreign Missions, opened a girls' school in their home in Canton. In the beginning, there were only eight girls at the school. By the end of the century, however, student enrollment multiplied by hundreds.[81] In 1860, the first Christian school for girls in Shantou was founded in the downstairs of the residence of American Baptist Reverend J. W. Johnson and his wife. The school was in operation until 1874 when Mrs. Johnson retired from the field.[82] According to a report from the Canton Missionary Conference, there were 236 Chinese girls enrolled in middle schools in Guangdong Province run by the missions in 1920.[83] Most of the girls were from affluent Chinese Christian families. According to a private survey in 1933, more than ninety percent of these girls were daughters of business men or professionals, and almost half of them had Protestant Christian parents.[84]

In addition to elementary and secondary education, Christian missions also established institutions of higher education in China. In 1906, North China Women's College (which later became part of Yanjing University) was founded by Dr. Louella Miner, a fervent missionary and advocate of higher education for women. After that, the number of women in Christian colleges in China steadily increased. In 1912, twenty students were admitted to North China Women's College, the only institution of higher education for women at the time. Two decades later, 1,261 female students were enrolled in seventeen Christian colleges in China. These women constituted twenty-two percent of the total number of students in Christian colleges. Almost half of these female students were in three institutions: Yanjing University had 223, the University of Shanghai had 206, and Guiling College for Women had 174.[85]

Clearly, Chinese women, who studied in mission schools and who were daughters of Chinese Christians, benefitted from their association with Christian organizations. They were able to enter the United States at a time when wives and daughters of Chinese laborers were barred from coming to America.

Between 1881 and 1892, according to Y. C. Wang, four Chinese female students sponsored by the American missionaries received their medical degrees from American colleges. These four Chinese women were believed to be the first Chinese women to study in America.[86]

In the following decades, according to immigration records, Chinese female students continued to arrive in the United States. In January 1900, a twenty-year-old Chinese woman named Mary Chan, daughter of Chinese Reverend Chan Sing Kai, entered America from Victoria in British Columbia, Canada, where she had lived for five years as a student. She was admitted to the United States by the Controller of Chinese and Collector of Customs at Victoria, British Columbia.[87] Whether she became a student in the United States is unknown, but she was probably one of the earliest Chinese female students to visit America.

In April 1914, Ng Gan Tong, a fifteen-year-old Chinese girl, was admitted as a student after American immigration officials denied her first application for admission as the adopted daughter of an American citizen of Chinese ancestry. Her educational background in South China Girls' School, a mission school in Canton, played a crucial role in her admission to the United States. In his letter to the Commissioner of Immigration at San Francisco, the American Consul General in Canton gave this argument in favor of Ng Gan Tong's admission as a student:

> . . . the applicant attended the South China Girls' School for a period of four years. This school is one of the recognized institutions of learning in Canton, and has a large number of Chinese girls in attendance. An examination of the record at the school shows that Ng Gan Tong attended from September 1909 to June 1913, or eight semesters, which corresponds to four years, pursuing the regular course of studies, viz, Bible studies, national reader, arithmetic, Chinese geography, Chinese history, hygiene, English, drawing and music, physical culture and needle work. This establishes the fact that she was a bona fide student. The photograph of applicant was positively identified by Miss Edna Lowry, Principal, and Rev. C. A. Nelson, missionary in charge.[88]

The immigration authorities also directed that after her admission, Ng Gan Tong would be "placed in a proper school" and that "adequate provision would be made for her maintenance and tuition."[89]

In 1916, the sisters Chan Ping On, Chan Pink Hong, and Chan Pink Ning, along with their mother, arrived in the United States to join their father, Chan Lok Shang. He was a minister in a Chinese

Methodist Episcopal Church in San Francisco, California, and a teacher in the school affiliated with the church. Although admitted as daughters of a teacher, they all clearly indicated their occupations as students at the time of admission.[90]

The most celebrated Chinese female students of this time who were associated with American missionaries were the Soong sisters, Eling, Chingling (later married to Dr. Sun Yat-sen, known as Mme. Sun Yat-sen), and Mayling (later married to Chiang Kai-shek, known as Mme. Chiang Kai-shek) Soong. They were the daughters of Charles Jones Soong, one of the earliest Chinese Christian ministers in Shanghai. Between 1904 and 1907, through arrangements by their father and his American missionary friends, the three Soong sisters successively arrived at Wesleyan College, a private women's college in Macon, Georgia. There they all started their college education at the age of fourteen and maintained outstanding academic records. Eling and Chingling returned to China after their graduation in 1908 and 1913 respectively, while Mayling transferred to Wellesley College in Massachusetts in 1913 to finish her undergraduate degree.[91]

Although Christian missionaries sponsored most of the Chinese female students of this period, a few came to America with scholarships from the Chinese government. According to Y. C. Wang's research, three women were awarded scholarships by Jiangsu province and one by Zhejiang province in 1907 for study in America.[92] Y. C. Wang's study also indicated that "by 1910 self-supporting female students abroad were competing on equal terms with male students for government scholarships."[93]

After the establishment of the Republic of China in 1912, the new government continued to send students abroad to study. During the years from 1912 to 1929, 1,268 Chinese students were sent to America through the auspices of Qinghua College.[94] Since Qinghua College was only open to men, beginning in 1914, ten scholarships were awarded every other year to female students from other colleges selected through competitive examinations. From 1914 to 1929, fifty-three female students were sent to the United States under the four-year scholarships.[95] In 1920 when Qinghua College temporarily canceled the awards, Chinese female students throughout China protested violently. This indicated intellectual Chinese women's strong desire for western education and equality between men and women.[96] In addition to national scholarships, the provincial governments also provided study abroad scholarships. The selection of scholarship students, however, was regulated by the central government, and all provincial students had to take two examinations, one at the provincial level and one in Peking. The central government also determined the number of scholarships to be awarded and the subjects to be studied.[97] As a result, the number of Chinese students in America increased to 1,446 in 1922, including 135 women.[98] Most of these female students obtained a western education at missionary schools in China and had a good command of the English language.[99]

※

Like other immigrant women, the early Chinese women mainly settled at the ports of arrival. In the nineteenth century, San Francisco was the major landing port. In 1870, of 4,574 Chinese immigrant women arrivals, 3,873 remained in the San Francisco area; in 1900, 3,456 out of 4,522 Chinese immigrant women arrivals settled in San Francisco.[100] Beginning in the 1940s, New York had the second largest concentration of Chinese women in the continental United States. Out of the total of 20,115 Chinese women in the United States, there were 12,255 in California, and 1,954 in New York.[101] In these urban settings, Chinese immigrant women, like their male counterparts, concentrated in the ethnic ghetto—Chinatown—and found themselves isolated and ignored by the rest of American society.[102]

The settlement patterns of the early Chinese immigrant women can be examined from two dimensions—social arrangements and physical arrangements. Socially, the wealthiest merchants, operating through their organization called the Chinese Six Companies, wielded control in San Francisco and eventually all other Chinese communities across the country.[103]

The Six Companies had primarily three functions. The first was its legal function. During the period of Chinese exclusion, the Six Companies not only negotiated with the American government as the formal representative of Chinese immigrants, but hired European American lawyers to defend Chinese immigrants involved in the exclusion cases as well. From the immigration records, one can easily find many cases in which white lawyers representing Chinese immigrants corresponded with the immigration authorities.[104]

The second and the most important was its socioeconomic function. As an informal form of government, the Six Companies demanded that Chinese immigrants register with them upon landing and pay fees and debts before departure for China. Their headquarters provided temporary lodgings for those just landing or awaiting ships to China. They arbitrated disputes among its members and provided social services to the needy.[105] In short, the Six Companies controlled almost every aspect of Chinese immigrants' lives.

The third was its cultural function. Culturally and emotionally connected with native land, Chinese immigrants diligently cultivated Chinese values in their young. To meet the community need, each company sponsored Chinese language schools, as indicated in the oral history interview of Mrs. S, which will be discussed in chapter 3.

In fulfilling these functions, Six Companies provided useful services to the Chinese immigrant communities, including women and children. As fraternal organizations, however, Six Companies completely excluded women from their activities.[106]

This pattern of social control was different from that in traditional China where the gentry-scholar class monopolized every level of government and despised and oppressed the merchant class. Secure in wealth and power, the gentry-scholar class had little incentive to emigrate. The lack of gentry-scholar class among Chinese immigrant societies made merchants, who were better educated and financed than most Chinese laborers, the natural leaders of the communities. The Six Companies soon became accepted by the Chinese immigrants as their formal representative to white Americans. The chairman of the Six Companies was called "the mayor of Chinatown" by outsiders. This dominance of merchants over the social and political life of Chinese workers combined well with the economic power to forge a mighty influence on everyday life in Chinatown. For Chinese immigrants in general, merchants became the dominant model of success. The wives of Chinese merchants were also accepted by American immigration authorities as decent and respectable Chinese women.

Although the social organization among Chinese immigrants in America differed from that in traditional Chinese society, both merchant class's social control over Chinese immigrant communities and the gentry-scholar class's dominance in China were characterized as patriarchal. The Six Companies, based on the origins of lineage and geographical locality, was the virtual transformation of the traditional Chinese patriarchal rule on American soil. Although standing on American land, Chinese immigrant women lived in the ethnic enclave and were subjected to the patriarchal rule of their husbands and the local government, the Six Companies.

Physically, the wealthy Chinese merchants and their families lived in four- to five-room apartments, possibly around the "Chinese Nob Hill" section on the 900 block of upper Clay and Sacramento Streets in San Francisco.[107] They might even have possessed "the ultimate community status symbol" of the time, a sofa.[108] Families of the most petty merchants, however, more likely lived in crowded rooms upstairs from their family businesses on Jackson Street in San Francisco.[109] The primary responsibility of the merchant wife was to bear children and raise the family. Due to the scarcity of women, the wives of merchants were closely guarded and highly valued commodities. Abiding by traditional customs, these women were seldom seen in the streets of Chinatown. Without English language and bound by Chinese tradition, the early Chinese immigrant women were excluded from larger American society and male Chinese immigrant society as well.

Just as their male counterparts in the United States lived in isolated societies, these Chinese women endured lonely, alienating, and even threatening surroundings. Most Chinese women of this period, having bound feet, could do little to defend themselves against physical attacks. Especially vulnerable were wives of merchants who were sheltered by their husbands and who seldom ventured out alone. An oral history interview conducted by Rose Hum Lee of the oldest woman in Butte, Montana's Chinatown depicted a vivid picture of what life was like for some merchant wives.

> When I came to America as a bride, I never knew I would be coming to a prison. Until the [1911] Revolution, I was allowed out of the house but once a year. That was during New Years when families exchanged . . . calls and feasts. We would dress in our long-plaited, brocaded, hand-embroidered skirts. . . . The father of my children hired a closed carriage to take me and the children calling. . . . Before we went out of the house, we sent the children to see if the streets were clear of men. It was considered impolite to meet them. If we did have to walk out when men were on the streets, we hid our faces behind our silk fans and hurried by. . . . When the New Year festivals were over, we would put away our clothes and take them out when another feast was held. Sometimes, we went to a feast when a baby born into a family association was a month old. Otherwise we seldom visited each other; it was considered immodest to be seen too many times during the year.[110]

A similar story was also told by Connie Young Yu, a historian and a writer in California. "[My] Great-Grandma seldom left home;

she could count the number of times she went out. She and other Chinese wives did not appear in the streets even for holidays, lest they be looked upon as prostitutes."¹¹¹

Though generally isolation from the outside world had been a part of the life for Chinese immigrant women, some Chinese women seemed to lead less restricted lives than others. When asked if her mother had a confined life in the United States, Mrs. S disagreed:

> In early time, women went to visit friends. My mother could go to everywhere and whenever she wanted. My mother had natural feet, . . . My mother was very independent. She didn't know English, but she could walk or take train to downtown shopping. She could take train to cross bridge to Oakland by herself. She could go anywhere.¹¹²

In summary, although restricted by financial constraints, traditional restrictions from China, and discriminatory American immigration laws, Chinese women emigrated to the United States with various motivations. As a sociologist said about half-a-century ago, migrations had their "inception in a condition of unrest and derive their motive power on one hand from dissatisfaction with the current form of life, and on the other hand, from wishes and hopes for a new scheme or system of living."¹¹³ Like immigrants from other lands, Chinese immigrant women were unsatisfied with conditions at home, and they were encouraged by hopes to have a new life to emigrate to the United States. Many came to this country to join their long-separated husbands. To them, the desire to join their spouses pulled them to the United States and provided them with enough strength to leave their native country and their beloved relatives and friends. Others crossed the Pacific Ocean for economic reasons. They saw America as a country full of opportunities where they could obtain what they could not get in their own homeland. Finally, some educated Chinese women arrived in America with a strong desire for personal fulfillment. Though differing in motivations, they shared one thing in common: the desire to start a new life in America. Upon arrival, however, most of them found that they had traded a restricted life in their homeland for another confined one on American soil. They were first detained at the immigration station on Angel Island for several months, and later confined in crowded quarters in Chinatowns indefinitely. Their lives seemed to have improved little by immigration.

Chapter 2

Nineteenth and Early-Twentieth Century Chinese American Women at Work

> They all lived in the rear of their grocery store, which also exported dried shrimp and seaweed to China. Great-Grandma . . . took care of the children, made special cakes to sell on feast days, and helped with her husband's work.
>
> —Connie Young Yu "The World of Our Grandmothers"

Most immigrant women saw clearly that their survival was inescapably linked with work. Generally, occupational choices were often restrained by the situation of a given woman, her education, her marketable skills, and her adaptability to the new environment. The time and destination of her immigration and the availability of employment in American labor market also determined her occupational choices. In the late-nineteenth and early-twentieth century, most immigrant women clustered in domestic work and related jobs in restaurants, laundries, hotels, or in needlework, clothing, or textile manufacture. While single women often found jobs in factory or domestic service, married women tended to work at home, having boarders, taking in sewing or laundry, or running small businesses from their homes.

During the earlier period of Chinese immigration, from the arrival of the first female Chinese in the mid-1830s to the 1940s when larger numbers of Chinese women entered America for the first time, Chinese women stayed mainly in menial jobs such as domestic service and prostitution or other service trades which the rest of the American population was unwilling to embrace such as laundry, restaurant, and grocery store businesses.

51

Although the job opportunities for Chinese immigrants appeared quite similar to those for other immigrant women, through a careful examination one can find at least three major differences between the two. First, even though both Chinese women and immigrant women of other ethnic groups worked in domestic services, the former were usually young slave girls purchased by their masters. They worked as indentured slaves for the families that owned them and were unable to choose their masters at their will. The latter were free individuals employed by families needing their services. They could move from one employer to another if desired. Therefore, the relationship between a Chinese domestic servant and her owner was not one of capitalistic employee and employer, but one of feudalistic master and servant. Second, although in the late-nineteenth century, women in the sex industry were from many different nationalities, most native-born women or European immigrant women worked as independent professionals or were employed by brothels. Some hawked their bodies sporadically to increase the family income. Chinese prostitutes, on the other hand, were kidnapped or sold to America, and forced into the industry. They had to sign contracts with brothel owners and received no pay during the approximately four-year servitude. Third, many young girls from eastern and southern European countries were employed by textile or other factories as unskilled laborers. Although at the very bottom of the scales of American working class, they could make more than their counterparts in domestic services. Early Chinese immigrant women, who were forced into prostitution or domestic servitude, had little chance to enter the industry.

Slave Girls

In the nineteenth and early-twentieth century, young Chinese girls arriving in the United States often started as house servants. As such, their lives were completely controlled by their masters and the treatment they received also varied from family to family. Some young girls were treated brutally, while others were regarded as members of the family. Lilac Chen, a servant girl, experienced both kindness and brutality from her different masters as she recalled later:

> Everywhere I had been they were very kind to me, except this last
> place. . . . Oh, this woman was so awful! They say she was a

domestic servant before and was cruelly treated. She used to make me carry a big fat baby on my back and make me wash his diapers. And you know, to wash you have to stoop over, and then he pulls you back, and cry and cry. Oh, I got desperate, I didn't care what happened to me, I just pinched his cheek. . . . She, his mother, went and burned a red hot iron tong and burnt me on the arm.[1]

Upon reaching a certain age, these young house servants either married a wealthy merchant or entered into several years of prostitution. According to Lucie Cheng Hirata's research, Chinese prostitutes comprised eighty-five percent of the Chinese women in San Francisco in 1860, seventy-one percent in 1870, and twenty-one percent in 1880.[2] Other writers, however, disputed Hirata's estimate, believing that the number of Chinese prostitutes was exaggerated and the number of Chinese wives underestimated, because census enumerators concealed the identities of individuals not engaged in prostitution, and suggesting instead that non-prostitutes may have comprised fifty percent of the adult females in San Francisco's Chinese population in 1870.[3] Even if we consider the latter's argument, there was one prostitute for every two Chinese women in San Francisco during the 1870s. Therefore, it is important to examine these women's lives closely.

Since virtually all of these women were illiterate, there was no direct account of their lives. A great deal of literature from crusading Protestant missionaries, many of them in San Francisco, has survived. The literature disclosed the terribly degrading conditions the young Chinese slave girls were forced to. They also applauded the courageous efforts to rescue these girls from servitude conducted by Donaldina Cameron and her colleagues from the Presbyterian Mission Home in San Francisco. Besides these early records of Chinese prostitution, the recent scholarly work has also revealed the miserable life these Chinese prostitutes led.[4] Some scholars have argued that Chinese prostitutes were not only victims of class and gender oppression, but also economic exploitation.[5] Others have asserted that Chinese prostitutes were not mere victims but unsubmissive individuals who fought their fate as well.[6]

These interpretations have provided valuable insight to our understanding of Chinese prostitution in nineteenth-century America. They were, however, narrow-focused in the sense that their observation and analysis were limited within the Chinese immigrant communities: Chinese prostitutes were oppressed and exploited by Chinese males and the patriarchal Chinatown authorities, and they attempted to challenge the establishment that enslaved them. They failed to see the Chinese sex industry in the United States from a broader and more comprehensive view.

Chinese prostitutes were not only victims of patriarchal rule and economic exploitation of Chinese immigrant communities, but victims of the exploitation of global capitalism. Geographical discovery and industrial revolution enabled capitalism to exploit the resources and markets throughout the world. Consequently, the nations with advanced industrialism would lure and attract laborers from the less developed countries. In the late-nineteenth century the United States emerged as one of the strongest industrial powers that naturally became the haven of individuals fleeing natural disasters, economic difficulties, and political and religious persecutions from their motherland. The new immigrants willingly or involuntarily became prey of American capitalism. As Chinese laborers were needed for the development of the American West frontier, Chinese prostitutes were indispensable for the maintenance of this army of cheap laborers. Thus, Chinese prostitution in nineteenth-century America, like any commercialized sex industry throughout the world in the past and present, was more a product of global capitalist development than a result of the Chinese patriarchal society.

As part of the global movement of laborers, most of the Chinese prostitutes in the late-nineteenth century were young girls from Hong Kong, Canton, and neighboring areas who were kidnapped, purchased, or stolen by procurers, and then smuggled to America.[7] Upon landing in San Francisco, these young Chinese women were delivered to Chinatown and locked in places known as the barracoons, where they were stripped and displayed for auction. Generally, the "fortunate" women were sold to well-to-do Chinese as concubines or mistresses. Some merchants considered experienced prostitutes ideal wives because they were attractive, sociable, and adept at entertaining guests. A small number were recruited to high-class establishments. They lived in upstairs apartments in Chinatown and were often patronized by a relatively stable client or clients. While they seemed to be well-treated, they could be sold at their master's will.

Except for those "fortunate" women, the rest of Chinese girls ended up in brothels of various grades, according to their attractiveness. During the typical four-year servitude, slave girls had to work for their owners without wages. Besides, they could only take off one month for their menstrual period during the four years, and

Figure 2.1. Chinese women in child slavery case, 1890s. Collection of the Library of Congress. Courtesy Ethnic Studies Library at the University of California, Berkeley.

they had to work for an extra year if they got pregnant.[8] These lower-grade prostitutes, according to Lucie Cheng Hirata, tended to attract white and Chinese customers, due to their comparatively low fees of twenty-five to fifty cents. The living conditions of these young women were miserable. Most of them lived in the street-level apartments. Their daily activities were restricted to these tiny rooms, usually four by six feet, and with a door that held the bared window facing a dim alley. A few pieces of furniture—a bamboo chair or two, a washbowl, and hard bunks or shelves covered with matting—were all the furnishings of the room.[9] The women were served two or three meals a day; the evening one usually consisted of a huge mound of rice and a stew of pork, mixed with hard-boiled eggs, liver, and kidneys.[10] Lilac Chen, a former slave girl, described the nightlife of these prostitutes when interviewed by Victor G. and Brett de Nee.

> This woman, who brought me to San Francisco, was called Mrs. Lee, and she kept the biggest dive in San Francisco Chinatown. Oh, she had a lot of girls, slave girls, you know. And every night,

Figure 2.2. Chinese slave girl behind celled room, 1900s. Collection of the Chinese Cultural Center, San Francisco. Courtesy Ethnic Studies Library at the University of California, Berkeley.

seven o'clock, all these girls were dressed in silk and satin, and sat in front of a big window, and the men would look in and choose their girls who they'd want for the night. . . .[11]

They were often mistreated by their owners and customers. Some owners occasionally beat them to death or shot them, and sometimes clients forced them to engage in aberrant sexual acts.

Under the harsh living and working conditions, these slave girls had low life expectancies. Many of them suffered from ailments, such as tuberculosis and venereal diseases, and died in their teens and twenties. According to the Chinese Mortuary Record of the City and County of San Francisco, among the over six hundred women listed between 1870 and 1878, most died in their teens, twenties, and thirties of tuberculosis, venereal diseases, and unknown causes. Since none of the women had their occupation listed in the record, a large number of them probably were prostitutes.[12]

In the mining camps, where conditions were more primitive and frightening than in urban brothels, prostitutes faced a worse fate. In 1875 there were eighty-four Chinese women on the Comstock Lode in Nevada, only nine of whom were not prostitutes.[13] These women "worked in public establishments and served a racially mixed clientele of miners and laborers." They were often called "Chiney ladies," "moon-eyed pinch foots," and "she-heathens" by their white customers.[14] Some Chinese prostitutes catered to whites by dressing in exotic silks and jewels. By and large, however, the lower-rank Chinese prostitutes dressed in plain cotton and worked for fees ranging from twenty-five to fifty cents per customer.[15]

In the isolated mining areas, Chinese prostitutes were also prone to ethnic crimes. In the 1870s, for instance, four Chinese prostitutes in Comstock Lode were kidnapped by rival tongs. Only one of the victims was later found alive on the railroad, inside a nailed crate being shipped from San Francisco to Reno.[16]

Some Chinese prostitutes escaped by running away or committing suicide. One prostitute in Nevada escaped from her owner and hid in the hills. When she was found, "both her feet had frozen and had to be amputated." She finally "courted death by refusing to take medicine or food." In Virginia City, Nevada, six Chinese prostitutes ended their miserable lives by committing suicide.[17]

A few fortunate prostitutes succeeded in escaping enslavement by taking court action and later enjoyed normal family life. Annie Lee was one of them. As a beautiful young Cantonese woman, Annie Lee was a prostitute owned by a member of the Yeong Wo Company in Idaho City around 1875. After she escaped to Boise to marry her lover, a young Chinese man named Ah Guan, her owner charged her with grand larceny for leaving Idaho City. When she was arrested and taken to court, she won the sympathy of the judge. In front of the judge, she clearly expressed her desire to end the enslavement and marry the man she loved.

The Judge said he would reject an interpreter and ask her questions himself. After administering the oath, the Judge asked her if she wanted to go back to Idaho City, or if she wanted to stay in Boise City. She answered, "me want to stay in Boise City."[18]

Finally, her case was dismissed and she returned to her husband.

According to the most widely accepted sociological definition, prostitution is often characterized as sex for extrinsic purpose, hire, promiscuity, and impersonality.[19] The higher the status of the prostitute, the less obvious her connection with any of these four characteristics.[20] Chinese prostitute-slaves were on the bottom of the social spectrum, as they attempted to attract as many customers as possible due to their absolutely low fees, and their patrons came mainly from the working class. Moreover, as slaves or servants indentured to brothel keepers, typically a four-year term, Chinese prostitutes kept nothing of what they earned and lived according to their owners' whim. Measured by those four characteristics, Chinese prostitutes ranked at the very bottom of the social scale of prostitution.[21]

It is instructive to compare Chinese and Japanese prostitutes in the late-nineteenth and early-twentieth century. Like Chinese prostitutes who were forced to be in this business, Japanese prostitutes in Hawaii, in most cases, were coerced into hawking their bodies. According to Joan Hori's study, they were sold to be prostitutes, however, not only by procurers, but also by their own husbands.[22] Some Japanese men sold their wives to other men for profits of $100 or $200. "The amount collected by the husbands rose from $50 to $100 to even $1,000, when some wives were bought to be resold to brothels."[23] Profits such as these resulted in more wives being brought to Hawaii to sell. Not all wives sold or prostituted, however, were victims or economic commodities; "some ran off with other more attractive or richer men, or left for the city" where money could be earned more easily than by working in the fields for thirty-five cents per day. "A prostitute earned fifty cents to a dollar per customer, and at least $4 to $5 in an evening." A good-looking and popular prostitute could make $20 per night. "Even after subtracting the cost of renting the shop, and buying clothes and food, a busy woman could have about $200 left at the end of the month."[24]

The working conditions of Japanese prostitutes also resembled those of Chinese prostitutes. Japanese prostitutes worked daily from seven o'clock in the evening to midnight. Their shops were usually shedlike buildings standing in rows along the street. Each building had a frontage of six feet and a depth of twelve feet, which held a low, small glass window. Through the window a guest could examine the women who sat inside and were lit dimly by hand lamps. If he chose a woman, he would enter the sleeping area which was behind a partition of wood.[25]

In contrast to Chinese and Japanese prostitutes, many Caucasian prostitutes worked as independent professionals. They did very well, especially during the boom days, when competition was limited and prices were high. One madam on the mining frontier, according to historian Julie Roy Jeffrey, made one hundred thousand dollars within less than a year.[26] These women were high-class prostitutes and considered their occupation a business. Obviously, Chinese prostitutes did not enjoy such a fate. Yet, regardless of racial and rank differences in the prostitution business, all prostitutes, as suggested by historian Ruth Rosen, regarded their trade as a form of work: an obvious means of economic survival which occasionally even offered some small degree of upward mobility.[27]

Like Chinese "coolies" who were indispensable for America's western development, these early Chinese prostitutes were an important labor force within Chinatown's economy. Lucie Cheng Hirata's study on Chinese prostitutes in nineteenth-century California has indicated that "at an average of thirty-eight cents per customer and seven customers per day, a lower-grade prostitute would earn about $850 per year and $3,404 after four years of servitude." Considering the average size of the brothel, which was about nine women in 1870, the owner could gross $7,650 per year. "Subtracting rent and maintenance of the women, the owner would end up with an average of no less than $5,000." Hirata has argued that Chinese prostitution played a vital role in maintaining a bachelor society, a convenient source of cheap labor for American capital. She has also suggested that many Chinese entrepreneurs utilized prostitutes not only in providing sexual services but also in working in the garment industry during the day, in order to amass capital for undertaking larger ventures.[28] Therefore, Chinese prostitutes were not only victims of sexual oppression, but also victims of economic and class exploitation.

Disturbed by the evil of prostitution, middle-class Protestant women joined together to try to establish female moral authority in the cities of the American West. While their projects took many forms, the most common was the establishment of rescue homes, institutions designed to provide a loving, home-like atmosphere in which unfortunate women rescued from predatory men might live under the watchful eyes of white, middle-class Protestant women.

The Presbyterian Mission Home in San Francisco, established by the Women's Occidental Board in 1874, was one such institution in the West.[29] Its directors, Margaret Culbertson and Donaldina Cameron, successfully conducted numerous rescue raids with help from police and used press coverage of the raid to turn public opinion against Chinese prostitution. Lilac Chen's story provided a graphic illustration of the rescue work. She was a slave girl in the biggest dive in the San Francisco Chinatown and later was sold to a vicious woman as a house servant. On one occasion, as discussed earlier in this chapter, her master burned her on the arm with a red hot iron tong. Then a white woman reported this case to the Mission Home and the Home sent people to rescue her:

> . . . . they described me much bigger than I was so when they came they didn't recognize me. And then the woman who reported to the mission said, "why didn't you take her? She's the girl," and then they came back again. But even then, they weren't sure that I was the one, so they undressed me and examined my body and found where the woman had beaten me black and blue all over. And then they took me to the home. Oh, it was in the pouring rain! I was scared to death. You know, change from change, and all strangers, and I didn't know where I was going. Away from my own people and in the pouring rain. And they took me, a fat policeman carried me all the way from Jackson Street, where I was staying, to Sacramento Street to the mission, Cameron House. So I got my freedom there.[30]

Chun Loie's story recorded by Margaret Culbertson, the first director of the Mission Home, also narrated this fight against "yellow slave trade." On March 25, 1892 she wrote:

> I received word in the afternoon that a little girl about 9 years old at the N.W. corner of Clay & Dupond Sts. was being badly beaten. I got the police went to the house and brot [brought] her to the home—she was in pitiable condition, two cuts from a hatchet were vizable [visible] on her head—her mouth, face and hands badly swollen from punishment she had received from her cruel mistress.[31]

Some rescued slave girls courageously testified in court, as documented in Carol Green Wilson's *Chinatown Quest*. Yute Ying, a ten-year-old slave girl in San Francisco, was brutally abused by her master. After she was rescued by Miss Cameron, she was called in front of the grand jury of San Francisco to testify the evils of the slave trade. She told the jury that even tiny children were brought to the United States as slaves. She greatly impressed the jurors by her quick, intelligent answers, and her neat appearance.[32]

Although the Mission Home could only shelter the limited number of Chinese slave girls from being physically abused and economically exploited, the rescue movement certainly contributed to the decline of the Chinese sex industry in California after the 1870s.

Merchant Wives

While single Chinese women were forced to be domestic servants or prostitutes, married Chinese women (most likely merchant wives) were confined at home as housewives. Although the total number of Chinese adult women decreased, those keeping house doubled from 753 (21 percent) in 1870 to 1,445 (46 percent) in 1880 according to census figures. Due to the pressure from the anti-prostitution campaign in California, many prostitutes married Chinesemen and became housewives. This increased proportion of married women in 1880 very likely reflected a number of former prostitutes.

Most of the married women were wives of merchants.[33] They usually lived in secluded areas, upstairs from their families' businesses. Their quarters were generally furnished with Chinese tables and chairs and decorated with Chinese ornaments.[34] Until they gave birth to a child, they were rarely seen outside their home.[35] After they had children, their major responsibility was raising children. Though merchant wives were the closest Chinese equivalent to the middle-class white women, Protestant women were struck by the former's situation and described the lives of merchants' wives as "extreme examples of domestic confinement." Mission workers reported that Chinese women were "so hemmed in by cultural prescriptions and by their own bound feet that 'very few of them are allowed to go on the streets, and the vast majority never leave their rooms'."[36]

Generally, rich merchants' wives had relatively easier lives. They did not have to perform daily house maintenance tasks of cooking, cleaning, and washing, since most well-to-do merchant families had house servants. They usually spent their spare time doing needlework, which could be used as presents for relatives and friends or as ornaments on caps for husband and children.[37]

Only well-to-do merchants' wives could live a leisurely life. The majority of married Chinese women confronted greater hardship.

As wives of laundrymen, restaurant owners, grocers, cooks, and laborers, these married women had to work side by side with their husbands, in addition to their daily household chores.

During the late-nineteenth and early-twentieth centuries, the laundering business had been a predominant occupation of the Chinese in the United States. After the 1870s, prejudice against Chinese immigrants from American society effectively cut them out of the rest of the labor market. Persecuted and harassed, the Chinese could not find jobs, and they were forced to rely on their own resources. When they were excluded from the gold mines in the hills, "they found an equally lucrative gold mine in the city." They realized that in setting up laundries, they did not have to seek jobs in established industries or incur the risk of heavy capital investment. All they needed for the business were a scrub board, soap, an iron, and an ironing board.[38] They would canvass a neighborhood, seek out a low-rent location, and open a business. An interview in Paul Chan Pang Siu's study revealed how this process worked:

> I don't know how the laundry became a Chinese enterprise in this country. But I think they just learned it from each other. After all, laundry work is not difficult; it requires no high skill. All one has to do is watch how others do it. It would not take long either.
>
> In the old days, some of those fellows were really ignorant though. They did not know even how to write down numbers. When a bundle of laundry was done, he had to put down the amount charged for the work. Being so illiterate, he could not write the numbers. He had a way though and what a way! See, he would draw a circle as big as half dollar coin to represent a half dollar, and a circle as big as a dime for a dime, and so on. When the customers came in to call for their laundry, they would catch on to the meaning of the circles and pay accordingly. It is indeed laughable.[39]

The Chinese laundry shop was not merely a place of work, but also a place for sleeping and cooking. According to Siu, the typical interior arrangement of the Chinese laundry consisted of four parts. First was the front section. It usually occupied one-third of the space of the house, functioning as the office-workshop of the laundryman. In this section, the laundryman ironed and labeled laundry, and waited on his customers. Here he kept the necessities for his business: the ironing bed, the abacus, the laundry shelves, the lock-counter, and secret cash drawer. Second, immediately behind the curtained doorway at the center of the house, usually between the laundry shelves, were the living quarters. Third, the drying room was located in the center or rear part of the house. In the center of the room was an old-fashioned coal stove, used for drying the wet laundry. About a dozen strong wires were strung across in parallel lines to put up the wet laundry. Finally, there was the rear section, where almost all the laundryman's machines were located, including the washing machine, washing sink, and steam boiler.[40]

This physical arrangement of a Chinese hand laundry in the late-nineteenth and early-twentieth century was not only typical in major urban Chinese communities of San Francisco, New York, and Chicago, but also common in remote small towns where the Chinese population was scarce. In Kirksville, a rural town located in the northeastern corner of Missouri, two Chinese men, Young Kee and Charlie Young, started a hand laundry in 1913. They worked in the laundry and lived behind their shop.[41] Clearly, to minimize costs and maximize savings, Chinese laundry operators had to work in crammed quarters and sometimes under hazardous conditions.

For a wife of a laundryman, her life was not easier than that of her husband. Her home was in the back of the laundry, where she slept, cooked, and tended her children. The quarters were humid and dim in all seasons. When she was not busy with her domestic chores, she was expected to help with the laundry work. Her daily life was characterized by long hours, drudgery, and intense loneliness. The only people she saw were customers who brought in their parcels and reclaimed them when they were finished. As depicted in Maxine Hong Kingston's *The Woman Warrior*, Brave Orchid, wife of a New York laundryman, worked at the laundry from 6:30 in the morning until midnight. She shifted her baby from an ironing table to a shelf between packages. The dust from socks and handkerchiefs choked her and made her cough everyday.[42] The wives of laundrymen were easily worn out from hard work and suffered physical weariness and emotional stress.[43]

Like laundries, restaurants were one of the most important businesses for the Chinese in the United States. Initially, Chinese restaurants started as a service for the bachelor communities of Chinese immigrants in isolated ranches, logging camps, mining towns, and other areas where Chinese men and women were willing to cook. When the Chinese eating places gradually drew a number of non-Chinese eaters, a few resourceful Chinese quickly realized that they could make cooking a business that would provide them a stable income. In the 1890s, Chinese restaurants sprouted in the United States in many places.[44] Most small Chinese restaurants were run as husband-wife businesses; the husband served as cook and dishwasher in the kitchen, while the wife worked as waitress, barmaid, and cashier in the front.

Some Chinese American women became successful proprietors despite the harsh environment. Sue Fawn Chung's case study of Gue Gim Wah provided a good example of the early Chinese businesswomen. In her article "Gue Gim Wah: Pioneering Chinese American Woman of Nevada," Sue Fawn Chung has chronicled the life of Gue Gim Wah, a pioneer Chinese American woman who settled in a small mining town in Nevada. Her story indicated that Chinese American women could survive tough environments and succeed. Gue Gim was born in 1900 in Lin Lun Li, a village near Canton, and brought to the United States in 1912 by her father, Ng Louie Der, a merchant in San Francisco. In 1916, Gue Gim married Tom Fook Wah, manager of a boarding house and restaurant in Prince, Nevada. In 1930, Gue Gim Wah began to help her husband run a boarding house for Chinese miners in the area. After she accumulated enough capital and experience, she opened her own restaurant at the Prince and Caselton Mine in 1942. She worked long hours during the war years. Since the mines operated three shifts a day, she worked and served all three shifts by herself. Besides long working hours, she worried about supplies, which were difficult to obtain. She collected food stamps from the miners in order to buy the necessary items, and this resulted in a good deal of bookkeeping and handling. She was so busy and tired everyday that sometimes she would fall asleep in a chair in her restaurant.

Engaged in her restaurant business for over half-a-century, Gue Gim Wah served the local Chinese and American communities as well. Her ability gave her regional fame and her fine cooking attracted many white patrons. During the war years, Herbert Hoover, one of Prince and Caselton area mine owners, became a great fan of hers. Whenever he was in the general vicinity, he would charter a special airplane to fly to her restaurant, Wah's Cafe. Her success was highly recognized. On October 31, 1980 in celebration of Nevada's 116 years of statehood, Gue Gim Wah was invited to serve as the grand marshal for the Nevada Day Parade in the state capital, Carson City. She was the first person of Asian ancestry and the second woman to be honored by the state.[45]

The grocery business ranked as a distant third occupation for Chinese immigrants before the 1940s, although it was one of the major enterprises of the Chinese in some southern and western states.[46] Chinese grocery stores provided Chinese ingredients for cooking and other goods for the need of Chinese communities. Unlike the Chinese restaurants, the Chinese grocery stores found their clientele primarily among Chinese and other Asian immigrants. They were mostly located in Chinatowns and Asian communities.

The operation of Chinese grocery businesses varied according to sizes. The larger Chinese firms not merely sold Chinese groceries, but also general merchandise. During the late-nineteenth and early-twentieth century, the larger Chinese firms usually had more than five partners with each owning a share from $500 to $1,500. They sold goods worth between $50,000 to $150,000 annually.[47] The following examples depict how big Chinese merchandise houses were operated. Sun Fat Company, known as the Chinese Bargain Store located at 2536 Main Street in San Francisco, was a merchandise house selling Chinese drygoods. It was established in the beginning of the century and reorganized in 1918. By 1921 the company had nine partners and seven of them actively participated in the operation of the business. Of the seven active partners, one served as manager with a share of $1,500, one as treasurer also

Figure 2.3. Employees of Kong Wo Sang Co., a Chinese store selling general merchandise in New Castle, California, 1926. Courtesy National Archives-Pacific Sierra Region, San Bruno, California.

with a share of $1,500, and the rest as bookkeeper and salesmen with shares ranging from $500 to $1,000. The manager received a salary of $70, the treasurer and bookkeeper $65, and the rest of the members $60 a month. All company members lived on the second floor over the store, where they ate and slept. A cook was paid $60 a month to cook for them.[48]

Similarly, Tong Sang Company, located at 383-385 9th Street of Oakland, was established in the late-nineteenth century selling gen-

Figure 2.4. Chinese merchant wife and child, 1920s. Collection of the Chinese Cultural Center, San Francisco. Courtesy Ethnic Studies Library at the University of California, Berkeley.

eral merchandise. In 1923, it had eighteen partners with each hold-ing a share of $1,000. Among them, eleven were active members, including a manager, a buyer, a broker, and eight salesmen. The company normally had an average annual business transaction of $150,000, and the profit allowed the company to pay its members a bonus of $100 each per year. Each member, including the manager, was paid $50 a month. The company hired a cook at $45 a month to cook meals for all the members. It also employed a white man to drive the company-owned truck for its delivery service.[49]

Different from the above two firms, the Henry Company of 670 Commercial Street in San Francisco was a wholesale busi-ness dealing with imports and exports. As of 1932, it had eighteen partners, and six of them were active. This included a manager with a share of $2,000, a president with a share of $4,000, and four salesmen with shares ranging from $500 to $2,500. The com-pany paid its members salaries from $55 (salesmen) to $75 (presi-dent and manager) a month. One member slept on the premises of the firm, and the rest only ate there and shared cooking responsibilities.[50]

While the larger firms seemed to have pooled capital and manpower, with each member having well-defined responsibilities

Figure 2.5. A Chinese girl and her young siblings outside of their family store, Kong Wo Sang Co. in New Castle, California, 1926. Courtesy National Archives-Pacific Sierra Region, San Bruno, California.

Figure 2.6. Map of Chinese firms on Jackson Street (partial), Chinatown, San Francisco, 1894. Courtesy National Archives-Pacific Sierra Region, San Bruno, California.

and receiving a regular salary, many smaller Chinese stores were run as family businesses with unpaid family members meeting the demand of labor needed for keeping the stores. As wives of grocers, the women worked along with their husbands, packing, stocking, and selling goods. As indicated in Connie Young Yu's family history, Chin Shee, Yu's great-grandmother, arrived in San Francisco in 1876 to join her husband, a successful merchant of a Chinese dryfood store. She lived in the rear of the store where she bore six children. She not only took care of her children, but also helped with her husband's business. All the hard work and responsibilities, Yu has noted, made her face appear "careworn" in middle-age.[51]

Most of the small grocers knew very little English, barely enough to tell customers the price of their goods. As a Hawaiian Chinese girl, Lily Chan noted, "they [her parents] did not know the English language, but they know enough as to keep a store."[52] Their businesses usually only made a marginal profit, for their clientele, mainly Chinese, were a minority. Their diligence, frugality, and shrewdness, however, enabled them to survive in the harsh environment.

Chinese women were not always passive and unpaid laborers of the family business; some women of energy and ability even had shares in business and became business partners of their husbands. Gee Guock Shee is a good example of a strong and capable early Chinese businesswoman (also see the previous chapter). She was born in San Francisco in 1873 and married Yee Ho Wo in San Mateo, California when she was eighteen years old. After her son was old enough to be left alone, she joined the family business, Yee Hing & Co., a store selling general merchandise. Being a woman, her name and interest were not mentioned in the business partners' list, although she had an equal share of $500 in the company. Jointly having the largest share in Yee Hing & Co., she and her husband were virtually the proprietors of the firm. As a saleswoman and cashier, she played a vital role in Yee Hing & Co. Everyday, she stood behind the counter looking after the business, took care of the money that came in, and had her husband enter the money into books. Apparently, she served as a manager, and her husband was the bookkeeper in the business. Gee Guok Shee was also responsible for the monetary transaction of the firm. She went to the San Mateo Bank regularly to deposit or withdraw money for the firm, though always accompanied by one of the male members of the company. Without any formal education, she was able to become a successful businesswoman. She impressed many people in San Mateo, including San Mateo Bank cashier Henry W. Hagan and the City Marshal M. F. Boland.[53]

Apart from the laundry, restaurant, and grocery businesses, the garment business proved to be a vital profession for early Chinese immigrant women. As was the case with Jewish immigrant women, it started as family sewing. In the late-nineteenth and early-twentieth century, married Chinese immigrant women sewed or mended clothes for Chinese bachelors at home to supplement their family income. The immigration documents from the Office of the Collector of Customs at San Francisco Port revealed that sewing was a common occupation for Chinese women in the late-nineteenth and early-twentieth century. Low How See, one of the earliest Chinese women in San Francisco, worked as a seamstress. "I worked in my room," she told the immigration official when she was called to the office of the Collector of Customs as witness for the entry of a Chinese woman on March 26, 1896. "My friend who know me well bring me work to do to my room."[54] Other married Chinese women Chun Shee, Jow Shee, and Tai See also indicated that they were seamstresses when asked about their occupation.[55]

Some even ran a tailor's shop in which both husband and wife were involved. The oldest Chinese woman in Butte, Montana reminisced:

> I made all my pin money sewing dozens upon dozens of [loose-fitting Chinese style] suits for the merchandise stores. I was always busy. The suits even went to men outside of Butte: they would send in their orders. As soon as I made a dozen, I would start on another. Practically all of the women of the community sewed like I did, or mended. We had all we could do.
>
> I made two kind of suits; washable ones for every day and woolen ones for special occasions. I never saw the men but my husband took orders at our store. He wrote down the measurements; I made the garments and sent them back through my husband. I saved several thousand dollars doing this until the [1911] Revolution.[56]

While some women set up a tailor business at home, more women went to a garment shop to work. Mrs. C's mother went to a sewing factory to work for ten years after her children grew older.[57] The garment shops in the late-nineteenth and early-twentieth century varied by size. The smaller ones had only a couple of workers. For instance, Sun Fat Company, a drygood store in San Francisco (discussed earlier in this section), also hired two women employees, Jow Shee and Wong Shee, to operate its sewing machines. Unlike the male employees of the company who were paid a monthly salary of $60, Jow Shee and Wong Shee were paid by the piece.[58] Apparently, San Fat Company not only sold Chinese groceries, but also owned a small garment factory. Many of the garment shops consisted of a dozen seamstresses, occupying one floor in a building crowded with sewing machines. The women were paid by the piece at a very low rate of a few cents each. Mrs. S reminisced about her mother's experience as a seamstress:

> My mother and some other ladies did sewing in a place. They [contractors] rented a store and set up machines. About a dozen women worked there. My mother worked during the day. She came back to cook lunch for us. The hours were very flexible . . . They were paid by piece. The pay was low, but it's still something.[59]

This "flexibility" of hours was one important factor to attract women to work in garment shops despite the low pay and poor working conditions. This still remains a common characteristic in today's major garment industry in New York, Los Angeles, and San Francisco bay area, which primarily employs Asian immigrant women.[60] In order to fulfill their household responsibility while increasing family income, these women considered the "flexibility" of garment shops a compensation for the low pay.

The sewing business, like the restaurant business, met the basic need of Chinese bachelors. Money made from sewing became a necessary part of the family income. As Roger Daniels has pointed out, the fact that many married Chinese women engaged in a sewing business "illustrates an important and often unnoticed factor in Asian American economic success: that is, the contribution made by Asian American married women at a time when most married women in this country were not in the labor force."[61]

Not only did married Chinese women sew as a business, but Chinese prostitutes were forced as well to sew in their free time during the day. As discussed in the previous section of the chapter, Lucie Cheng Hirata's study has revealed that the prostitutes in nineteenth-century California were assigned to sewing and other forms of work during the day while they had to hawk their bodies at night.[62]

Like other ethnic women in the garment industry, Chinese garment women workers also attempted to unionize to improve their working conditions. Records showed that Chinese women garment workers engaged in strikes in the 1930s. The most publicized strike of Chinese women workers came in early 1938 when the Chinese Ladies Garment Workers Unions selected San Francisco National Dollar Stores as its target. When the strike occurred, the National Dollar Stores paid its Chinese garment women workers between $4 and $16 per week; union wages for the same work ranged from $19 to $30 per week.[63] In November 1937, the workers presented their demand for better pay to the owner but failed. Angered by the owner's uncompromising position, the workers organized the International Ladies Garment Workers Union (ILGWU) Local 341, known as the Chinese Ladies Garment Workers Union. This event indicated that at least by 1937 Chinese women garment workers had organized in an independent local union chapter, and had taken collective action, as opposed to the conventional view of Chinese women being invisible in the American union movement. Jennie Maytas, an organizer for the ILGWU, later noted:

> . . . we organized the Chinese into a separate local, but not because we believed in segregation. We offered to the Chinese that they could either have a separate local or they could come in with 101 [the San Francisco local of ILGWU], but if they thought that this would prove to their Chinese people that they were autonomous, that we weren't meaning to take any advantage away from them to give to white workers, they could have a local of their own . . . They wanted their own local.[64]

On February 26, 1938, the 108 members of the ILGWU Local 341 began to picket the factory and three Dollar Stores. The strikers received moral and financial support of the community and the ILGWU. After thirteen weeks of picketing, an agreement was signed on June 8, 1938. It provided a five percent increase in weekly wages, pay for Labor Day, and a $14 per week minimum wage.[65]

Students

Academic life was a large part of Chinese female students' experiences in America. Just as most Chinese male students concentrated in such practical fields as business administration, chemistry, and engineering, most Chinese female students also chose courses that would be useful in their future careers. According to a survey by the China Institute in America, the top ten courses of study chosen by Chinese female students were, in descending order, (1) education, (2) sociology and chemistry, (3) home economics, (4) English, (5) general arts, (6) music, (7) history, (8) psychology and nursing, (9) mathematics, and (10) biology, art and archaeology, and medicine.[66] Many Chinese female students showed outstanding academic performance.[67] Mayling Soong, the third Soong sister, for example, majored in English literature with a philosophy minor at Wellesley College in Massachusetts (1913–1917). In her senior year she was named a Durant Scholar, the highest academic honor conferred by the college.[68]

The pioneer Chinese female students also participated in extracurricular activities such as YWCA programs, prayer meetings, and club meetings.[69] The Soong sisters, especially Mayling, were very active outside of their classrooms. They went to church regularly, joined the tennis club, and traveled around the country during the summers.[70]

More importantly, some Chinese female students were concerned about their country and were conscious of their future roles in China. In 1911, Chingling Soong, the second Soong sister, wrote an essay for the college magazine, *The Wesleyan*, entitled "The Influence of Foreign-Educated Students on China." She recommended a western type of government in China and suggested that returned Chinese students had improved the quality of Chinese officialdom.[71]

Similar to the Chinese women garment workers, the Chinese female students of this period also began to show their political clout and became an important part of Chinese student organizations. The Chinese students in American universities and colleges organized local student clubs as early as 1911. On the basis of these clubs, a national Chinese student organization called the Chinese Student Alliance was formed later. The Alliance held a conference for Chinese students each summer and had "annual," "quarterly," and "monthly" publications that reported the news of student activities and presented substantial articles reflecting Chinese students' thinking and ideas.[72] Chinese female students not only participated in the activities of the Alliance, but also declared in the Alliance's publications their positions on political issues in China. They were especially concerned about China's future and the women's liberation movement there. In June 1922, Rosalind Mei-Tsung Li, a Chinese female student, published an article entitled "The Chinese Revolution and the Chinese Women" in *The*

Chinese Students' Monthly. Li criticized rigid Chinese social etiquette and morals and Christian dogmas as well. She called for Chinese girls to rid themselves of social restrictions and to renew their lives.

> The chief difference between the Chinese men students and the Chinese women students in America is, so far as my intuition can tell, that the former have no ideals and the latter have. . . . The amazing uniformity of personality of Chinese women students in America shows that they have all been dominated by the same ideals. As I analyze them carefully, I find that there are two: Correctness and Usefulness. . . .
>
> The uniform yellow of Chinese social etiquette and morals is very much like frost in April. Added to all this, most of us have had the privilege of a regimented education in a missionary school where our own puritanism is made doubly, nay triply, "Grundyish" by the Old Testament and the American frontier tradition. We were bound in our homes and society and killed, cured, and ossified in the missionary school. The wonder is that we still walk.
>
> If the Chinese Revolution is to be something which our descendants shall be proud of, it must mean a renewal of life. Of course, it cannot renew life in China if it does not touch the broad and populous realm of the womanhood of China.[73]

Chinese female students' quest for emancipation in political, professional, and personal realms were part of the general effort for "enlightenment" by modern Chinese intellectuals at the time. Their articulating bold criticism of social norms was in striking contrast to other Chinese immigrant women, who at this time were still subjected to all the traditional restrictions on women and were unaware of women's emancipation. Though a small proportion of Chinese women in the United States, these Chinese female students very likely projected a different and more positive image of Chinese women in America during the early years of their presence.

Many of the pioneer Chinese female students returned to China after the completion of their education or training, and became prominent in their professions. The first four recorded Chinese female students who received medical degrees from American colleges became the earliest women doctors in China upon their return.[74] Other Chinese female students also became pioneers in their professions in China. Ms. C's mother, for instance, received her degree in sociology from Denision University in Ohio in 1930, after which she returned to China and taught English at several leading universities. In 1936, she and her husband established South China College in Hong Kong. During the Japanese occupation of Hong Kong, the couple moved the college to China. Prior to the Communists' takeover of China in 1949, they moved the college back to Hong Kong again. In 1949, she began to teach at Chung Chi College (the present Chinese University of Hong Kong), and later became the Dean of Women's College there.[75]

Similarly, the Soong sisters utilized their education in America by devoting their lives to Chinese politics. Chingling Soong returned to China after receiving her degree in philosophy at Wesleyan College in 1913. She served as Sun Yat-sen's personal secretary and assisted his revolutionary career. After Sun Yat-sen's death, she continued to support her husband's cause and became a highly revered Chinese woman leader. Mayling Soong had the same ambition as her sister. After her marriage to Chiang Kai-shek, president of the Republic of China, in 1927, she assisted Chiang's political career as his personal secretary and interpreter. As a leader of Chinese women, she led the Women's Department in Chiang's government in the 1930s. As an envoy of Chiang, she visited the United States during World War II to gain American support for the Nationalist government.[76]

Farm Wives

While the Chinese immigrant women in urban areas engaged in the above occupations, their counterparts in rural settings shared farming with their husbands in addition to their domestic duties. In order to escape the anti-Chinese sentiments, after the passage of the Chinese Exclusion Act in 1882, many Chinese men moved to remote rural areas and their women followed them.

Anti-Chinese legislation, however, continued to plague the Chinese in rural areas. During the last two decades of the nineteenth century, American farmers organized to protect their interest. Frustrated midwestern and western farmers found the prohibition of landownership by aliens an easy solution to their economic difficulties, and they consequently launched an alien land law movement.[77] Between 1885 and 1895, twelve states in the midwest and west passed alien land laws. Indiana first passed a comprehensive alien land law in 1885. Illinois, Colorado, Wisconsin, Nebraska, and Minnesota followed Indiana's example in 1887. The Iowa legislature passed a similar law in 1888. Two years later, Washington

joined the movement. In 1891, Kansas, Texas, and Idaho also
adopted alien land laws. In 1895, Missouri became the last state to
participate in the alien land movement of the nineteenth century.[78]
Although the nineteenth century alien land movement was aimed
primarily at large absentee landowners from Europe and most of
the alien land laws were repealed by the legislatures of these states
by the end of the century, it set an example for the later alien land
law in California. Beginning in 1913, this law prohibited "aliens
ineligible to citizenship," namely, Chinese, Japanese, Koreans, and
Asian Indians, from owning land. In Washington, a similar law
was passed in 1921. Chinese farmers, however, managed to till
land by vesting title or lease in the name of their American-born
children.

Most of the Chinese who engaged in farming were in California, Oregon, Nevada, Washington, and Arizona. In California most
farmers produced fruits, potatoes, vegetables, wheat, rice, and cotton, while in Oregon they planted hops, mainly in the Willamette
Valley. Chinese cotton plantations were concentrated in Arizona.[79]
According to the 1910 U.S. Census, of a total 17,200 Chinese farmers, 11,986 were in California, 799 in Oregon, 783 in Nevada, 706
in Washington, 605 in Arizona, 473 in Idaho, 404 in Montana, 166
in Mississippi, 146 in New Mexico, 113 in New York, and 107 in
New Jersey. Only 706 of them had their own farms. Most leased or
had share of land with white landowners. Mar Goon Sow, for example, a Chinese farmer in Sacramento River, owned a share of
$1,000 of a 160 acre piece of land on which he worked since 1900.
From his share he could earn $800 a year and send about ten
percent of his earnings to China to support his wife and children
there. After his children in China died of illness, he arranged for
his wife, Chan Shee, to come to America to join him.[80]

Following the traditional division of labor, most farm wives
engaged in housework. They cleaned the houses, cooked the meals,
raised the children, and even took in boarders to help with the
family income. In addition to their own housework, they gardened
and tended livestock. Some of the Chinese farmers' wives took part
in farm work. In Georgiana, California, a farm family was headed
by Gee Chom, aged thirty-seven. The family included his wife Kee,
aged twenty-three, "who had been in the United States since she
was five years old and was one of the few women working as a farm
laborer" in 1900.[81]

This expansion of women's labor was more common and noticeable in Hawaii. Unlike the mainland immigrant laborers, Chinese

laborers in Hawaii were encouraged to bring their wives, who were paid to work in rice plantations. Women were "paid an advance bonus of $20 and were required to do light labor, such as cane cutting and stripping, in exchange for free passage, room and board, and a monthly wage of $3."[82] These farm wives worked shoulder to shoulder with their husbands. After the three to five year contract, these Chinese laborers could buy a small farm to cultivate. This process was exemplified in the family history of a high school student in Hawaii:

> The call for labor [in Hawaii] was sent to China in 1890. My father answered it to escape the monotony and lack of opportunity in the home land. He, his wife, two sons and a daughter left the old home and his mother for Macao in 1891. They were [for] four months in the sailing vessel, finally landing at Mahukona in Hawaii. They were taken by train straight to their quarters in the Hawaii plantation. The camps were long rows of rude structures housing several families each. Each family was assigned to a room which was used for dining, sleeping and entertaining. After the three years of labor, my father bought a farm in Halawa. . . .[83]

However, not all Chinese laborers who worked in rice and sugar plantations were fortunate enough to become landowners. In fact many remained wage laborers of rice or sugar plantations for their entire lives and were never able to establish families in Hawaii.[84]

With a strange environment, poor living conditions, and endless drudgery, life was tough for these Chinese wives. But it was much harsher for widowed Chinese women. They often had the double burden of single motherhood. Moreover, handicapped in language and isolated by the white communities, widowed Chinese women had to confront more hardship than the white widows. The same high school student quoted earlier in Hawaii wrote:

> Hard time as I have never experienced before I experienced after the death of my father. My brother had to leave school and go to work; my sister did too to stay at home to look after the house and care for younger ones while my mother looked after the animals. . . . A year after my father's death, my mother sold what we owned and came to Honolulu where her two children were, thinking that she might give us better opportunities.[85]

Compared to the Chinese immigrant women in urban Chinatowns, where they were isolated and discriminated against, the Chinese women in rural areas were better integrated and assimilated into local American society. In these areas, due to the absence of large Chinese concentrations, Chinese were forced to mix with others in the population. May Seen, a pioneer Chinese woman in Minnesota, acculturated very well in the local larger society. "As the only Chinese woman living in Minnesota for many years, she became acquainted with the upper class women of the Lowry Hill area in Minneapolis, where her husband delivered laundry in a colorful horse-drawn wagon. Among the women who took an interest in her was Maybeth Hurd Paige, the first woman in the Minnesota legislature."[86] Mary Mammon, a dancer in a Chinese nightclub, recalled her childhood: "I was born in a small town in Arizona. We have to mingle with all other population there, which were most whites. Our traditions were American traditions and our Chinese traditions were not really that strong."[87] Noel Toy, another dancer in the same Chinese nightclub, had a similar experience. "We were the only Chinese family there [a small town in San Francisco bay area]," she told an interviewer, "so consequently I don't know too many Chinese. I was brought up purely Caucasian, Western. When I went to a junior college, I saw an Oriental woman. I said, an Oriental! My gosh, an Oriental woman! I never thought myself one."[88]

White Americans in rural areas were more curious and less hostile to Chinese than their counterparts in big cities. This more friendly environment helped accelerate the assimilation of Chinese American women into the larger society. In 1915 Gue Gim, at the age of fifteen, married Tom Fook Wah, a forty-three-year-old Chinese bachelor in Prince, Nevada. She helped her husband with cooking and serving in his boardinghouse restaurant. Realizing that education was important for her adjustment to a new world, she attended the local Prince School. The children at the Prince School were very warm toward her and helped her with English. In addition to the regular classes, her teacher gave her individual instruction in English. To satisfy the schoolchildren's curiosity about her background, the teacher organized a special program called "A Trip to Asia" in November 1917. Many parents and friends attended the special event and learned about Asian culture. Gue Gim Wah's positive educational experience at the Prince School helped her have a close relation with white American society. She became good friends with Mary Thomas, daughter of Leonard G. Thomas, who was the superintendent of the Combined Metals Reduction Company of the Prince Mine. The friendship between the two women lasted for a lifetime.[89]

These rural Chinese immigrant women showed industry, frugality, friendliness, and competence that earned the respect of their white neighbors. Polly Bemis was the most famous Chinese woman in Idaho history. Her legendary story and her romance with Charlie Bemis were written about in different versions.[90] Polly, originally named Lalu Nathoy, was born into a poor peasant family in Northern China on

Figure 2.7. Polly Bemis with hens in Idaho. Courtesy Ethnic Studies Library at the University of California, Berkeley.

September 11, 1853 and spent her childhood in poverty. When she was eighteen, she was sold to bandits for two bags of seeds by her father.[91] Resold in America for $2500, Polly became a slave of Hong King, a Chinese saloon owner in Warren, Idaho in 1872. She later married Charlie Bemis who bought her freedom in a poker game.[92] With her knowledge of Chinese herbs and her caring nature, she nursed many neighbors' ill children. She even performed surgery to save Charlie Bemis' life.[93] After their marriage in 1894, the couple bought a ranch on the Salmon River.[94] On their farm, Polly grew plums, pears, cherries, strawberries, blackberries, corn, clover, watermelon, and all kinds of garden vegetables. She also raised some chickens, ducks, and a cow. She even became an adept fisherwoman.[95] Polly Bemis survived the harsh frontier life and was adored by the local people because of her pleasant and friendly personality. All of her guests left her boardinghouse with fruit and vegetables they could carry and good memories of her hospitality and generosity.[96]

A similar story unfolded in Oregon. In a lumber camp at Wood, Oregon, a fourteen-year-old Chinese girl married a fifty-year-old Chinese cook in the 1910s. She grew up in San Francisco and had only two years of elementary education. But, within these two years, she learned American ways and assimilated into the local community very well. She was beloved by the women in the camp. Occasionally, she could cure some of her neighbors' ailments by using Chinese herbs.[97]

In Hawaii, as in rural communities on the mainland, many Chinese had close social relationships with Hawaiians. Most Chinese residents during the nineteenth century learned enough Hawaiian to communicate, and many had Hawaiian wives and families.[98] These early intermarriages and patterns of cohabitation perhaps explained the absence of Chinese prostitution and the better assimilation of Chinese immigrants in Hawaii.

With various expectations, Chinese immigrant women in the nineteenth and early-twentieth century discovered that America was not a place full of gold. They also found that they could not enter the industrial labor force like Irish and Eastern European women did. Though restricted by the limited occupational opportunities, these Chinese immigrant women found means of survival through their determination and hard work. Laundry, restaurant, grocery store, sewing, and farming work were basic means of livelihood for these women. Prostitution was also a way of survival. Though excluded from the American labor force, these Chinese women found jobs within their ethnic communities. Their work insured the survival and independence of Chinese communities and their members as well.

Chapter 3

Defining Home and Community

> My father spent many years to save money for his marriage. So when he had enough money to support a family, he was already a middle-aged man. He went to Guangdong, China, to marry my mother when she was sixteen.
>
> —Isabella Chan Chang

Immigrant experiences in a new country could very likely result in changes in family life and family structure for immigrant women. Once in a different environment and a completely new culture, the female exodus found that the relationships between them and their husbands and children were more or less altered. Like women in other immigrant groups, Chinese immigrant women also experienced changes in their family life and family structure.

Although restricted by Confucian ideologies and racial discrimination, early Chinese immigrant women managed to participate in social gatherings such as traditional festivals, family celebrations, and religious activities. Some women were involved in community politics and even concerned about national issues in China.

Family Life

Family Structure

Due to the uneven sex ratio among Chinese immigrant communities and the lack of sources on early Chinese immigrant women, the study of Chinese immigrant families in America has lagged. Most studies of Chinese communities in America have either overlooked the aspect of family life in Chinese immigrant history or treated it in very terse text.[1] This situation continued until the publication of several specialized studies on Chinese families in America during the 1980s. Evelyn Nakano Glenn's essay "Split Household, Small Producer and Dual Wage Earner: An Analysis of Chinese-American Family Strategies" was the first significant study of Chinese families in America.[2] In this work, she asserted that there were three distinct immigrant family types which emerged in different periods in response to particular political and economic conditions: split household, small producer, and dual-wage worker. From 1850 to 1920, the split-household family was the predominant form. In the split-household family, production would be separated from other functions and carried out by a member living far away. The other functions—reproduction, socialization, and the rest of the consumption—would be carried out by the wife and other relatives in the home village. The presence of the second type of Chinese families was evident in the major United States Chinatowns by the 1920s. These families were started primarily by small entrepreneurs such as laundrymen, restaurant owners, and grocers. All family members, including children, worked without wages in a family business.[3] In the third type which appeared after the 1960s, wives and husbands became more or less coequal breadwinners. "The existence of these distinct types," Glenn has concluded, "suggested that characteristics often interpreted as products of Chinese culture actually represented strategies for dealing with conditions of life in the United States."[4]

Similarly, David Beesley has challenged the prevalent notion that no family existed among the early Chinese immigrant laborers in his article "From Chinese to Chinese American: Chinese Women and Families in a Sierra Nevada Town."[5] From census and other data, Beesley has found evidence that some of the Chinese laborers in a Sierra Nevada town with regular income had wives or women with them.[6]

The above studies have confirmed the existence of family life among the early Chinese immigrants. However, such questions as whether women's role in Chinese immigrant families had changed and how the changes occurred still remain unanswered. In this section I argue that in most Chinese immigrant families, women became not only sole female heads of the households but also providers of their families. In performing the above roles, women participated in decision making in family affairs.

First, the structure of Chinese immigrant families gradually shifted as women became the sole female heads of households. A traditional and predominant Chinese family was an extended family in which several generations lived together under the same roof and was ruled by the patriarchal familial authority. Once married, a Chinese woman—the daughter-in-law of her husband's family—had to serve and please every family member, especially the parents-in-law, in order to conform to the social norms of model daughter-in-law, wife, and mother. This predominant family pattern of three generations in one household, however, was not transplanted into America, and Chinese immigrant families in America were mostly nuclear ones. No complete three-generational families were recorded in the 1880s or in all the following censuses. Standing on a strange and sometimes hostile land, Chinese immigrant women and young wives especially discovered that for the first time they headed their households. Having suffered the pain of leaving a familiar surrounding, seasickness for a month, and prolonged interrogation and detention at an American immigration station, they now found that they were no longer subjected to their mothers-in-law and they could work with their husbands to support their families. "It's better to be a woman in America," Helen Hong Wong of San Francisco, California said. "At least you can work here and rule the family along with your husband. In China it's considered a disgrace for a woman to work and it's the mother-in-law who rules."[7]

Chinese immigrant women were not only joint household heads, but also family providers. Although most Chinese women had worked at home in northern China and in the fields in southern China to supplement family income throughout Chinese history, Chinese immigrant women's participation in family economic activities or wage-earning work were essential and indispensable for the survival of their families in the United States. In this sense, their new role could be seen as co-providers of the families, though they were not necessarily making fifty percent of the family incomes. Their contributions to their family economies can not be easily calculated by mathematical means. To most Chinese immigrant women, the focus of their lives was survival through hard work, which was quite different from their lives in China. As an immigrant woman commented in Maxine Hong Kingston's book *The Women Warrior*:

> This is terrible ghost country, where a human being works her life away. . . . I have not stopped working since the day the ship landed. . . . In China I never even had to hang up my own clothes. I shouldn't have left, but your father couldn't have supported you without me. I'm the one with the big muscles.[8]

As noted in the previous chapter, the work conducted by Chinese immigrant women was vital for their family economy. Their wage-earning and nonwage-earning work made survival possible for Chinese immigrant families in a strange land. Therefore, their roles in the family were not only as producers of children but also as providers of a bowl of rice.

This new role reinforced Chinese women's position in families and they began to share decision-making with their husbands. When working jointly with their spouses, immigrant women generally had more input in family affairs and decision-making, as was the case with Irish immigrant women. Historians have found that Irish immigrant men generally experienced a decline in status and power within their families as a result of migration, which pushed women into more authoritative roles than they had experienced in Ireland. The comparatively open range of economic options for many young Irish women made them more influential in family and community.[9] The similar changes were also evident among Chinese immigrant women. For most Chinese immigrants, a family was a basic productive unit, in which husband and wife formed a work team and they were indispensable to each other. The equal sharing of responsibilities enabled the wife to have a higher voice in family decision-making.

In the same light, it is instructive to draw parallels between white frontier women and Chinese immigrant women. In the middle- and late-nineteenth century, the hardships of frontier life forced the husband and wife to work together as a team in order to survive. As a result of this work sharing, the line dividing the actual activities of men and women blurred and, in some cases, disappeared. When women were both practically and emotionally involved in the family economy, their power in the families increased. Therefore, the activities of these self-reliant frontier women defied a number of nineteenth-century stereotypes about women.[10] Similarly, the majority of early Chinese immigrant women whether they lived in urban communities or rural areas, had to raise families and help with husbands' businesses or work in the fields and tend gardens and livestock. Moreover, Chinese immigrant families in urban areas often lived in the back of their family businesses. As in the cases of Gue Gim Wah, Chin Shee, and some other urban Chinese immigrant families, many small Chinese entrepreneurs had converted the rear part of their stores into family quarters.[11] The overlapping of family life and work life made a wife's involvement in family business inevitable. Meanwhile the expansion of the female sphere enhanced Chinese immigrant women's sense of self-esteem and self-confidence. They consequently became more comfortable in sharing family decision-making with their husbands. For both white frontier women and Chinese immigrant women, survival required the involvement of all members of the family. At the same time, the new environment, though unfamiliar and frightening, had fewer cultural restraints than their old societies. Therefore, both internal migration and external emigration provided women with a favorable climate for the expansion of the female sphere.

During the late-nineteenth and early-twentieth centuries most Chinese immigrant women, however, were still careful to pay homage to ideas of male authority. Although immigration elevated a woman's position in her family as she became sole female head and co-provider of the family, moving from China to America did not shake her belief in family solidarity that could only be maintained when a wife was subordinate and compromising. As one Chinese girl in Hawaii noted, her father "was the dominating head of the family," even though her mother played an important role in her family life.[12]

Similar attitudes toward male authority also existed among Italian immigrant families in Buffalo in the late-nineteenth and early-twentieth century. Italian immigrant women preserved their traditional view of marriage and found comfort and security in fulfilling their customary roles in a strange land.[13] Like Italian women, German-speaking immigrant women in the midwest were also continuously subjected to male dominance as they did in the old world, although their contributions to the family economy in the new world had earned them a certain degree of respect and authority.[14]

Individual cases among Korean immigrant women in the early-nineteenth century show a similar pattern of male dominance in the family. Mary Paik Lee, a Korean immigrant women, recalled that her father was the decision-maker of the family, even though her mother worked equally hard to help make the ends meet by taking boarders or laundering for others.[15]

Marital Relation

Very commonly, the family structure for many Chinese immigrants included a married couple in which the husband was usually older than his wife. David Beesley's investigation, involving twenty-seven married Chinese couples in a Sierra Nevada town, has indicated that the average age of the women was twenty-two, while the average age of the men was thirty-one.[16] The documents

from Immigration and Naturalization Service and oral history interviews also suggest the age gap between a married couple being
a common feature of many Chinese immigrant families.

The most obvious and primary reason for this age gap between
marital partners was the American immigration policies before 1943.
These policies effectively reinforced the sexual imbalance among
Chinese immigrants by restricting the entry of Chinese women.
The Page Law of 1875, although applied to women of any race and
nationality engaged in prostitution, was specially designed to single
out Chinese women. The Chinese Exclusion Act in 1882 effectively
banned the entry of Chinese laborers and the wives of Chinese
laborers who were already in the United States. As a result, from
1906 to 1924, only an average of one hundred fifty Chinese women
per year were legally admitted.[17] The Immigration Act of May 26,
1924, based on the ruling of the Supreme Court in the case of
Chang Chan et al v. John D. Nagle on May 25, 1924, excluded
Chinese alien wives of American citizens of Chinese ancestry. Consequently, no Chinese women were admitted from 1924 to 1930.[18]
In 1930, an act relaxed this ban by allowing the entry of alien
Chinese wives as long as the marriage was legally effective before
May 26, 1924. Under this provision, about sixty Chinese women
were admitted each year between 1931 and 1941.[19]

The second reason was the enforcement of anti-miscegenation
laws in many states, which prevented Chinese men from marrying
women outside their own ethnic group.[20] Anti-miscegenation laws
in the United States evolved as a reaction of white society toward
possible racially mixed marriages between whites and blacks resulting from the introduction of black slaves from Africa. In 1661,
Maryland passed the first anti-miscegenation law to prohibit marriages involving white females and black males. Following Maryland, thirty-eight states in the Union passed similar legislation.[21]
In 1850, California lawmakers adopted a miscegenation statute to
prohibit black-white marriages, which was later included in Section
60 of the new Civil Code in 1872. A drastic evolution of anti-
miscegenation laws in California in 1880 also outlawed Chinese-
Caucasian marriages along with black-white marriages. In the same
year, the California legislature introduced Section 69 of the Civil
Code, which restricted the issuance of marriage licenses to unions
between a white and a "Negro, Mulatto, or Mongolian."[22] Although
the generic term "Mongolian" refers to Chinese, Japanese, Koreans, and many other ethnic groups in Asia, the law was designed
to target Chinese, echoing the anti-Chinese cry along the West

Coast. In 1905, to make Sections 60 and 69 consistent and to deal with the fear of the Japanese, another group of Mongolian people, the California legislature amended Section 60 to make marriages between whites and Mongolians "illegal and void."[23] The above anti-miscegenation laws were enacted by the involved states until 1967, when they were finally declared unconstitutional.

Third, the noticeable age difference between Chinese husbands and wives was also due to the financial disability of Chinese men. Many of them worked for almost their entire lifetime to save enough money for a marriage. Consequently, American-born daughters of Chinese families were in demand as prospective brides. Finally, the patriarchal nature of Chinese families determined that a marriage was often a social and economic arrangement between the families of the bride and groom rather than a romantic union between two individuals.

One such marriage arrangement involved a fourteen-year-old second generation Chinese girl in San Francisco in the early 1910s. She was to be married according to her parents' plan. She had to choose between two men, but she had never seen either of them in person. She had only seen their photographs, so she took her parents' advice. One was young, about twenty, and her parents put it this way: "This man is young, he has his way to make, and he has a large family of brothers and sisters. You would be a sort of slave to all of them. This other man is fifty years old, but can give you everything, he has no family. 'Better to be an old man's darling than a young man's slave.'" They told her, too, that a young man would not be content. He would be running around with other women; it was far safer to take an older man, who would settle down. Following her parents' advice, she married the older man, a cook in a lumber camp at Wood, Oregon. The marriage turned out to be an unhappy one.[24]

Another case of arranged marriage involved Gue Gim Wah. At the age of fifteen, Gue Gim married Tom Fook Wah, a forty-three-year-old Chinese restaurant owner in Prince, Nevada who was her father's old friend. Tom Fook Wah was born in the mining town of Marysville, California in 1871. Because his parents died after his birth, he was taken back and raised in China by his aunt. He was readmitted to America in 1892 at the age of twenty-one. After first working as a cook for an American family in Marysville, he opened a boardinghouse in Prince, Nevada. Tom began to settle down and wanted to find a wife by 1915. While visiting his friend Ng Louie Der in San Francisco, he noticed Gue Gim going in and out of their family store and decided to propose marriage to her. He asked to marry Der's daughter and Der, "noticing that the time of marriage had come for Gue Gim and that Tom was a good prospect, agreed." Tom and Gue Gim were married in 1916.[25]

The age difference produced unhappiness in many Chinese immigrant families. Being in almost different generations, each spouse in the marriage had different attitudes, patterns, and values of life. Usually, these young Chinese girls grew up in America and attained some education in American public schools; consequently they were more Americanized than their ill-educated China-born husbands.

In the case of the fourteen-year-old Chinese girl from San Francisco, she was very attractive and had a good disposition, while her husband was suspicious, jealous, and had a horrible temper. She was influenced by American ways even though she only attended the public school for two years, while he was very traditional and resented all her American behavior. As a result, this Chinese girl's life was one long tragedy with him.[26]

In addition to the age gap between married couples, bigamy was another problem that plagued the Chinese immigrant family life. Some Chinese merchants, according to Peggy Pascoe's study, had more than one wife. In these cases, the households were contaminated by "the dark coils of that hydra-headed monster polygamy" and threatened by the explosive undercurrent of jealousy, which was the inevitable outcome of a polygamous marriage.[27] Even with such accounts, polygamy has remained largely unnoted in Asian American studies. The reasons for this void were complex. The most obvious reason, however, has been the absence of documents. The practice was illegal, and consequently no one would admit committing polygamy. In the extended history of Chinese immigration, polygamy resulted in the denial of entry to America of many Chinese immigrant women and caused inevitable problems within many Chinese immigrant families.

The most common form of polygamy was concubinage, which was a natural product of the patriarchal society in traditional China and some other cultures. The origin of concubinage in China was obscure, but it certainly was related to the patriarchal nature of the society, in which only a male heir could secure a family's name to be passed down, keep its fortune intact, and have its social and economic status in the community unchallenged. Confucian teachings systematized the patriarchal beliefs and formalized them into cultural institutions that ruled Chinese society and individuals.

According to the Confucian ideal, "a man without a son was not a dutiful son."[28] A man therefore could legitimately have a concubine or concubines if his wife failed to produce him a male heir. The institution of concubinage was further strengthened and developed during the Song dynasty when urban development and economic prosperity reduced the significance of women's participation in economic activities, and enabled wealthy Chinese gentry-landowners and merchants to enjoy a more leisurely lifestyle.[29] Together with other valuable possessions, concubines signified a man's social status and economic power. Many wealthy Chinese men therefore acquired concubines more as a display of their fortune and power than as objects for their sexual pleasure.

Though this centuries-long feudal practice of polygamy had been challenged several times in Chinese history during the Taiping Rebellion (1850–1864) and the May Fourth Movement of 1919, it was not outlawed until 1950 when the government of the People's Republic of China issued the Marriage Law that legally prohibited polygamy and concubinage.[30] In what was perhaps China's most famous twentieth-century novel, *The Family* (originally published in 1933), Ba Jin (Pa Chin) vividly portrayed a typical feudal patriarchal wealthy Chinese family, the Gao family. Grandfather Gao, the patriarchal family head, and some of his wealthy friends all had concubines.[31]

Polygamy was also an unavoidable ramification of immigration. Before the 1940s, when a more favorable immigrant policy allowed more Chinese women to enter the United States, most Chinese men in the United States had left their families in China. Some of those married Chinese men had two wives, either both in China, or one in China and another in the United States. There were also cases in which, unsatisfied with the arranged marriages by their parents, Chinese men left their families. They later found mates at their will, but never filed legal divorces with their first wives. These practices confused American immigration officials, who consequently denied the entry of Chinese women who were suspected to be involved in a polygamous marriage. The famous Lee Lung case was an example of the tough reaction from the United States immigration office.

Lee Lung, a successful Chinese merchant in Portland, Oregon, went to China in October 1898 with the intention of returning to America with his family. On April 3, 1900, Lee Lung arrived back in Portland, Oregon, from China. The Collector of Customs at Portland permitted Lee Lung to land without hesitation due to the fact that he was an American resident. However, he refused to let his wife, Li Tom Shei, and his nine-year-old daughter, Li A. Tosi, enter the country on the ground of polygamy (Lee Lung had, prior to this marriage, another wife living in China). As a result, Li Tom Shei and Li A. Tosi were held in the detention center for a year. Meanwhile, Lee Lung who, as an affluent merchant, could afford the legal expenses, underwent tedious petitions and appeals.[32] It is unknown if Li Tom Shei and Li A. Tosi were finally released and permitted to land. Yet, it is clear that polygamy made the entry of Chinese women to the United States more difficult than that of Chinese men.

In some cases the married couples were not only involved in polygamy, but also entangled in slave smuggling because of the shortage of money. In 1920, Lum Quong, a Chinese American man from San Francisco, returned to China for a visit. He agreed to bring back a Chinese slave girl for a San Francisco dealer, a woman who paid him in advance. In fact, he was looking for a Chinese wife, and married a woman in her native village. The marriage was not a success, and he therefore left his wife and went to Hong Kong. In Hong Kong he saw Sing Choy at her foster father's store, and proposed marriage through a matchmaker. He concealed the fact that he was commissioned and paid to buy a slave. After six months in Hong Kong, the couple prepared to return to America. Lum Quong's sister-in-law then appeared, asking Sing Choy to send money to her husband's first wife. Shocked and distressed, Sing Choy told her parents about Lum Quong's deception and they questioned him. "He promised," the girl told the court later, "that I was to live respectably in America as his wife. . . ." The couple finally sailed to America. After arriving in America, Lum Quong wept when he informed his wife of his promise to buy a slave. He said that he could not repay the money he had received, and that he was being harassed as a result. He tried to borrow money from a kinsman but failed. After they had lived in San Francisco for only three months, Lum Quong surrendered Sing Choy to the dealer. The woman was forced into prostitution, and "bound to work for three years to repay the money her husband had received."[33]

Chinese women were not always passive and oppressed parties in marriages. Some Chinese women ran away from unhappy marriages and found mates at their will. In the 1910s, an American-born Chinese girl from Portland married a Chinese man in Butte, Montana at her parents' insistence. Her marriage became so intolerable that she deserted her husband, returned to Portland, and ran away with another Chinese man. According to later reports, she was happily settled in Shanghai.³⁴ Another Chinese woman in Butte, Montana, the mother of nine children, eloped with her husband's clan relative. Her relatives in Butte "disowned" her for they regarded her act as a shame to her clan. The husband attempted to arouse community opinion with the intention of gaining revenge. Fortunately, "the incident occurred at a time when the community's spirit was disheartened by the war in China." Failing at revenge, the husband left the city and settled in a coastal Chinatown with his two eldest children. The remaining younger children followed their mother to Chicago.³⁵

Despite anti-miscegenation laws, a small number of interracial marriages existed among Chinese Americans. For those Chinese men who married non-Chinese women, the intermarriage usually occurred among small entrepreneurs or laborers. The racial and ethnic background of their wives varied from region to region.³⁶

In the South, most Chinese men were laborers from California or Cuba recruited to the South by railroad companies or sugar plantations. They found wives among black women, and Irish or French immigrant women. The 1880 census for Louisiana indicated that among the 489 Chinese in the state, thirty-five were married, widowed, or divorced. Of the married Chinese men, only four had a Chinese wife. The remaining Chinese men married non-Chinese women, among whom four had married mulatto women, twelve black women, and eight white women, including six of Irish or French immigrant background.³⁷

In the Midwest, interracial marriages occurred among Chinese small entrepreneurs and laborers. In Minneapolis and St. Paul, there were at least six interracially married Chinese men in the early-twentieth century. They were laundry and restaurant owners and cooks. The women they married were often Irish and Polish women, whom worked as vegetable washers in Twin Cities restaurants.³⁸

In New York City, census and contemporary newspapers revealed an interracial marriage pattern of Chinese men and Irish women consistent through the last decades of the nineteenth century. *Harper's Weekly* and other magazines and newspapers frequently featured stories of "Chinamen" and "Hibernian" women in which Irish women praised their Chinese husbands.³⁹

Hum Bing's marriage was representative of the interracial marriages among Chinese men. Hum Bing emigrated from Taishan in Guangdong Province in 1880 and settled in Wilmar, Minnesota, a railroad center west of Minneapolis. He operated laundries and a hotel in Wilmar and Minneapolis. He married an Irish woman from Canada who had previously been married to his closest friend. His friend was a fellow Chinese railroad worker in Montana who had been killed in an accident. Partly due to his desire to assimilate and partly due to the influence of his non-Chinese wife, Hum was remarkably acculturated.[40]

Compared to Chinese men, few Chinese women of this period married men outside of their racial group with the exception of Polly Bemis (discussed in the previous chapter) and a few others due to cultural prejudice from both larger American society and Chinese immigrant communities. This situation was exemplified in Suey Sin's story and Mrs. S's family history.

Suey Sin (meaning "water lily" in Chinese) was a beautiful Chinese girl working in the film industry in Los Angeles in the 1920s. There she played minor roles in movies and met a handsome white actor. Their relationship started in the casual studio way and soon developed into a romance. However, the actor's mother and sister objected to the relation, and the actor never had the courage to stand against his family's will to not marry her.[41] Unlike Suey Sin, Mrs. S had never dated Caucasian men because intermarriage was considered unacceptable in her community at the time. Born into a Chinese immigrant family in San Francisco in 1917, Mrs. S was an obedient daughter. Like most of her peers in Chinatown, she attended public school and Chinese language school, and learned sewing from her mother at home. She did not date until she met her future husband, Mr. S, then a language technician for the Office of War Information in San Francisco. They were married in 1946. "Most of us," Mrs. S reminisced, "married Chinese. Intermarriage was not popular [in Chinese community then], since you have a big Chinese population there."[42]

The size of most Chinese families was large, though it varied according to the class status of the male head of the household.[43] Many well-to-do Chinese men wanted to raise a big family to financially secure their future and emotionally alleviate their loneliness as immigrants. Mrs. C's family history was exemplary. As the daughter of an affluent Chinese merchant in Boston, Mrs. C recalled, "there are nine children in my family. My father knew that he was alone in this country. He did not have any relative here. So he wanted to have many children as security in his old age."[44] Similarly, Mrs. S's merchant family from San Francisco consisted of seven children, including four boys and three girls.[45] Like Chinese merchants on the mainland, some Chinese farming families in Hawaii also tended to be large in size. Lily Chan, a farmer's daughter in Honolulu, wrote, "our family was a very large one, comprising of five brothers and four sisters, so my father had quite a hard job feeding and clothing us. . . ."[46] It was a hard job too for her mother to keep such a big family. Cooking, cleaning, and childraising was drudgery for these early Chinese immigrant women.

Second-Generation Women

At the turn of the twentieth century, due to the small number of Chinese women in America, out of a total 89,832 Chinese in the population, there were only 2,353 who were native-born or second-generation Chinese girls. This figure increased to 3,014 in 1910, 5,214 in 1920, and 10,175 in 1930. With the increased immigration of Chinese women during and after the World War II and the birth of Chinese American children, the figure reached 14,560 of a total Chinese American population of 40,262 by 1940.[47]

Similar to other immigrant children, most second-generation Chinese American girls growing up in the early-twentieth century followed Chinese traditions at home in their daily life. As one Chinese girl noted: "The food [we eat] . . . are rice, meat and fresh vegetables. In my family, my mother and I was dressed in Chinese costume, which was high collar and long sleeve."[48] Many second-generation Chinese girls also sewed at home, one of the domestic duties considered necessary to be passed to daughters by Chinese mothers. Mrs. S, a San Francisco-born second-generation Chinese woman, "learned sewing from mother" and sewed all her clothes.[49]

Although most Chinese immigrant families lived in simple or substandard housing with little furniture, they kept their homes as clean as they could. A Chinese girl at McKinley High School in Honolulu wrote in 1926:

> My home was a little house with two rooms, a parlor and a bed-room. In this house there were only two windows. Our kitchen and lavatory were outside of the house. The lavatory and bathroom were used by several families. . . . The furniture were old but they were kept clean by my mother who dusted them daily. We had very few pictures and decorations in the house. A few calendars and photographs were the only decorations in the house. . . .[50]

As in eating, dressing, and housekeeping, Chinese immigrant women preserved their cultural traditions in child-rearing. Valuing traditional Chinese culture and customs, Chinese women taught their children, especially their daughters, as much of the Chinese language and Chinese ways as possible. Most early Chinese immigrant women had no formal education in China and knew little English. The children of Chinese immigrant families learned and spoke English in public, while they spoke a Chinese dialect with their parents at home. As Mrs. C recalled her childhood in Boston: "I spoke Cantonese to my parents. My father didn't want us to speak English at home. To preserve our Chinese language, we went to Chinese language school after public school, from five-thirty to eight-thirty, five days a week and Saturdays too."[51] Mrs. S's childhood in San Francisco resembled that of Mrs. C and her reminiscence provided a detailed picture of the typical Chinese language schools in major urban Chinese communities.

> I was born and raised in San Francisco. Being in a city like San Francisco, after we got to American school, we attended Chinese language school. In language school they taught Cantonese. We learned Chinese in Cantonese. [The Chinese language school operated] from five to eight o'clock in the evening from Monday to Friday, and ten to one on Saturday. We paid one dollar a month for tuition. I went to a Chinese language school called Nanqiao Xuexiao (South Bridge School). The school was built by [Chinese] organizations in that district. The Chinese Benevolent Association owned many properties. Income from properties was used to built school. . . . [The school was run by] Benevolent Board of Director, selected by the Benevolent Association. They met several times a year. All of them were men. The teachers were men and women. Some were [college] students. They went to school during the day and came to teach after their school. Some [Chinese language] schools were connected with Methodist Church. Catholic Church also had a [Chinese] language school. . . I quitted Chinese school in junior high. Chinese school usually goes to high school level. You do whatever the others do. The class was getting smaller and smaller [as the level went up].[52]

Growing up in a society different from their parents, some Chinese girls did not take their family traditions very seriously. As a Chinese girl in Hawaii said in the 1920s: "I have often made fun of the customs of my racial group. Some of the customs which I did not like were the serving of tea to visitors, forbidding to call the visitors by their first names; and the marriage customs."[53]

Strict family upbringing, heavy household responsibilities, and limited educational opportunities were universal constraints to many second-generation Chinese American girls. As a Chinese college girl in San Francisco complained in the 1920s: "We were brought up more strictly than most girls, even according to Chinese ideas, and my sister and I have kept those habits, never going to dances, or having company, always working."[54]

Following Chinese tradition, Chinese immigrant parents valued education as a tool for upward mobility in American society. However, like their counterparts in China, these Chinese parents believed that formal education was only appropriate and important for their sons. Daughters were often expected to stay at home to learn domestic skills or work to supplement family income while their brothers attended school. A Chinese girl at McKinley High School in Honolulu in the 1920s said: "They [her parents] believe that girls should not have as much education as the boys, and that the girls must stay at home and work while boys go out and play."[55] Many Chinese girls had only a few years of elementary education and spent their teen years performing domestic chores of cooking, cleaning, sewing, and taking care of younger siblings. They also helped with their family businesses or worked in tobacco factories to increase family income.[56] A Chinese girl student in San Francisco recalled the reason her sister decided to get married at the age of fourteen. "She felt that she could not stand it to keep on with such heavy work. As the eldest daughter she had always been overworked, never had any time to herself."[57]

While many Chinese parents retained traditional attitudes toward their daughters' education, others gradually realized the social and economic value of education for their daughters as the entire society was experiencing an attitude change toward women.

Table 3.1

School Attendance (5 to 20 Years), by Race and Sex for the United States, 1910–1940 (Percentage)

Census Year	Native M	White F	F-B M	White F	Black M	Black F	Other Race* M	Other Race* F
1940	76.3	73.1	59.7	53.4	70.2	68.1	82.6	80.4
1930	74.9	72.3	58.9	51.8	65.3	63.0	75.1	79.6
1920	67.5	66.7	47.7	42.8	57.9	58.8	63.6	67.0
1910	62.5	62.0	40.4	38.4	48.5	50.4	48.3	59.7

Source: Census of the United States 1940, Population Vol. II, Characteristics of the Population, 37–39.

* Chinese were included in "other race," in which Japanese and Chinese comprised the majority.

This parental attitude change was reflected in school attendance. According to the 1940 census, since 1920 a higher percentage of Chinese girls between the ages of five and twenty had attended school than had white girls and Chinese boys (see table 3.1).

As a result of formal education, the second-generation Chinese women adopted western ways and resembled their American peers in many aspects. To become "hundred percent Americans," they dressed like Caucasian flappers, attended parties, and participated in school bands and sports.[58] Some young Chinese college girls even took dancing and singing lessons. Some were recruited by Forbidden City, a Chinese nightclub in San Francisco, as professional dancers or singers for the "Oriental" floor show. "We did this in 1930s and 1940s," France Chun, a singer in Forbidden City, recalled, "We were a shock to the Chinese community and a confusion to the Caucasian people."[59]

As the second-generation Chinese girls became more westernized and independent, they began to challenge the parental authority. They attempted to control their own lives, and make decisions themselves on important issues such as marriage and career choices. Some second-generation Chinese girls sought refuge in missionary homes or eloped in order to avoid arranged marriages. When such a misfortune was about to happen to a Chinese girl in San Francisco, she decided to escape from her father's control and seek help from Miss Cameron's Mission Home:

> My father ... bought my ticket to China. ... I told him all the time that I wouldn't go, and finally, the night before the boat sailed, I told him that if he insisted, I would go up to the mission and throw myself on their protection. But he did not believe me. ... I was in the care of relatives, who believed ... that I ought to go, and that I ought to get married, the sooner the better. But I was resolved not to marry, to have a education instead. My sister had asked me to see Miss Cameron about her own trouble and I told my relatives I had to go there for that purpose, and went, the next morning, before the boat sailed.[60]

Some girls openly expressed their views on marriage. A high school girl in Honolulu wrote, "I would prefer to marry a Hawaiian-born member of my own race. Because his ideas would agree with me, while a foreign-born member might differ from me entirely and then there would be conflicts."[61] Edna, a Chinese farm girl, was happily married to a young man of her own choice, only after she had firmly refused to marry an older man whom her mother had planned to be the husband.[62]

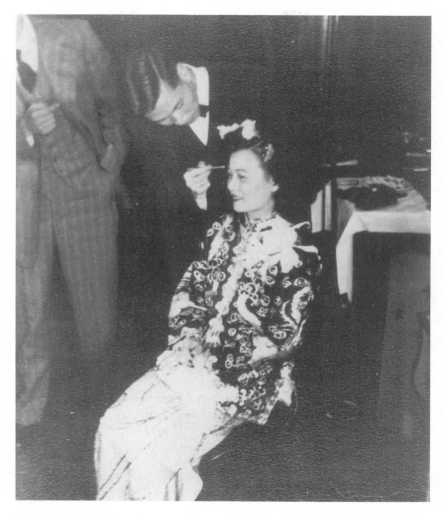

Figure 3.1. Wedding of a second-generation Chinese woman in San Francisco, 1946. Huping Ling Collection.

During their high school years, many Chinese girls dreamed of professional jobs, especially teaching, which was one of the few occupational options then available to career women. Lily Chan, a second-generation Chinese girl of McKinley High School in Honolulu, recalled that "since I was twelve years old, I began to thinking of a vocation. I have always wanted to teach. . . . my father and my mother also want me to be a teacher."[63]

While the ethnic traditions at home impeded efforts by second-generation Chinese women to become westernized, continued social prejudice also prevented their participation in the larger society. Despite their ability to speak English and gain a higher education, many second-generation Chinese women felt that they could not easily mingle into mainstream society. Many felt that they became "marginal" women, belonging to neither culture. As Janie Chii, a second-generation Chinese girl, noted in an article entitled "The Oriental Girls in the Occident" in 1926:

> The second-generation Chinese girl . . . is a thing apart from her sister of the older generation who was bound by the traditions of many centuries. Freed from old restraints, yet hampered by many new problems which she meets in her daily living, she is still an uncertain quantity. Consciously and unconsciously she reflects the conflict within her caused by her Chinese heritage and American environment. She has broken her link with the East. She has not yet found one with the west.[64]

The conflict between Chinese heritage and American environment also affected the mother-daughter relationship within Chinese American families. American-born Chinese girls were more exposed to western customs than to Chinese ways and imitated their western counterparts. On the contrary, their immigrant mothers who were brought up by Chinese traditions preferred to raise their daughters according to Chinese cultural values. Therefore, a cultural and generational gap inevitably existed.

Although illiterate or less educated, most Chinese immigrant women were able to bring a complete set of cultural values from China to America. Their daily activities and behavior were defined according to the Chinese Confucian mechanisms of subordination. The first set of these restrictions was "the Three Obediences" in which a Chinese woman should obey her father before marriage, her husband after marriage, and her son when widowed. Secondly, "the Four Virtues" included virtues that a woman should know her place in the universe, be reticent in words, be clean of person and habits with a view to please the opposite sex, and fulfill her household duties. When Chinese immigrant women used these traditional values to cultivate their American-born and educated daughters, they confronted confusion or rebellion from their offspring.

Some Chinese girls felt baffled when their Chinese upbringing at home contradicted their western education in American public school. A Chinese high school girl in San Francisco complained in 1924:

My parents always tell me that a girl should be quiet, obedient, and respectful to all who are senior to you. But at school, I am told to ask questions and even disagree with teachers. I don't know whom I should listen to.[65]

Other girls challenged the authority of their parents. Jade Snow Wong's story exemplified those rebellious second-generation Chinese girls. Jade Snow Wong was the fifth daughter of a Chinese immigrant family in San Francisco. Ever since her early years, she learned to be obedient to her parents and to defer to her brothers. As she grew older, however, her personal aspirations began to clash with her parents' expectations when she first tried to date a boy of her choice and later decided to go to college.[66] As a result, she moved out of her parents' home and completed her education on her own by working as a housekeeper.

In addition to different educational backgrounds, the loss of ancestral language for the American-born daughters also contributed to cultural and generational conflict. While many American-born daughters were taught to speak Chinese at home, they were not able to express their feelings well or understand their parents' emotions completely in Chinese. As Jing-mei Woo, an American-born Chinese daughter in Amy Tan's *The Joy Luck Club* complained, "my mother and I never really understand one another. We translated each other's meanings and I seemed to hear less than what was said, while my mother heard more."[67] This loss or insufficiency in their native language together with cultural difference contributed to the generational gap.

Community Involvement

Social and Cultural Involvement

Though most Chinese American women's lives were confined to their families or to Chinatowns, many tried to step out of their homes to participate in various social activities in the Chinese community. The social gatherings gave them a sense of joy and identity so meaningful in their restricted lives. Special holidays or family anniversaries helped to relieve their daily stress.

Traditional festivals provided Chinese American women, especially the early immigrant women, with opportunities to meet friends and relatives. The oldest woman in Butte, Montana's Chinatown recalled that during the Chinese New Year, long-confined Chinese women put on their best dresses and jewelry, visited each other, and exchanged information about their families and friends.

> The women were always glad to see each other; we exchanged news of our families and friends in China. We admired each other's clothes and jewels. As we ate separately from the men, we talked about things that concerned women.[68]

Other occasions such as the celebration of a newborn also gave these women chances to get together. "Sometimes," the same woman recalled, "we went to a feast when a baby born into a family association was a month old."[69]

Like social gatherings, religious activities provided an emotional outlet for Chinese immigrant women. In Chinatowns, one can find both Christian churches and non-Christian temples. This co-existance of different religions has been seen as an interesting and distinctive phenomenon among Chinese and probably some other East Asian peoples. Unlike many Europeans, the Chinese showed an affinity for syncretism, a remarkable acceptance of different religions. Because of this, some individuals could closely or loosely associate with more than one church. This flexible attitude toward religion enabled Chinese immigrant women to benefit from their connections with different churches.

In large Chinese communities, women usually had more opportunities to establish contacts with native-born women from various churches. As described in Amy Tan's *The Joy Luck Club*, when Suyuan Woo first arrived in San Francisco, the Refugee Welcome Society gave her two hand-me-down dresses. The society consisted of a group of white-haired American missionary ladies from the First Chinese Baptist Church. Because of these gifts, Suyuan Woo and her husband felt obligated to join the church.[70] In churches and church-sponsored activities such as English classes, cooking classes, sewing classes, and social gatherings, Chinese immigrant women had opportunities to find jobs, make social contacts, and sample some American ways of life. This certainly helped their adjustment to the new environment.

Even though the missionaries were primarily white, they fervently recruited religious workers among enthusiastic Chinese women followers. Some Chinese women started by visiting church and later became devoted religious workers.[71] Others were rescued from slavery and educated by missions, and therefore completely committed to missionary work. Lilac Chen, for example, was "rescued" as a young girl by Donaldina Cameron in the 1910s and later worked as an interpreter for many years at the Presbyterian Mission House in San Francisco's Chinatown. When interviewed by Victor and Brett de Bary Nee, Lilac, at the age of 84, recalled her work in the Mission House:

> The work I did with Miss Cameron was called rescue work. We would find the Chinese girls who were sold to work in the dives, or as domestic servants, and bring them to Cameron House so they could be free. Sometimes people reported to us or sometimes the slave girls themselves would slip a note under our front door and we would find it, and go to the place where the girl wanted to be rescued.[72]

Although Christian churches assisted Chinese immigrant women in adapting to American society, they were far less indispensable to Chinese women than to Korean immigrant women. A number of studies on Korean immigrant women have emphasized the importance of church to Korean immigrant women. In the early immigrant history of Korean women, churches not only provided spiritual comfort, but met the social and psychological needs of immigrants as well. Since more than forty percent of the Korean immigrants were Christians prior to their immigration to America, churches had virtually served as grassroots organizations that would band immigrant women together.[73]

In addition to the above differences, the Christian churches played different roles in the adaptation of Chinese and Korean immigrant women. Christian churches served as windows of the mainstream American life to Chinese immigrant women and attempted to accelerate their Americanization. In contract, churches among Korean immigrants functioned as community organizations that resembled the patriarchal social structure in Korea and consciously preserved Korean ethnic tradition. Therefore, these churches impeded the Americanization of Korean immigrants.[74]

Apart from traditional festivals, gatherings of friends, and religious activities, musical life in Chinatown also provided Chinese women an opportunity to go out for some enjoyment. The 1920s brought substantial economic prosperity to the American society. Coinciding with such affluence, there was an upsurge in theatrical activity in San Francisco's Chinatown, which had a special impact on the social life of Chinese women. The young women of the community "made the Cantonese opera an occasion for the display of their latest gowns and accessories in the Western mode." The opera soon changed the evening life of Chinatown. "Before the opera came [in the 1920s]," Ronald Riddle has observed in a recent study, "the Chinese people stayed home in the evening and social intercourse was within the family. . . . After the opera came the young people began giving supper parties and inviting friends to each other's houses."[75]

Mrs. S remembered much the same thing in her account of cultural life in San Francisco's Chinatown as a child:

> There were two [Cantonese] opera houses [in San Francisco Chinatown]. The performance usually was in the evening. Old people would go there. That was before [the age of] the movies. Cantonese opera was performed and troupes from China were invited, especially at Saturday night. They started at seven o'clock and admission was one dollar. But by nine o'clock, if there still were seats left, they would sell the tickets for twenty-five cents. Women would go to opera too.[76]

Beginning in the 1920s, social dancing gained popularity among the younger Chinese as local Chinese youth followed national trends. This reflected the acceptance of Western customs among the younger Chinese women. One reporter wrote in 1929:

> Not long ago the windows of Chinese shops bore huge posters showing a young Chinese girl, flapper type, dancing with a Chinese young man in formal clothes. The headline ran:
>
> "Chinese Collegiate Shuffle!"
>
> What would old John Chinaman think, could he see one of these lively dancing parties of the Chinese students of the San Francisco district, jazz music, bright costumes, beautiful young women, gaiety on every hand. "Everything but hip flasks," someone said of the dance.[77]

Political Involvement

Politically, Chinese American women remained less visible than women of other ethnic groups, particularly Italian and Irish women, until the 1960s. Irish women made special contributions to the early American union movement. Mary Harris Jones, universally known as "Mother" Jones, was a good example. Irish-born and a mother and wife of an immigrant family, she emerged as a union organizer in the 1870s. She was responsible for helping organize the most significant strikes in the history of the American union movement for nearly half a century. These strikes included the great rail strike in Pittsburgh in 1877, the Haymarket massacre in Chicago in 1886, the rail strike in Birmingham in 1894, the national coal strikes of 1900 and 1902 (where she organized the miners' wives to march with mops and brooms), the West Virginia coal strike of 1912–1913, the New York garment workers and streetcar strikes of 1915–1916, and the great steel strike of 1919.[78]

In addition to Mother Jones, a group of Irish women unionists were also noticed by the public, while the majority of Irish working women supported the union movement enthusiastically. As Hasia Diner has noted in *Erin's Daughters in America*, "Irish-American women in all sorts of occupations . . . seemed willing to risk public disapproval and disdain in order to secure their economic lives. . . . While a handful of Irish women crossed over from trade unionism to a more radical economic analysis . . . the vast majority viewed their trade unionism instrumentally. They worked because women worked if they did not marry. If trade unionism improved their earning power, then the social stigma that it carried mattered very little."[79]

Similarly, Jewish immigrant women in the garment industry actively participated in strikes to improve their condition. In October 1909, the Executive Board of Waist Maker's Local 25, consisting of six Jewish immigrant women and nine Jewish men, pressured the International Ladies Garment Workers' Union (ILGWU) to call a general strike for the entire New York shirtwaist industry. Between November 1909 and February 1910, more than 20,000 shirtwaist workers picketed outside the factories of lower Manhattan, demanding a 52-hour workweek, paid overtime, the abolition of fines and inside subcontracting, and union recognition. By the end of the strike, most employers accepted all or some of the strikers' demands. Jewish immigrant women played a significant role in this general strike.[80]

In contrast to Irish and Jewish immigrant women, Chinese women were confined at home or in a Chinatown community. Obviously, the lower visibility of Chinese women in the union movement was largely a result of limited opportunities for Chinese women to work in factories outside of Chinatown. Besides, other internal barriers including psychological constraints, cultural restrictions, and patriarchal and structural impediments, hampered political activism among Chinese American women.[81]

Though Chinese women were less visible and active than some groups of ethnic women in American mainstream politics, they were not as silent in their own communities. As early as the 1910s, a modest movement for women's emancipation developed in China and the United States. In China, western ideas like freedom and democracy were introduced by western-educated Chinese scholars. These ideas stimulated the enthusiasm of educated young Chinese for modernization in China. They believed part of modernization involved elevating Chinese women's social status within Chinese society. As a result, anti-footbinding societies, girls' schools, organizations for women's rights, and the increased participation of women in public affairs became visible in major cities of China. Some young women initiated work-study programs which organized women to study abroad, especially in France, where they could obtain western experience and knowledge in order to help the Chinese revolution and modernization.[82] At the same time, progressives and feminists in the United States pressured the federal government to provide women with increased opportunities for education and participation in public life. Many middle-class American women became enthusiastic social reformers involved in temperance, settlement house work, and suffrage movements.[83] What were the responses of Chinese women in America to the changes taking place in China and the United States? Some writers claimed the social awakening of Chinese American women was evident in the 1910s. Although most were not active participants in mainstream politics, Chinese American women did support women's right to an education, gainful employment, and political participation.[84]

In the social awakening movement, some Chinese female students were especially active. They spoke against the earlier system of slavery that bought girls from impoverished parents in China and then sold them to brothels as prostitutes or to wealthy Chinese families as concubines or servant-girls. In 1902, Sieh King King, a sixteen-year-old student from Tianjin, gave a speech in front of a Chinatown theater. She condemned the slave-girl system and called for equality for men and women.[85] In the 1920s, many second-generation Chinese girls also expressed their resentment at the slave-girl system: "It's like stocks, like an investment," one said.[86]

Some Chinese women also delivered speeches to raise the consciousness of Chinese women in America, and encouraged them to join the revolutionary efforts in China.[87] In 1904, Zhang Zhujun, a Chinese intellectual woman, spoke to San Francisco's Chinatown audience. She urged Chinese women to unite and fight against the oppression of women in China and to support her organization's efforts to open schools for girls and provide relief for widows and orphans.[88] Wu Fengming, another young Chinese intellectual woman, delivered many speeches from 1903 to 1905 at rallies in Oakland and San Francisco in California, Baltimore in Maryland, and other places around the country. In her speeches, she spread revolutionary ideas, attacked the monarchists, and called on Chinese Americans to support the revolutionary cause.[89] In 1911, two women graduates of the University of California in Berkeley, J. Jung and B. Loo, according to the *San Francisco Call Bulletin*, "stepped to the front at a public meeting and in speeches of fire and patriotism called to their countrymen to win the ballot in China by the sword, to overthrow the Manchu dynasty and instill a republican form of government in its place."[90]

After the Japanese invasion of Manchuria in 1931, Six Companies called an emergency meeting on August 21, to which ninety-one Chinese organizations throughout America sent representatives. The meeting resulted in the founding of the China War Relief Association of America, which ultimately included forty-seven chapters in the western hemisphere. The most urgent business of the association was to raise money for the war effort in China. One effective means of raising money was the "Bowl of Rice Movement," which was the collective effort on the part of Chinese Americans to raise funds and collect supplies to send to China during the war. The association also encouraged a boycott against the Japanese goods. Joined by Koreans, the association twice held anti-Japanese parades in New York in 1938 and picketed the shipyards of Los Angeles (January 1939), Everett in Washington (January 1939), and Astoria in Oregon (March 1939). Through Rice Bowl Parties, parades, and various cultural programs, the association raised millions of dollars for China's effort in World War II.[91]

Like their male counterparts, Chinese American women participated fervently in the war effort. Many women took part in the Chinese Women's New Life Movement, which was inaugurated in 1934 by Chiang Kai-shek's Nationalist government and directly led by Mme. Chiang Kai-shek. Based on traditional Chinese values, the movement aimed at moral reform. During World War II, the movement supported China's war effort by engaging in such war relief activities as fundraising, blood donation, and first aid.[92]

Chinese women in major Chinese communities were especially active in these war relief activities. Responding to Mme. Chiang's call, four women organizations in San Francisco, including the Women's Patriotic Association, the Women's Association, the Square and Circle Club, and the YWCA, jointly sponsored fundraising shows in June 1943. These organizations urged Chinese Americans to study the Chinese language and culture, and to associate with American charitable organizations to support China's war effort.[93] The New York chapter of the Chinese Women's New Life Movement was also active, as revealed by *The Chinese Nationalist Daily*, a newspaper in the Chinese language published in New York. On January 25, 1944 (the Chinese New Year Day according to the Chinese Lunar Calendar), women joined the Lion Dance parade organized by the New York chapter of the China War Relief Association of America to raise funds for Chinese war refugees.[94] By the end of 1944, Chinese in the United States had purchased more than twenty million war bonds.[95] From 1938 to 1947, an average of seven million dollars per year was remitted to China from the United States. "This vast sum was sent for the living expenses of family members residing in China, for investment in land and real estate," and more importantly, "for contributions to the war effort."[96]

In addition to fundraising, Chinese American women participated actively in obtaining blood donations for China's war effort. The New York Chinese Blood Bank was established in July 1943. Lin Siru, daughter of the prominent Chinese writer Lin Yutang, served as the secretary of the Blood Bank. Many other local Chinese women were also involved in it. From July 1943 to January 1944, blood received by the Blood Bank was enough for 1,757 soldiers. In answer to a request from General Joseph W. Stilwell, the Blood Bank sent agents to Yunnan Province in China, engaging in war relief in the Yunnan-Burma theater of war.[97]

Many Chinese American women in this period also became members of various women's organizations. Inspired by the western ideas of individualism and women's rights, Chinese American women stepped out of their homes to join women's organizations such as the Young Women's Christian Associations (YWCA). By 1921, there were three Chinese Young Women's Christian Associations in America. The YWCA sponsored various services, such as cooking classes, English classes, vocational training classes, recreational activities, and social gatherings. Other women's organizations such as the Square and Circle Club organized its members to work in raising funds for scholarships, orphanages, nursing homes, and flood and war relief in China.

In addition to joining women's organizations, Chinese American women began to practice their voting rights. Tye Leung, an interpreter for the U.S. Immigration Services in San Francisco, became the first Chinese woman to vote in an American presidential election in 1912.[98] Encouraged by the Chinese YWCA and the

Square and Circle Club, Chinese American women in San Francisco "began to register to vote and campaign for political candidates in the early 1930s."[99] In 1949, Chinese women in Boston's Chinatown founded the Boston Chinese Women's Club. Under the jurisdiction of the Chinese Consolidated Benevolent Association (CCBA), the Women's Club was a social as well as political organization.[100]

※

Immigration had an enormous and sometimes devastating impact upon family life and family structure of Chinese immigrants. While Chinese immigrant women intended to preserve their cultural heritage, they experienced changes in their family lives. Their indispensable role within the family economy made them, for the first time, sole female heads and co-providers of the households. Consequently, the husband-wife relationship among Chinese immigrant families was often more equal than in their home country.

On the one hand, Chinese immigrant women enjoyed the new freedom and opportunities provided by immigration; on the other, they regretted the lack of Chinese cultural atmosphere in the United States, which they considered crucial for their children's upbringing. The preservation of their cultural heritage, however, caused objections from their American-born and western-educated children. This generational and cultural gap inevitably produced tension and conflicts among Chinese American families, which became a popular topic in much Chinese American fiction.

Since the late-nineteenth century, various social activities and community organizations in Chinese communities eased the Chinese immigrant women's transition from the old society to a new culture. They also offered an outlet for emotional depression resulting from the stress and difficulty of immigrant life. Social gatherings in the Chinese American communities were more meaningful than those in the old society, which only functioned as cultural institutions to enrich people's cultural lives. Having been transplanted into the new country, these social activities not only served as facilities of cultural lives, but also as a means of survival. Although most Chinese women were absent from mainstream American politics, some young Chinese intellectual women made a great effort to raise women's consciousness and ask support for political movement and war effort in China. Many also enthusiastically took part in the war relief activities in Chinese communities, and joined social and political organizations for Chinese American women.

Part Two

※

Postwar Chinese American Women, 1943–1965

Chapter 4

Postwar Chinese American Women

World War II proved to be a turning point for Chinese American women. The repeal of the Chinese exclusion acts in 1943 helped increase a more family-oriented Chinese American population by allowing more Chinese women to enter the country under such special laws as the War Bride Act and the G. I. Fiancées Act. The American war effort created job opportunities for Chinese American women in the larger society. Different from Chinese women in the earlier period, postwar Chinese women moved upward professionally. They became clerical workers, sales personnel, or professionals such as professors and technicians, in addition to working in the four historically predominant occupations of Chinese males and females as well—the laundry, restaurant, grocery, and garment businesses.

Repeal of Chinese Exclusion Acts

Anti-Chinese sentiment abated during World War II, when China became a member of the Grand Alliance and public images of the Chinese gradually changed. A more favorable attitude in America toward China and Chinese Americans continued after the war. Facing pressures from the public and other interest groups, Congress repealed a large number of exclusion laws, which for years had denied Chinese Americans' fundamental civil rights and legal protection.[1] On December 17, 1943, Congress passed an act to repeal all Chinese exclusion acts since 1882, permitted Chinese aliens in the United States to apply for naturalization, and allotted a preference up to 75 percent of the quota given to Chinese immigrants.[2]

In spite of the repeal of the Chinese exclusion acts, the Chinese immigrant quota designated by the American government was only 105 per year. This figure was one-sixth of one percent of the number of the Chinese in the United States in 1920 as determined by the census of that year.[3] Nevertheless, non-quota immigrants were allowed to immigrate. More Chinese scholars came to teach in the United States, an average of about 137 each year, in comparison with ten per year during the previous decade. More important, under the War Bride Act of December 28, 1945 and the G. I. Fiancées Act of June 29, 1946, alien wives and children of veterans and American citizens were permitted to enter America as non-quota immigrants. During the three-year operation of the War Bride Act, approximately 6,000 Chinese war brides were admitted.[4] Thus, in 1947, the number of Chinese immigrants entering the United States climbed to 3,191, most of whom came on a non-quota basis.[5]

Many women also came under other laws. The Displaced Persons Act of 1948 and the Refugee Relief Act of 1953 allowed several thousand Chinese women to immigrate to America. The former granted "displaced" Chinese students, visitors, and others, who had temporary status in the United States, to adjust their status to that of permanent resident. The latter allotted 3,000 visas to refugees from Asia and 2,000 visas to Chinese whose passports had been issued by the Chinese Nationalist government which lost its power in mainland China in 1949.[6] On September 22, 1959, Congress passed an act under which more Chinese on the quota waiting list obtained non-quota status.[7] Thus, by 1960, the number of Chinese in the United States, as reported by the 1960 census, had reached 237,292. This included 135,549 males and 101,743 females, of whom 60 percent were native born.[8]

Among the women who immigrated in this period, many were so-called war brides who had hastily married Chinese American veterans before the War Bride Act was to be expired in 1949. In her article, "The Recent Immigrant Chinese Families of the San Francisco-Oakland Area," Rose Hum Lee described the war bride. "The most publicized case of 'getting married quick' was of the ex-soldier who enplaned to China, selected his bride, was married, and landed at the San Francisco airport the evening before his month's leave of absence expired. His bride came later, a practice applying to many others whose admission papers could not be processed rapidly."[9]

Whereas during the 1930s an average of only 60 Chinese women entered the United States each year, in 1948 alone, 3,317 women

Table 4.1
Chinese American Population and Sex Ratio, 1900–1990

Year	Total	Male	Female	Ratio of Sex
1900	89,863	85,341	4,522	18.9:1
1910	71,531	66,858	4,675	14.3:1
1920	61,639	53,891	7,748	7.0:1
1930	74,954	59,802	15,152	3.9:1
1940	77,504	57,389	20,115	2.9:1
1950	117,629	77,008	40,621	1.8:1
1960	237,292	135,549	101,743	1.3:1
1970	431,583	226,733	204,850	1.1:1
1980	806,040	407,544	398,496	1.0:1
1990	1,648,696	821,542	827,154	1.0:1

Source: U.S. Census of Population.

immigrated. During the period from 1944 to 1953, women comprised 82 percent of Chinese immigrants to America. For the first time, the number of Chinese women and families in the United States noticeably increased. The male/female ratio dropped from 2.9:1 in 1940 to 1.8:1 in 1950, and 1.3:1 in 1960 (see table 4.1).

Motives and Means of Immigration

Compared to the early Chinese immigrant women, Chinese women who came after World War II were different from their early counterparts in many ways. Most early immigrant women came to the United States for familial reasons, as family members or as slave girls sold by their poor parents in China. On the contrary, postwar Chinese immigrant women emigrated for individual reasons such as education and job opportunities. While the majority of early immigrant women were driven by the lack of economic opportunities in China, many postwar Chinese immigrant women were pushed to emigrate by dramatic political change in China. While most early immigrant women were virtually illiterate or poorly educated, many postwar immigrant women had a better education and were exposed to Western culture prior to their emigration. These distinctive characteristics of the postwar Chinese immigrant women partially explained the occupational change and upward social mobility of Chinese American women in the postwar time. These differences in immigrant motivations and patterns also affected the degree of their assimilation.

Personal fulfillment was a motive for some Chinese women, especially students and professional women, to emigrate to the United States. The stories of Dr. Jianxiong Wu, Mrs. D and Ms. C exemplify those who came to America for further education and personal fulfillment. In 1912, Jianxiong Wu was born into an intellectual family in Liu He, a small town near Shanghai in Jiangsu province. She had her elementary education at Mingde School, a private school in her home town established and operated by her father, and was deeply influenced by her father's dedication to education. She received her Bachelor of Science from the National Central University in Nanjing, China. She came to the United States in 1936 on a Nationalist government scholarship to pursue her graduate studies under Ernest Lawrence, the director of the radiation laboratory at the University of California and a Nobel Laureate in 1939.[10]

Mrs. D was born into a well-to-do family in Guangzhou [Canton], Guangdong province, China in 1919. She attained her bachelor's degree in geography at Xiangqin University of Guangdong in 1941 and was a winner of the national college thesis competi-

Figure 4.1. Chinese female in front of the International House in Chicago, 1948. Huping Ling Collection

Figure 4.2. Chinese female students at the University of Wisconsin, Madison, 1947. Huping Ling Collection.

tion. Since then, she had always wanted to gain further education in geography. Wars and social upheavals in China delayed her plans for further education in geography. She first worked as a researcher at the National Geography Research Institute in Chongqin, Sichuan, jointly supported by the war-time Nationalist government and British government. With the Communist victory imminent, Mrs. D moved to Taiwan in 1947, along with her aunt, a prominent woman general of Chiang Kai-shek's Nationalist Army. Mrs. D taught geography courses at the Teacher's College of Taiwan until 1952 when the Nationalist government of Taiwan initiated a program to grant scholarships to individuals for study in the United States after five years of service to the government. Mrs. D grabbed this opportunity and was awarded one of the eight yearly governmental scholarships of $500, enough for her trip to America. Meanwhile, she applied to the University of Oregon in Eugene and was accepted with a scholarship. In early 1953, she came to America to pursue graduate study in geography at the University of Oregon, where she was the only female student in the department at the time.[11]

Ms. C was born in Kowloon, Hong Kong, in 1938. Both her mother and father had obtained higher education in the United States and were well-known educators in China. In 1955, when she was seventeen years old, she decided to get her college education in the United States. Her father provided her traveling expenses from the proceeds of his books on elementary, secondary, and higher education. A benefactor in the United States supplied $18,000, enough for her four-year education at Berea College in Kentucky.[12]

Political repression was another important factor pushing Chinese immigrant women to the United States. While the policy change in America encouraged Chinese immigration, the political transformation in China turned the previous elite class into émigrés, which significantly changed the profile of Chinese immigrants. After a twenty-two-year civil war between Chiang Kai-shek's Nationalist government and Mao Zedong's Communist Party, the latter finally seized power and founded the People's Republic of China in 1949. Afraid of the coming political persecution, many wealthy Chinese industrialists and high ranking officials of the Nationalist government transferred their family fortunes to the United States. Chen Yuan-tsung was similar to Guan Ling-ling, the heroine in her autobiographical novel *The Dragon's Village*. Chen was born and raised in a wealthy and influential family in Shanghai. In early 1949 when the People's Liberation Army (PLA, led by the Chinese Communist Party) troops were crossing the Yangtze River, there was a rumor in Shanghai that there would be a blood bath in the city after the changeover. Chen's family, like many other wealthy and pro-Nationalist families, fled the city for Hong Kong and later for the United States.[13]

Some Chinese women were sent to the United States by their wealthy families to be beneficiaries of their assets on the eve of the Chinese Communist Party's triumph. Ms. Y was one of such women. She came to America in 1949 supported by her affluent family in Beijing. She then enrolled at a prestigious university on the East Coast to study Chinese language and literature.[14] Similarly, Ms. W came to America to escape the Communist takeover in 1949. She was born in an interior city, Taiyuan, Shanxi, where her family had accumulated considerable wealth. In 1948, when the Communist troops were approaching Taiyuan, her family immediately transferred all their assets to the United States, where they had relatives and friends, and sent Ms. W and her grown-up brothers to America to inherit the family wealth. Upon arrival in America, Ms. W and her brothers all enrolled in prestigious universities in the New England area and later became scholars in physics and chemistry.[15]

In the late 1940s, when the political situation in China was about to change dramatically, some former Nationalist government officials and diplomats working in the United States stayed after their terms of service were completed.[16] Bette Bao Lord's father was one of these former Nationalist officials. He was a Chinese diplomat whom the Nationalist Government of China had assigned to work in New York City in 1946. He took up his position and brought his family, including young Betty. Though he had not planned to stay in America initially, he decided to remain when the Communist Party took over China and expelled the Nationalist Government in 1949.[17]

Different from the early Chinese immigrant women who were predominantly from impoverished rural areas in Guangdong province, many postwar Chinese immigrant women came from wealthy families in large cities in north, central, and south China. While the most early immigrant women were illiterate, many of the postwar women had attended colleges or universities in China and had been exposed to Western culture before their immigration. Equipped with better education and special training in China, many of the postwar women had better employment opportunities than did their earlier counterparts.[18]

New Employment Opportunities

In addition to cracking the door of Chinese immigration, which significantly increased the number of Chinese immigrant women, World War II provided new employment opportunities for Chinese American women. Like their counterparts from other ethnic groups, many Chinese American women found jobs for the first time in private companies, civil service offices, and professional fields. The new work opportunities also helped many to break down racial barriers and launch new careers outside Chinatowns during and after the war.

Some American-born Chinese women entered the entertainment industry during wartime. Forbidden City, a Chinese nightclub in San Francisco, attracted many talented young Chinese women to work. In 1938, Charlie Low, a shrewd and farsighted Chinese businessman, opened Forbidden City. In the first years, business was not very good. After the United States entered World War II in 1941, the business of the Forbidden City became brisk. This was caused by the increased occupational opportunities due to

America's war effort, and the consequently increased family income that enabled people to enjoy entertainment. Americans poured into Forbidden City to taste exotic food and enjoy the oriental floor-show. The actresses recruited by Charlie Low were mostly American-born, college-educated Chinese girls. During the war years, around one hundred young Chinese women worked in this establishment.

These young performers confronted suspicion from both Chinese and white communities. While the Chinese community thought something was wrong with them, Caucasian audiences questioned their talent: Can Chinese dance? They don't have rhythm. They are bow-legged.[19] They were also described as being different in attitude from their counterparts in the more standard nightclubs by contemporary observers:

> . . . the night-club idea still is so new that there is, among the girls, none of the hard-boiled sophistication that is the trademark of their white sisters in Eastern American cities. They're more like a bunch of college kids having a good time—and in fact, more than two thirds of them are graduates of Western universities.[20]

These devoted young Chinese women, however, worked hard and won appreciation from their audiences. Dorothy Toy, the leading dancer of the club, recalled proudly, "We were much better than the Caucasian dance team." During the boom days, Forbidden City entertained 2,200 visitors a day.[21]

Some other Chinese American women even broke military barriers and found employment in the U.S. Army. After the United States entered the war in 1941, approximately twelve thousand Chinese Americans enlisted in the armed forces. Among them, there were Chinese American women serving as pilots, officers, and nurses. Hazel Y. Lee of Portland, Oregon took flying lessons and qualified for the Women's Airforce Service Program (WASP). In November 1944, her plane had an accident and crashed in Great Falls, Montana when she was carrying out a mission. She was severely injured and died in a hospital a few days later.[22] Similarly, Helen Pon Onyett, an Army nurse to the North African campaign, served on landing ships by tending wounded soldiers. During her thirty-five-year military career, she was promoted to the rank of colonel and awarded eight major decorations.[23]

In the postwar period, more and more Chinese American women joined the labor force. In the 1940s, 22.3 percent of them worked outside the home, while 39.5 percent of white women worked. The percentage for the former increased to 30.8 in the 1950s and 44.2 in the 1960s. However, the percentage for white women labor dropped to 28.1 in the 1950s, and then rose to 33.6 in the 1960s (see table 4.2). The higher percentage of Chinese American women compared to white women in the labor force was due partially to the economic need and partially to the higher percentage of college-educated Chinese American women.

During the postwar years, most Chinese immigrant women were still confined to menial jobs within Chinatown because of limited knowledge of English and minimal job skills. On the other hand, their college-educated daughters could now get clerical jobs. This young generation, however, found, according to a Fair Employment Practices Commission transcript, that most employers shared the opinion "that Oriental women had been trained to be subservient to the man at home, and therefore would make good secretaries."[24] This cliché was partially true because traditional Chinese women were expected to follow the "Three Obediences" and other moral codes. The upbringing of the second generation Chinese women would naturally affect their performance and behavior in the work place. Although some had benefitted from this new stereotype of Chinese American women as obedient secretaries in finding clerical jobs in companies, they were also hampered by the same stereotype for further advancement, especially for promotion to managerial level.

Table 4.2
Percentage of Chinese American Women in the Labor Force Compared with White and Black Women, 1910–1990

	Chinese Women	Black Women	White Women
1910	32.5	54.7	40.9
1920	14.1	38.9	37.7
1930	16.0	38.9	39.3
1940	22.3	37.8	39.5
1950	30.8	36.6	28.1
1960	44.2	41.5	33.6
1970	49.5	48.0	42.0
1980	58.3	52.9	49.4
1990	59.2	59.2	56.3

Source: U.S. Census, 1910–1990.

Though plagued by the stereotypical images of uncomplaining and efficient office workers, many Chinese American women made endeavors to enter new fields of art, science, and literature. Rose Hum Lee was an outstanding example of these women. She was born on August 20, 1904 in Butte, Montana. She received her bachelor's degree from the Carnegie Institute of Technology in 1942. Her graduate work was completed at the University of Chicago where she earned a master's degree in 1943 and a doctorate in sociology in 1947.

Lee was actively interested in improving racial and human relations. She served on the Education Committee of the Chicago Commission of Human Relations and with the National Conference of Christians and Jews. In 1959, she was National Secretary of the Society for the Study of Social Problems.

In 1960, Lee published her exhaustive research in her book, *The Chinese in the United States of America*. In this work, Lee questioned why the Chinese had not yet assimilated into the American mainstream. Chinatowns were understandable as a reaction to the hostility of white America, she claimed, but made no sense once that hostility had abated. Chinatown leaders had a vested interest in segregation, she suggested, but the Chinatown masses were being exploited by these interests and should escape them by unrestricted entrance into American society.[25] In 1961 Lee took an extended leave from Roosevelt University to return to the West and take up residence at Phoenix College in Arizona. She died in 1964.

Some prominent Chinese American women even entered advanced scientific fields. Jianxiong Wu's success was a good example. After receiving her doctorate in physics at the University of California, Berkeley in 1940, she taught at Princeton University. In 1943, she went to Columbia University to work on the development of the atomic bomb with the Manhattan Project. In 1957, Wu joined a group of scientists from the National Bureau of Standards in Washington, D.C. and tested the proposal by two male Chinese American physicists, Zhenning Yang [Chen-ning Yang] and Zhengdao Li [Tsung-dao Lee], of parity violation in weak interactions within the atomic nucleus. That same year, Zhenning Yang and Zhengdao Li won the Nobel Prize in physics. This work not only brought worldwide acclaim to Yang and Li, but professional fame to Wu as well.[26]

Unlike their predecessors, who were predominantly in domestic services and clerical work, Chinese American women in recent decades broadened their work sphere by entering the technical, sales, and professional fields. From table 4.3, one can see the change in the occupations of Chinese American women (see table 4.3).

Many professional women originally came from China as students as discussed in the previous chapters. During and after World War II, more Chinese female students came to the United States as a result of the Nationalist government's policy to promote foreign study (see figure 4.1). According to a survey by the China Institute in America, the number of Chinese students in America increased from 706 in 1943 to 3,914 in 1948.[27] The ratio of females to males increased from 1 to 6 in the 1930s to 1 to 3 in the 1940s and 1 to 1.5 in the 1950s (see table 4.4).

Table 4.3
Major Occupations of Chinese American Women: 1920–1990 (Percentage)

1920		1930	
Domestic Service	39.3	Domestic Service	39.3
Manufacturing	24.0	Manufacturing	24.0
Trade	16.7	Trade	15.3
Clerical	7.4	Clerical	11.2
Other	14.0	Other	13.0
1940		1950	
Domestic Service	29	Clerical, Sales	39
Operatives	26	Operatives	21
Clerical, Sales	26	Domestic Service	18
Professional	6	Professional	11
Other	13	Other	12
1960		1970	
Clerical, Sales	38	Clerical, Sales	32
Operatives	21	Operatives	23
Professional	17	Professional	19
Domestic Service	10	Domestic Service	15
Other	14	Other	12
1980		1990	
Technical, Sales	40	Technical, Sales	33
Managerial, Pro.	25	Managerial, Professional	28
Operators, Laborers	18	Service	12
Service	14	Operators, Laborers	11
Other	3	Other	16

Source: U.S. Census: 1920–1990.

Table 4.4
Chinese Students in American Colleges and Universities
by Year of Entry, 1900–1953

			All Chinese Students*			
	Male Students		Female Students			
Year of Entry	Count	Percentage of Total Chinese Immigrants	Count	Percentage of Total Chinese Immigrants	Sex Unknown	Chinese Immigrants (Not including Students)†
1900	3	0.24	—	—	0	1247
1901	12	0.49	—	—	2	2458
1902	7	0.42	1	0.06	0	1649
1903	4	0.18	1	0.05	0	2209
1904	18	0.42	2	0.05	1	4309
1905	24	1.10	—	—	1	2166
1906	55	3.56	4	0.26	1	1544
1907	69	7.18	1	0.10	1	961
1908	64	4.58	6	0.43	7	1397
1909	58	2.99	3	0.15	8	1943
1910	90	4.57	6	0.30	11	1968
1911	77	5.27	7	0.48	6	1460
1912	69	3.90	4	0.23	6	1765
1913	109	5.18	14	0.66	15	2105
1914	155	6.20	16	0.63	19	2502
1915	172	6.47	17	0.63	24	2660
1916	143	5.81	19	0.77	19	2460
1917	136	6.08	21	0.93	16	2237
1918	183	10.20	26	1.45	20	1795
1919	219	11.15	20	1.01	22	1964
1920	322	13.82	26	1.12	47	2330
1921	304	7.58	40	1.00	43	4009
1922	307	6.97	49	1.11	47	4406
1923	351	7.04	32	0.69	43	4986
1924	322	4.61	32	0.46	29	6992
1925	279	14.40	37	1.91	33	1937
1926	266	15.20	42	2.40	33	1751
1927	233	15.84	50	3.40	19	1471
1928	237	17.95	43	3.26	26	1320
1929	286	19.78	34	2.35	20	1446
1930	248	15.61	40	2.51	28	1589
1931	170	14.78	33	2.87	24	1150
1932	121	16.13	22	2.93	15	750
1933	74	50.00	17	11.49	13	148
1934	120	64.17	29	15.50	23	187
1935	147	64.20	35	15.28	30	229
1936	166	60.81	38	13.91	26	273
1937	157	53.58	38	12.97	24	293
1938	157	25.61	64	10.44	14	613

Table 4.4 *(Continued)*

			*All Chinese Students**			
	Male Students		*Female Students*			
Year of Entry	*Count*	*Percentage of Total Chinese Immigrants*	*Count*	*Percentage of Total Chinese Immigrants*	*Sex Unknown*	*Chinese Immigrants (Not including Students)†*
1939	104	16.20	48	7.48	6	642
1940	140	21.77	55	8.55	11	643
1941	138	13.76	64	6.38	18	1003
1942	114	63.69	32	17.88	4	179
1943	158	243.07	50	76.92	10	65
1944	204	408.00	52	104.00	14	50
1945	408	574.64	82	115.49	53	71
1946	422	167.46	164	65.08	62	252
1947	780	24.44	340	10.65	74	3191
1948	846	11.75	320	4.44	108	7203
1949	672	19.68	297	8.70	47	3415
1950	422	32.97	221	17.27	20	1280
1951	318	59.44	205	38.32	22	535
1952	317	120.53	192	73.08	14	263
1953	191	36.17	97	18.37	17	528

* China Institute in America, A *Survey of Chinese Students in American Colleges and Universities in the Past Hundred Years* (New York, 1954), 26–27.

† U.S. Bureau of the Census, *Historical Statistics of the United States, Colonial Times to 1970*, Part I (Washington, D.C., 1975), 107.

Like their earlier counterparts, most Chinese female students of this period worked hard and enjoyed academic success. Oral history interviews provided a glimpse of their life in America. Having sailed to the United States in 1952, Mrs. D studied in the department of geography at the University of Oregon for a master's degree. She recalled her experiences in Eugene, Oregon:

> My life in Oregon was fun. Since my scholarship only covered my tuition, I had to support myself. A friend of mine introduced me to an American couple, Mr. and Mrs. Alvin C. Stockstad who operated an appliance store in Eugene. The Stockstads provided room and board for me, and in turn, I would work one hour a day to cook and to clean house for them. I never cooked in China and did not know how to cook in the beginning, but they taught me. They also showed me how to use vacuum cleaner. I broke a cup when I was washing dishes and wrecked the glass door of the

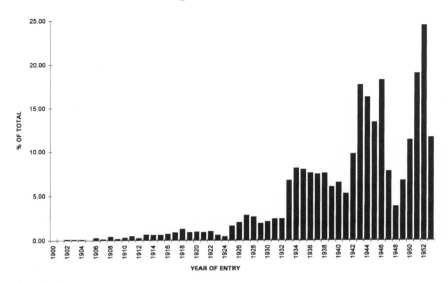

Figure 4.1. Chinese Female Students as a Percentage of Total Chinese Immigrants, 1900–1953.

fire-place when I was cleaning it. I told them what I did and was going to quit the job. But the Stockstads told me, "We hired you because you are honest and sweet." It was true. I treated them like my parents. Every time when I heard their car enter the garage driveway, I would run to the door to greet them and help them to take off coats, and they were so pleased. The friendship between us grew so strong that the Stockstads bought my wedding dress and airline tickets for my honeymoon when I got married.

I was the only women in the geography department [at the University of Oregon at the time], but I got good grades in all my classes. In the beginning, I had difficulty in English and oftentimes could not follow lectures. I had to read the textbook before and after classes. Mrs. Stockstad also volunteered to edit my papers. I conducted a personal art exhibit of my paintings in traditional Chinese southern style in the University gallery in January 1954, which attracted a good local crowds. Several local newspapers reported the event and Dr. Wallace Baldinger, professor of art at the University of Oregon commented on my works.[28]

Similarly, Ms. C's college years were challenging yet rewarding:

I came to the United States for my undergraduate work in 1955 when I was seventeen-year-old . . . In the first year at Berea [Col-

Figure 4.3. Chinese student and her host family, Eugene, Oregon, 1953. Huping Ling Collection.

lege], I was very shy, because I could not speak English and I looked different . . . But I could get along with my classmates and roommates and did not feel lonely. I was behind in English, but I got high scores in math and other science courses . . . I stayed at Berea from 1955 to 1957. Then I transferred to the University of Chicago . . . Using the money from my benefactress and the money I earned in summer, I was able to support myself. [In 1960], I entered the graduate program at the University of Chicago with a scholarship. I never felt I was discriminated. I was always the only female in my class. I was treated like a queen. I felt I was special.[29]

Ms. R. also came America in the 1950s to major in library science at the University of Oregon. Several decades later, she still clearly remembered how hard she worked for her degree. Oftentimes, she would work overnight in her tiny bedroom, with books and papers spread all over the floor. She did not have time to cook; she ate sandwiches and drank coffee while reading or writing. She felt she was working like a mad person.[30]

Many of these women completed their education smoothly and found employment in academic and professional fields in America. Ms. C's case was illustrative. After completing her doctoral degree in chemistry at the University of Chicago, she became a research fellow in several leading American research institutions. Finally she joined the faculty at a midwestern university as a member of the chemistry department.[31]

Family Life

The dramatic change in the male/female ratio among Chinese American population during the postwar years made family life more important to Chinese Americans than ever before. More sexually balanced and family oriented Chinese American communities began to replace the old predominantly bachelor Chinatowns.

Though more Chinese women obtained occupational opportunities than before, the majority of Chinese women still remained at home as housewives, like their counterparts from other ethnic groups. As mothers and wives, they continued to cling to their Chinese heritage and pride. They believed that taking care of a home and cultivating the young were more important and rewarding than having a job or living independently. The persistence of traditional attitudes among Chinese American women was perhaps best reflected in the upbringing of their children.

Chinese children appeared better adjusted to school than the children of other ethnic groups. Generally, they were less apt to fight with other children and were more compliant to the teachers' commands. Philip Vernon reported that IQs on verbal group tests of Chinese children were 97. This was a little below the white average, but their mean IQs on the nonverbal and spatial tests were superior in arithmetic, history, geography, and, surprisingly, spelling.[32]

There were many Chinese sayings that reminded Chinese women to devote their entire lives to cultivating their children and to tie their future lives to the achievements of their children. Such examples were "hoping your sons become dragons (dragons symbolize ruling powers and authorities)," "parents should be blamed for the evildoing of their children," "raising children for one's future happiness," and "a mother's honor and well-being depend on her children."[33] These deeply rooted conceptions encouraged Chinese American women to make sacrifices willingly for the future of their children and to regard their children's achievements as their own success and security.

Mrs. D's life history was exemplary. In 1952, she came to America to pursue her graduate degree in geography at the University of Oregon. After her marriage in 1954, she quit school to move to a small midwestern town where her husband was employed as a professor of physiology at a medical school. Then she enrolled at a midwestern university in the town to major in fine arts. Due to the arrival of her son, Weysan, in 1955, she withdrew from school again. Weysan's education became a top priority of her

Figure 4.4. Chinese intellectual women and their families, Kirksville, Missouri, 1958. Huping Ling Collection.

life. Unlike many Chinese immigrant women who insisted on their children speaking Chinese at home, Mrs. D wanted her son first to learn perfect English in order to facilitate his assimilation to American society. For this reason, Mrs. D hired a local woman to be her son's babysitter and to teach him English. Concerned that her son might pick up her own accent or incorrect grammar, she consciously and consistently avoided talking to her son in English. As a result of the strict training, Weysan had an excellent mastery of the English language and spoke without an accent. A straight-A student, Weysan graduated from the local high school as an honor student and was granted a four-year scholarship to Cornell University at Ithaca in New York to major in premedicine.[34]

Although many immigrant women were confined in menial jobs due to their limited English-speaking abilities and marketable skills, they hoped their children would have better educational and occupational opportunities. No matter how hard their life was, they never neglected child-raising. Therefore, Chinese American youths' academic achievements were in a large degree attributable to their mothers' efforts.

While many postwar Chinese women found a sense of accomplishment in cultivating their young, others felt adjustment to the new environment difficult.[35] This was especially true for older women and those who had been separated from their husbands for many years. Lee Wai Lan came to the United States in 1946. During the Sino-Japanese war, she was a war refugee in China who ran from village to village with her children to hide from the Japanese. After enduring a lot of hardship, Lee sent her four children to her husband in Cleveland, Ohio, and later she was reunited with them. What shocked her the moment she arrived was that her husband had a white mistress and her teenage children refused to acknowledge her as their own mother.[36]

A similar story can be found in Maxine Hong Kingston's book, *The Women Warrior*. Moon Orchid, a Chinese immigrant woman, came to the United States to join her husband at the age of sixty-eight. He had become a successful neurosurgeon in California and married a young Americanized Chinese woman. Cultural shock and emotional hurt together made her collapse, and she eventually died in an insane asylum in California.[37]

The deterioration of traditional family relationships, the pressure of American life, and the poverty in Chinatown contributed to a rise in the percentage of suicides by Chinese women. According to Stanford Lyman's study, the percentage of suicides by Chinese women in San Francisco increased from 17.5 percent of total suicides in the 1950s to 28.3 percent in the 1960s. Most of the suicides were married, unemployed, and relatively older immigrant women.[38]

In contrast, those highly educated Chinese students and professionals experienced better adaptation to the new society. Some of them had chosen mates outside of their ethnic group and maintained successful marriages. Ms. R, for instance, came to the United States from Beijing after World War II as a student majoring in library science. After completion of her degree, she was employed as a university professor and married an Italian American man who worked at the same campus as a librarian. With appreciation of each other's cultural heritage, they enjoyed a happy marriage.[39] Similarly, Ms. C met her husband, a European American chemist, at her work place, and they had a happy family life since then. As she noted:

> I am very happy about my marriage. If you work with somebody, then you might develop relationship with him, which was what happened to us. My husband appreciate Oriental culture. He has great knowledge of Chinese history and geography. He made the whole thing smooth.[40]

Interracial marriage certainly did not always result in social acceptance and economic upward mobility. Not every Chinese woman who married a non-Chinese did so because the interracial marriage had such a practical socioeconomic function. All women interviewed had equal or higher academic degrees and satisfactory professional lives compared to their husbands. Marrying a member of the majority of the society, however, was probably a good indicator of a Chinese intellectual woman's better cultural adaptation and social assimilation.

Social Activities and Community Work

In order to cope better with the difficulties created by the immigrant life, postwar Chinese immigrant women developed different types of social gatherings and community services. One important type of social gathering was in clubs comprised of close friends. This kind of social interaction often occurred among Chinese immigrant women who came from well-to-do Chinese families. Having led an easy and affluent life in China, these Chinese women gathered frequently to spend their leisure time playing Mah-jong, eating fine Chinese food, and gossiping about one another's families and friends. After their immigration, they transplanted this familiar social institution to the New World in order to ease their isolated and lonesome immigrant life. As depicted in Amy Tan's *The Joy Luck Club*, Suyuan Woo was a Chinese immigrant woman from a rich family in Shanghai. With three of her friends, An-mei Hsu, Lindo Jong, and Ying-ying St. Clair, she started "the San Francisco version of the Joy Luck Club" in 1949. They gathered regularly to play Mah-jong games, share Chinese delicacies, and chatter about their children.[41]

Significantly, these social gatherings were not only places where these women could have fun, eat Chinese food, and enjoy gossiping, but they were also enclaves where they could preserve their cultural habits, reminisce about old times, exchange information, and give emotional comfort to one another. In their gatherings, they insisted on maintaining old customs and parochial habits. They wore, Tan noted, "Chinese dresses with stiff stand-up collars and blooming branches of embroidered silk sewn over their breasts."[42] They met in one another's houses, where "too many once fragrant smells" from Chinese cooking have been "compressed onto a thin layer of invisible grease."[43] After Suyuan Woo died, the other three remaining aged women made an effort to get in touch with her daughters in China. Then they arranged for Jing-mei Woo, Suyuan Woo's American-born daughter, to visit China and meet her Chinese sisters there, which had been Suyuan Woo's long-cherished wish.[44]

Moreover, some Chinese female students or professionals were also enthusiastic participants in local Chinese community activities, especially those who settled in small university towns. Mrs. T's story was a good example. A native of Shanghai, Mrs. T came to the United States in 1947 to study library science at the University of Oregon and later settled in the university town of Eugene, Oregon. Being an active member of several local organizations such as the American Association of University Women, the Red Cross, and the Human Rights Commission, she was among those who organized the Eugene Chinese Benevolent Association. After her retirement, she devoted even more time and energy to community activities. She generously assisted many Chinese scholars and students in easing their adjustments to the new environment.[45] Like Mrs. T, Ms. C was active among Chinese student communities in a midwestern university town. She made efforts to participate in

all major activities organized by the Chinese students and to provide financial and moral support to the needy students.[46] Similarly,
Mrs. D was also very involved in the local Chinese community.
After her marriage to a Chinese professor at a midwestern medical
school, she settled in the small university town. Remote from any
major Chinese communities, Chinese students and faculty members there found friendship and support among themselves. Mrs. D
was a magnet for all Chinese students and faculty members:

> I like to be with people, and I always have friends to come to see
> me. On weekends or holidays, Chinese students and professors
> would come to my house to read Chinese newspapers, exchange
> news, and try new Chinese cooking recipes. Somebody joked that
> my house is a "Chinese Club." Many students still wrote to me or
> sent me gifts long after their graduation.[47]

Chinese women not only participated in activities in Chinese
communities, but some also became enthusiastic community workers

Figure 4.5. Chinese teacher and Chinese students from Taiwan at Northeast
Missouri State University, 1964. Huping Ling Collection.

after World War II. Sociologist Stacey G. H. Yap's work, which focuses on a group of Chinese women community workers in the Chinatown in Northville, Massachusetts, has revealed this fact.[48] Yap suggested that the development of community work was not recent but had undergone three historical stages: "the pioneering stage that began in the 1940s, the professional stage that began in the late 1960s, and the activist stage that began in the mid-1970s."[49]

According to Yap, four types of women became involved in community work: volunteers, professionals, officials, and activists. Each type "reflects differences in the relationship community workers have with the community and their approach to community." The volunteers, Yap has noted, only spent a small amount of time of two to five hours a week to work on community affairs because of their family responsibilities. In contrast, the new community workers were trained professionals, working full time in the community organizations and were more visible than volunteers. Their major responsibilities ranged from budget planning and approval, fundraising decisions and projects as well as program action. Finally there were the activists, who emerged in the late 1960s and early 1970s. Viewing Chinatown as a product of social and political discrimination against Asians, they were dedicated to the equal rights movement in the Chinese community.[50]

These community workers helped newly-arrived Chinese immigrants. They contributed individually to the needy people by giving away clothes or providing services that were necessary for helping the immigrants. Jean, a community worker in Northville, talked about the community work her family did:

> Community work probably goes back to my mother; we used to bring old clothes to refugees from China. She was a very generous person, she would give her clothes that she herself made and would give to these refugees coming in. . . .[51]

Oftentimes, such community activity was associated with church work, and the community workers were also devoted religious believers. Mimi, a community worker in Northville Chinatown who worked in the community for almost forty years, starting in the post-World War II period, recalled:

> I do mostly social services for people like interpreting, translating, helping people to write letters and I am very involved in church

work too. I feel that I've [got] to help because the Lord sends us into this world to do a mission. . . .[52]

In summary, during postwar years, many social changes occurred in American society, which resulted in the transformation of job opportunities for Chinese American women. The growth of the Chinese American female population and the widening of the job market made Chinese American women more visible in the larger society. No longer confined in domestic services or occupations only available in Chinatowns, they moved into clerical, sales, operative, technical, managerial, and professional occupations. This upward occupational mobility of Chinese American women helped change the previously prevalent images of Chinese women as exotic showpieces, sinful prostitutes, and docile clerks. It also contributed to the formation of a new stereotype for Chinese Americans as the "model minority" in the 1960s.

The influx of postwar immigrants aggravated the existing problems in Chinese communities. To ease the problems, some Chinese women volunteered to help newcomers, and later professional community workers appeared. In the ethnic enclave, community work proved to be valuable for the stability of the Chinese community.

Part Three

Contemporary Chinese American Women, 1965–1990s

Chapter 5

New Turning Point

Most scholars of Chinese American studies have agreed that World War II was a turning point for Chinese Americans.[1] Other scholars have related the phenomenal increase of the Chinese American population to the abolition of the discriminatory and anti-Chinese immigration quota system on October 3, 1965, or have claimed the 1965 immigration law opened the way for the second wave of Asian immigration.[2] Few of them, however, have attributed the noticeable educational, occupational, economic, political, social, and psychological changes since the 1960s to the social reform movement in the 1960s and the 1965 immigration law. In this chapter, I will argue that dramatic changes occurred in Chinese American women's educational, occupational, political, and psychological experiences since the 1960s, and all of the changes directly or indirectly were related to the social reform movement in the 1960s and the liberalization of American immigration policies in 1965. I will also examine the motives and means of immigration of the Chinese immigrant women since the 1960s and the socioeconomic conditions for them in the United States.

Educational and Occupational Achievements

In the 1960s, the civil rights movements pressured the Kennedy administration, and especially the Johnson administration, to pass legislation to ban discrimination in employment, education, electoral politics, medical assistance, and housing on the basis of race, color, religion, sex, or national origin. The Civil Rights Act of 1964 outlawed racial discrimination in all public accommodations and authorized the Justice Department to act with greater authority in school and voting matters. Its Title 7, "Equal Employment Opportunity," banned discriminatory hiring in companies with more than twenty-five employees on the grounds of race, religion, gender, or national origin. This legislation was one of the great achievements of the 1960s. Although, as many acknowledged, the civil rights movement was predominantly a black movement, other minorities including the Chinese also benefitted from it.

One of the changes inspired by the civil rights movement was the curriculum reform in higher educational institutions. The growing Asian American communities since 1965 demanded a change in the structure of universities. In the late 1960s, Asian American communities and scholars launched the Asian American studies movement. In 1968, San Francisco State University spearheaded the first Asian American studies program. Other schools in California soon followed. By the early 1970s, Asian American studies programs or courses were established at colleges and universities throughout the United States.[3] Most of the Asian American studies programs intended to raise Asian American students' ethnic consciousness and self-awareness, and to develop research on Asian Americans.

In the 1980s, a new wave of interest in Asian American studies swept the East Coast, and the institutionalization of Asian American studies program took place among a number of universities. In 1987, Wellesley University, Boston University, and the University of Massachusetts at Boston incorporated new courses on Asian Americans into their curricula. Cornell University, Brown University, and Yale University also developed Asian American studies programs or courses in the same year.[4]

The Asian American studies movement continued in the 1990s when some schools in the Midwest adopted courses on Asian Americans. In 1992, the author developed Asian American studies courses at Truman State University (then Northeast Missouri State University) in Kirksville, Missouri. By now, Asian American studies programs have evolved into a nationwide movement.

The educational achievements of Chinese Americans were very impressive. The *San Francisco Chronicle* of December 1, 1983, for instance, made the following comments: Asian Americans are today held to be among "the most economically successful minority group in the country. . . . Exceeding all other groups in income and education. . . . ethnic Asians are the state's [California's] fastest growing minority and have begun to influence the state's education system, economy and government out of proportion to their numbers."[5]

Chinese Americans' educational achievements were noticeable not only in California, but throughout the United States. According to the 1970 U.S. census, school enrollment rates of the Chinese compared favorably with those of the Japanese, the Filipinos, and the total United States population. The high enrollment of both men and women between 18 and 24 was particularly impressive (see table 5.1). Chinese American women college graduates also composed the higher percentage since the 1950 compared with black women, white women, and white men (see table 5.2).

Educational achievement of Chinese Americans largely contributed to their economic success. Many national publications recorded the academic achievements of Chinese American students in universities. They assumed that the educational levels of adult Chinese had a direct bearing on their occupational and income status. In 1970, 31 percent of Chinese women in the 25–34 age group were employed in professional and technical positions, as

Table 5.1
School Enrollment Rates of Total U.S., Japanese, Filipinos, and Chinese by Sex and Age, 1970 (in percentage)

	7–13 Yrs.	14–17 Yrs.		18–24 Yrs.	
		M	F	M	F
Total U.S.	97.3		92.5		32.2
Japanese	97.5	96.3	96.2	55.6	48.4
Filipinos	96.1	92.9	92.6	27.5	23.2
Chinese	96.4	95.3	95.2	70.8	58.2

Source: U.S. Census of Population, 1970.

Table 5.2
Chinese American Women with Four or More Years of College Compared with Other Groups, 1940–1990 (in percentage)

	1940	1950	1960	1970	1980	1990
Chinese Am. Women	3.7	7.8	12.5	16.5	25.6	35.0
Black Women	1.2	2.2	3.3	4.6	8.3	11.7
White Women	4.0	5.3	6.0	8.4	13.3	18.4
White Men	5.8	7.6	10.3	15.0	21.3	25.0
Chinese Am. Men	2.8	8.5	18.2	30.8	43.8	46.7

Source: U.S. Census, 1940–1990.

opposed to only 17 percent in 1960. More Chinese American women in 1986 were in the professional (25 percent) and technical/sales (40 percent) sectors of the work force. That year, the median income of Chinese American women ($11,891) was slightly higher than that of white women ($10,512).[6]

Taking advantage of the favorable situation, some Chinese American women of strong personality and talent attained national prominence. Connie Chung's rise in the broadcasting industry exemplified the successful Chinese American women's experience. In 1971 Connie Chung was hired by the Columbia Broadcast System (CBS), one of the major national television networks. She clearly indicated that CBS hired her and other minority women only because of the pressure from the Federal Communication Committee demanding the hiring of minorities. Once hired, however, she rapidly demonstrated her dedication and capability through her excellent performance in the 1972 presidential campaign and the Watergate incident. She soon became one of the few famous women news anchors on a national television network.[7] Setting an example of exertion and success, Connie Chung has been the pride and admiration of Chinese Americans.

In the following decades, other Chinese American women continued to become successful in the fields of arts and sports. In the early 1980s, Maya Lin, a talented and serious artist, emerged as a promising architect. In 1981 when she was only a twenty-one-year-old undergraduate at Yale, her design for the Vietnam Veterans Memorial in Washington, D.C. was selected as the winner from 1,420 entries. Many Vietnam veterans felt that they could finally get rid of the nightmare of the war when they saw the Memorial, despite some commentators' criticism of her work due to her age, gender, and race. The critics charged that she was too young to understand the cruelty of Vietnam War and therefore her work was only "a shameful black crack." They believed her design was chosen because the selecting committee deliberately looked for a design by an Asian.[8]

Maya Lin was born in a Chinese immigrant family in Athens, Ohio in 1959. She was encouraged to pursue her love for the arts by her father, a geneticist and the dean of fine arts at Ohio University, and by her mother, a professor of English and Asian literature also at Ohio University. Growing up, she did not play with dolls. Instead, she enjoyed anything she could get her hands on, such as silversmithing and foundry casting. After creating the Vietnam Veterans Memorial in Washington, D.C., Maya Lin completed the Civil Rights Memorial in Montgomery, Alabama in 1989, and the Museum for African Art in Manhattan in 1993. Beginning in 1994, she turned her interest to architecture and sculpture. In this same year, she renovated two houses, one in Williamstown, Massachusetts, and the other in Santa Monica, California. She also used 43 tons of broken glass to make Groundswell, three pieces of landscape sculpture at the Wexner Center for the Arts, in Columbus, Ohio. She envisioned Groundswell to be a geode "cutting the earth and polishing the earth."[9] Her clear vision and creativity enabled her to become, in one author's words, the "only heroine" in American architecture.[10]

Michelle Kwan emerged as a shining star in figure skating in 1994 when the thirteen-year-old skater was bumped from the Olympic figure skating team in favor of Nancy Kerrigan. Rather than being bothered by the matter, she concentrated on preparing herself for future opportunities. Daughter of a Chinese immigrant family in Torrance, California, Michelle Kwan started skating when she was a five-year-old. Her parents, owners of a family Chinese restaurant, wholeheartedly supported her career. They scheduled her training and schooling, and accompanied her to every meet. After years of hard work, Michelle Kwan appeared at the World Figure Skating Championship Contest in Edmonton, Canada, on March 23, 1996 with a completely new and mature image. The more decisive factor to her winning, however, was her mature and flawless skating. Using a tiny technical edge, a triple toe jump, in the last seconds of her performance, she defeated the defending champion, China's nineteen-year-old Chen Lu, and became the world ladies champion.[11]

Participation in Mainstream Politics

In addition to educational and professional achievements, Chinese American women became more involved in American mainstream politics since the 1970s. This was partly due to the valuable training ground of minority and women's political movements. It was also partly due to the increase of the Chinese American population and the growth of the Chinese American middle class, which reinforced Chinese Americans' political clout and improved the image of Chinese Americans from illiterate "coolies," or "sojourners" to a highly-educated "model minority." Like their male counterparts, some Chinese American women entered American politics, holding posts first at the local level, then at the state level, and finally in the federal government.

March Fong Eu, a pioneer Chinese American woman in mainstream politics, started her political career by serving on the California School Board in 1956. She was elected California's secretary of state in 1974.[12] Jean King served as lieutenant governor of Hawaii from 1978 to 1982, and became the highest-ranking Chinese American woman ever to hold a state office.[13] Lily Chen was the first Chinese American woman in the nation to be honored to serve as mayor in Monterey Park, California in 1983.[14] Judy Chu, another Chinese American woman, was elected as the mayor of Monterey Park in 1990 and in 1994.

On September 15, 1988, Qianwen Chen won election as representative of the New York State Democratic Party in the Sixty-First District of New York City, becoming the only Chinese American representative in this district. The Sixty-First District covered Lower Manhattan, where the Chinatown community was located. Having graduated from the City College of New York, she had been an activist in Chinese communities in New York City. She was enthusiastic in providing Chinese community social services and fighting for benefits for Chinese communities. She also maintained close associations with other ethnic minority groups. All of these merits helped her to win the election.[15]

Kexin Zheng was president of the San Francisco chapter of the Organization of Chinese Americans, a national group, founded in 1973, which promoted civil rights, culture, and education for Chinese. On October 20, 1990, she was elected president of the organization at the meeting of the Board of Directors. She became the youngest and the first woman president of the organization. Once in office, she urged the organization to participate in American mainstream politics and to obtain equal rights in education and employment.[16]

In the 1990 race, there were twenty-two Chinese Americans, among whom fourteen won election to various government offices. March Fong Eu won her fifth term as California's secretary of state. Following in her footsteps, Meilian Liu became the second Chinese female secretary of state in Nevada. Mengshi Deng was elected the judge of the city of San Francisco.[17]

In addition to serving the local governments, Chinese American women entered the federal government. On April 19, 1989, Elaine Chao was appointed Assistant Secretary of Transportation. This appointment made Chao the highest female official, the first

Chinese American federal secretary, the highest federal government officeholder among first generation immigrants, and the youngest such departmental officer. Born in Taipei in 1953, Chao emigrated to the United States with her parents at the age of eight. With a degree of Master of Business Administration from Harvard University, she worked in several banks. In 1983, after an intense competition, she was selected as a "White House Scholar" and began her government career. Due to her achievements, she was chosen as one of the ten most outstanding youths in the United States in 1987.[18] After her appointment, she became an active and powerful spokeswoman for Asian Americans. For instance, she strongly opposed the "quota system" in the hiring of government agencies and educational institutions prevailing in recent years. She claimed that the prejudiced quota system was against the basic principles of the U.S. Constitution and created false equality. She also stated that well-qualified women and minority professionals did not need the protection of a quota system.[19]

Chinese American women politicians not only entered the federal government, but also served as the U.S. ambassador to foreign countries. Julia Chang Bloch became the first U.S. ambassador of Asian descent in American history when she was appointed as the U.S. ambassador to Nepal in September 1989. Julia Chang Bloch was born in China in 1943 and emigrated to the United States with her family in 1951. She received an undergraduate degree from the University of California at Berkeley and a master's degree from Harvard University in government and East Asian regional studies. She first worked for the Peace Corps in Southeast Asia, and later for the Agency for International Development (AID), rising to head its Asia and Near East Bureau. Upon her arrival in Kathmandu in 1989 where a revolution just occurred, she organized the evacuation of nearly 2,000 Americans and won the trust of both the palace and revolutionaries.[20]

Attitude Change of the Younger Generation: More Appreciation of Chinese Heritage

Changes also occurred in the familial life of Chinese American women. Although cultural and generational gaps existing since the 1920s still survived within Chinese American families, the close mother-daughter attachment began to catch social attention. Wayne Wang's 1985 film *Dim Sum* vividly portrayed a loving and touching mother-daughter relationship in which there was a mutual reliance and attachment between the mother and daughter. Though having lived in the United States for forty-five years, Mrs. Lum, the mother, remained illiterate in English. In order to take care of her mother, Geraldine lived with her mother when most of her peers moved out of their parents' homes or got married. When she finally moved out, she visited her mother almost every day to help her cope with daily chores. These included cleaning and writing checks which Mrs. Lum was not able to do. Meanwhile her mother cooked fine Chinese food for her, a skill in which Geraldine did not excel.[21]

Moreover, in the past three decades, younger Chinese began to appreciate and attempted to understand their cultural heritage. This change of attitude toward Chinese cultural heritage was clearly revealed in Jade Snow Wong's two autobiographical novels. Wong appeared as a rebel against Chinese tradition in her first novel *Fifth Chinese Daughter*, published in 1945, in which one could feel the author's pain of being torn between two cultures and two generations. Yet, thirty years later, she reevaluated her cultural tradition and showed appreciation and a gratefulness to her parents for their persistence in passing on her Chinese heritage. She expressed this feeling in her second autobiographical novel *No Chinese Stranger*: "... because of my father's discipline and education in my heritage, I did not feel a Chinese stranger [when I visited China in 1972]."[22] Historian Roger Daniels has explained that Jade Snow Wong's attitude change and other Chinese youths' recognition of the virtues of Chinese culture reflected "a change brought about, at least in part, by an increasing sense of security about the place of Chinese Americans in our national life. Such feelings were doubtless heightened by President Richard Nixon's China trip and by the acknowledged success of more and more Chinese in American life."[23]

In 1980, a Chinese girl from San Francisco wrote to "Dear Diane," Diane Yen-Mei Wong, who was the former San Francisco Chinatown Youth Center Executive Director. The girl expressed her desire to learn Chinese and encouraged other Chinese youth to preserve their family's language.

> When I was little, my parents tried to force me to learn Chinese, but I always resisted. I guess that I was too concerned about being 100% American like all my friends.
>
> Now that I'm 25, I realize that maybe I should've listened to my mom a little more. I've never been able to share my feelings

with my parents or talk with my grandparents. Since they are getting older, I feel like I'm missing out on all of what they have learned.

I've decided to take language classes myself, but I just wanted to encourage other young people to try to maintain their family's language. Don't succumb to the pressures that I felt about trying to be American. You can be an American and bilingual, too.[24]

This trend was stimulated by the achievements of Chinese American youth in higher education and work. The outstanding academic performance of Chinese American youths made educators and behavioral scientists believe that there must be something inherent in Chinese culture that promoted academic excellence.[25] The new and successful experiences of Chinese Americans since the 1960s impelled them to look at their heritage in a positive way.

There was a parallel to this cultural recognition among other immigrant groups. The so-called Hansen Thesis revealed this immigrant cultural phenomenon. Historian Marcus Lee Hansen's hypothesis was captured in the aphorism that "what the son wishes to forget the grandson wishes to remember."[26] In a speech on "The Problem of the Third Generation Immigrant" presented on May 15, 1937 at the annual meeting of the Augustana Historical Society in Rock Island, Hansen argued that each generation—the pioneers themselves, their children, and their grandchildren—faced a special problem rooted in and characteristic of its social position within the overall population. The problem of the first generation was to make the adjustments necessary to survive economically, to function within an alien culture, and to learn about democracy. The challenge of the second generation was "to inhabit two worlds at the same time." The problem of the third generation was properly interpreting the history of the first two.[27]

Motives and Means of Immigration Since the 1960s

In addition to the social reforms in the 1960s, the 1965 Immigration Act and the consequent influx of new Chinese immigrants contributed to the transformation of Chinese American society. The 1965 Immigration Act, officially called An Act to Amend the Immigration and Nationality Act of 1924, abolished the 1924 quota system and set up three immigration principles of family reunification, the need for skilled workers, and the admission of refugees.

According to these principles, the visas were allocated among quota immigrants from the Eastern Hemisphere in the following percentage: (1) twenty percent of total annual visas to unmarried children of citizens of the United States, (2) twenty percent to spouses and unmarried children of permanent residents, (3) ten percent to professionals, scientists, and artists with "exceptional ability," (4) ten percent to married children of citizens of the United States, (5) twenty-four percent to siblings of citizens of the United States, (6) ten percent to skilled and unskilled workers in occupations "for which a shortage of employable and willing persons exists in the United States," and (7) six percent to refugees.[28]

The architects of the 1965 Immigration Act intended to make the immigration policies appear more humanitarian and impartial to applicants on the one hand, and more beneficial to the United States on the other. The new law allowed 20,000 quota immigrants from every country in the Eastern Hemisphere to be admitted to the United States each year, regardless of the size of the country. It reserved seventy-four percent including twenty percent in preference 1, another twenty percent in preference 2, ten percent in preference 4, and twenty-four percent in preference 5 of the total 170,000 visas annually allotted for the Eastern Hemisphere for family reunification. The lawmakers anticipated that European immigrants would continue to be the cohort of new immigrants, since there was a very small percentage (0.5 percent of the total U.S. population in the 1960s) of Asian Americans in the country.[29] Two occupational preferences (preferences 3 and 6) allowed the United States immigration authorities and the Department of Labor to select carefully only applicants with special training and skills who would fill the vacuum in the American job market. In the years following this act, the Chinese American population increased dramatically. In addition, the male/female ratio, as seen in table 4.1, finally approached parity.

The majority of new immigrants came to the United States for economic reasons. The influx of Chinese refugees from Vietnam since 1975 and immigrants from Cuba, Jamaica, and other Caribbean islands were lured by economic opportunities in America. In addition to laboring immigrants, a large number of professionals (the better-educated and the wealthier from China, Taiwan, Hong Kong, and Southeast Asia) also arrived since 1965. These new immigrants benefitted from the 1965 Immigrant Act, which gave priority to refugees, to those who had close family members in the United States, and to applicants who had skills, education, and capital.

    After the normalization of the Sino-American relationship in
1979, some Chinese who had family members in the United States
were allowed to come to America as immigrants. Since many of
them came for economic reasons and were determined to settle,
they brought their families as allowed by U.S. immigration policies. Some resigned their professional jobs in China and started
from scratch in the United States. Mr. C was a scientist in China
and immigrated to the United States in 1981. At the age of 47, he
enrolled in the department of geology at a midwestern university
to work on his master's degree. His wife and children joined him
two years later. Mrs. C tried very hard to adjust to her new life; she
learned English and obtained her driver license. She finally was
able to work for an optical company as a technician, earning a
$25,000 annual income for her family.[30]

    Like many other postwar immigrants, many Chinese immi-
grant women entering America after 1965 were driven to immigration for political reasons. The constant political campaigns since
the Communists took over in 1949, particularly the Cultural Revolution from 1966 to 1976 and the Tiananmen Incident on June 4,
1989, destroyed many Communist believers' careers and faith,
threatened their lives, and forced them to become immigrants or
exiled émigrés. Like Guan Ling-ling, the heroine in her autobiographical novel *The Dragon's Village*, Cheng Yuan-tsung sincerely
believed in the Communist Party, and decided to stay and work for
the people in a new China when her wealthy family fled to Hong
Kong in 1949. During her participation in the land reform movement, she re-educated herself according to the Party's rules. She
criticized herself at the "criticism and self-criticism" sessions.[31] Like
other intellectuals and government officials, she suffered a great
deal during the Cultural Revolution, which changed her belief in
Communism. She left China, arrived in the United States in 1972,
and taught Chinese language and literature at Cornell University.
She felt that she had more academic freedom in America, where
she became actively involved in scholarly discussions on contemporary Chinese literature and art in the 1970s. In August 1974, she
participated in an important discussion on Chinese literature of
the 1930s and 1940s at a workshop held at Harvard University.

    Similar to the Cultural Revolution, the Tiananmen Incident
and the following political purge chased some prominent intellectuals and political dissidents out of the country. Among these Chinese, there were a few women. Chai Ling, a prominent student
leader of the 1989 democracy movement in China, was one of the

activists wanted by the Chinese government. After almost one year of hiding, she was smuggled through Hong Kong to France. Later, she arrived in the United States and gave speeches at various rallies. She condemned the Communist hardliners, appealed for political reform, and called for a human rights movement in China.[32]

Many others came to the United States after 1960 for a better education and personal fulfillment. Among this group of immigrants, students from Taiwan formed the first wave of large-scale student immigration. Taiwan had a separate immigration quota of 20,000 per year, so Chinese from that island doubled the immigrant ranks. In the 1960s, there was a study abroad craze in Taiwan while universities and colleges were closed in Mainland China due to the Cultural Revolution. It seemed desirable for graduates of universities and colleges to pursue graduate studies abroad, especially in the United States.[33] From 1950 to 1974, a total of 30,765 students were approved by the Chinese Ministry of Education of Taiwan for advanced study in the United States.[34] In the following decades, the number of Chinese students from Taiwan increased rapidly. Between 1979 and 1987, approximately 186,000 students came to America to continue their education.[35]

The study abroad movement had roots in success of the post-war Taiwan economy. In the 1950s and 1960s, Taiwan experienced economic growth accompanied by structural and demographic changes. There was a dramatic rise in the relative significance of the nonagricultural sector, particularly in manufacturing. Industrial development required more highly-educated and well-trained personnel. Meanwhile, a demographic transition from high to low fertility, coinciding with a shift in income distribution toward greater equality, changed people's attitudes toward child-raising; higher incomes and fewer children enabled parents to support their children's desire to obtain an advanced degree in the United States.[36]

Ms. L was a graduate of Cheng Gong University majoring in English literature; Ms. M was a graduate of Danshui University majoring in French literature; Ms. R was a graduate of Providence College, a private Catholic college, majoring in western languages; and Ms. S was a graduate from National Taiwan University majoring in economics. These women and many others followed the national trend to come to America for a further education during the 1960s and 1970s.[37] Ms. M's decision to come to America was typical:

> We think that we just followed the trend . . . At my time that type after college to go to abroad was a fashion. So every college gradu-

ate, if they had financial capacity, or they could get admission from the school in the U. S., everybody would like to go.[38]

After the 1970s, the study broad craze from Taiwan spread to the Chinese mainland. Since the establishment of the People's Republic of China (PRC), the government, like its predecessors, relied on foreign counties to train its specialists. The Soviet Union was the only foreign power friendly to China during its first decades; therefore, the Chinese government kept sending students to Russia, until the 1960s when the relations between Moscow and Beijing openly broke. Starting then, Mao Zedong led China into a reclusive existence by advocating self-sufficiency and self-reliance. During the decade of the Cultural Revolution (1966–76), international exchange programs were virtually suspended and few were sent abroad to study. Only 1,629 students who primarily studied foreign languages were allowed to study abroad.[39] Following the Sino-American reconciliation in 1972, the government of the PRC once again began to view foreign study as a shortcut to the acquisition of world-level scientific and technical knowledge. The decision to initiate scholarly exchange was made in 1978, even prior to the normalization of relations between the United States and the People's Republic of China in 1979. Since then, this cultural exchange has remained a vital link in the relationship between the two countries.

Similar to what had happened in Taiwan twenty years ago, study abroad became extremely popular in the PRC simply because one would be better off with an American graduate degree. For middle-aged and established scholars, study abroad became a criterion for promotion.[40] For young university or college graduates, an advanced degree from a foreign institution, especially from one in the United States, symbolized the beginning of a promising career in China.[41]

Study in America for many of these people, however, meant not only academic improvement but also material gain, in terms of the savings they could make from their meager scholarships, stipends, or other income. These savings were small by American standards, but to many Chinese they were significant in modernizing their daily life. They could equip their families with modern electronic gadgets when they converted their savings into Chinese currency at a very favorable exchange rate.[42] Still many others simply wanted to find an opportunity to stay in America by studying there.[43]

Motivated by their various dreams and expectations, more and more Chinese students and scholars have entered the United States since 1979. According to official Chinese records, from 1979 to 1988 there were 36,000 Chinese students studying in the United States; thirty-seven percent of them were self-supporting.[44] According to American sources, this figure was even larger. Jesse Chain Chou's study has indicated that there were 63,000 students and scholars from the People's Republic of China during the same time period.[45] The Immigration and Naturalization Service estimated that there were 73,000 Chinese students in June 1989.[46] In a statement on December 2, 1989, President George Bush announced that "as many as 80,000 Chinese have studied and conducted research in the United States since these exchanges began."[47]

In contrast to government-sponsored students and scholars (J-1 visa holders), self-supporting students (F-1 visa holders) were financed either by the U.S. institutions or by their relatives in the United States.[48] They usually hoped to earn a graduate degree first, then find a job, and eventually become a permanent resident in America. The survey of over two hundred Chinese students' spouses conducted by the author indicated that ninety percent of F-1 students hoped to stay in the United States after the completion of their education. The path toward their dream, however, was rough, even for those who came to the United States with financial support from their American relatives. They were legally guaranteed at least one year of financial aid from their sponsors, but, in fact, most of them had to earn their living and tuition from the very beginning. In 1988, Ms. Z arrived in the United States from Shanghai to work on a master's degree in education at a midwestern university. Although she came to America as an F-1 student sponsored by her relatives in the United States, she had to be self-reliant. She worked in the university cafeteria, library, and in whatever job allowed by her visa status until she was granted a scholarship by the university in the following year.[49]

The sex-ratio among Chinese students from the PRC remained uneven. Since 1979, according to Leo A. Orleans' study, only less than twenty percent of the J-1 students were female, while female F-1 students did not even exist until 1983 (see table 5.3). In fact, this small percentage of female Chinese students in America reflected the students sex-ratio in Chinese higher education. In most Chinese universities or colleges, the percentage of female students varied from ten percent to forty-five percent, depending on the field of study. Generally, female students in Chinese universities amounted to roughly ten percent in the pure sciences and engineering schools, thirty percent in medical schools, and forty to forty-five percent in the humanities.[50] In short, female students were underrepresented in all subjects, especially the sciences, within the Chinese higher educational system. This disparity was a complex historical phenomenon. Traditional values and gender discrimination in secondary education and admission policy of higher education worked together to discourage women from pursuing higher education. Logically, this small percentage of female university students in China resulted in an even smaller percentage of female students studying abroad.

In addition, as a general rule, the Chinese government viewed sending students in the pure sciences and engineering as the first priority in its educational program. Chinese authorities have always been reluctant to spend the nation's foreign currency reserve on students in the humanities, for they believed that only those individuals who had special training in advanced science and technology could immediately benefit the country.

The more genuine reason behind this pragmatic policy was the fear that western ideology and philosophy would harm the Chinese socialist system. Though publicly calling for China's Four Modernizations (modernization of agriculture, industry, science and technology, and national defense), the new Chinese government had actually inherited the official belief from Qing dynasty of *"zhongxue wei ti, xiyue wei yong"* (meaning "Chinese learning for fundamentals, western learning for practical application").[51] As a result of this restricted study abroad policy, female students have always remained a minority.

Table 5.3
Percentage of Women among Chinese Students and Scholars, 1979–1985

Year	J-1 Scholars	J-1 Students	F-1 Students
1979	14	13	n.a.
1980	16	18	n.a.
1981	15	18	n.a.
1982	17	18	n.a.
1983	18	17	37
1984	20	19	45
1985	24	20	41

Source: Leo A. Orleans, *Chinese Students in America: Politics, Issues, and Numbers*, Washington, D.C.: National Academy Press, 1988), 98.

The uneven gender distribution among Chinese students began to change in 1985. In this year, the Chinese government revised its policy regarding cultural exchange programs, making it more flexible and less restrictive than before. More students and scholars in the humanities were selected to study in the United States, and consequently more female students were allowed to cross the Pacific Ocean, as a result of the relatively higher percentage of female students in the humanities. By the end of the 1980s, female Chinese students comprised thirty percent of all Chinese students in the universities and colleges in the United States.[52]

The relaxation of official Chinese policy also contributed to another demographic change. Starting from the early 1980s, many Chinese students began to arrange for their spouses to join them, something never officially permitted before. In December 1986 to accept the reality and to regulate the procedure, the Chinese government modified its policies on the study abroad program. In a document titled "State Education Commission Provisions on Study Abroad," the government agreed that "since the time of studying abroad for the graduate students is relatively longer, the application of their spouses for visiting them abroad should be handled . . ."[53] The same document also stipulated:

> If, during the visiting period, the spouse of the graduate student has obtained foreign scholarship or subsidiary funding and applies for studying abroad she/he can report to her/his employing unit for approval during her/his visitation abroad, thus becoming a public- or self-funded student studying abroad through proper procedure.[54]

Since the formulation of this policy, more Chinese women joined their student husbands, and similarly, some Chinese men joined their student wives. According to the author's survey of over two hundred Chinese students' spouses, more than ninety percent came to the United States after 1987. Ninety-five percent of the wives of students were university and college graduates. Many came to America with the plan of being a dependent first (it was much easier to enter the United States as a dependent of an already-admitted student than as a student), and then with the secondary goal of being admitted to an American institution for a graduate degree.[55] These women became potential students, and many of them did in fact fulfill their secondary goal of studying in the

Figure 5.1. A group of Chinese students from the People's Republic of China, 1987. Huping Ling Collection.

Figure 5.2. Wedding of Chinese students, 1987. The bride was from Taiwan, and bridgegroom from the People's Republic of China. Huping Ling Collection.

United States.[56] The presence of Chinese student wives balanced the uneven sex distribution among Chinese students. In the 1990s, the gender ratio of females to males became three to four in most universities and colleges.[57]

Unlike the early Chinese immigrant women who came mainly from a few village districts in the Guangdong Province in southern China, a majority of the new immigrants came from Taiwan, Hong Kong, and other areas of China. In recent decades, one could hear Putonghua (or Mandarin), various types of Guangdongese (Hong Kong, Canton, and village dialects), Fujianese, Hakka, Shanghainese, and Taiwanese in Chinatowns across the country.

Also, unlike the early Chinese immigrant women who predominantly concentrated in menial jobs, the new Chinese immigrant women gravitated toward a wide variety of occupations. They were restaurant helpers, factory workers, seamstresses, food store proprietors, office workers, government employees, college students, artists, teachers, and professionals such as engineers, professors, and lawyers.

There was, however, a parallel between the old and new Chinese immigrant women. Like their counterparts from a century ago, the new Chinese immigrant women tended to settle in urban areas and in various Chinatowns located in the major cities of the

Table 5.4
Ten Preferred States of Residence for Chinese: 1980

State	All Chinese	% of Total	Foreign-Born Chinese	% of Total Foreign-Born
1. California	325,882	40.1	174,421	39.5
2. New York	147,250	18.1	96,135	21.8
3. Hawaii	55,916	6.9	10,183	2.3
4. Illinois	28,847	3.6	16.772	3.8
5. Texas	26,714	3.3	16,486	3.7
6. Massachusetts	24,882	3.1	14,650	3.3
7. New Jersey	23,432	2.9	13,591	3.1
8. Washington	17,984	2.2	9,716	2.2
9. Maryland	15,037	1.9	8,617	1.9
10. Pennsylvania	13,769	1.7	7,939	1.8
Total	679,713	83.8	368,510	83.4

Source: U.S. Bureau of the Census, *1980 Census of the Population, Supplementary Reports* (Washington, D.C.: Government Printing Office, July 1981) and "Foreign-Born Immigrants: Chinese—Tabulations from the 1980 U.S. Census of the Population and Housing," mimeographed report, Washington, D.C., October, 1984.

United States. There they were able to find work easily (even without adequate language skills), obtain Chinese ingredients for preparing favorite foods, and engage in social interaction with people who spoke the same language and had the same customs and traditions. Table 5.4 shows the ten states where the largest number of Chinese resided in 1980. As can be seen, California was the preferred place for new Chinese immigrants, and New York was the second most attractive. In fact, New York seemed to be a particularly popular place of residence for the foreign-born Chinese. Following New York, Illinois, Texas, Massachusetts, and New Jersey became the other popular destinations for the new immigrants, indicating a different settlement pattern of Chinese immigration since 1965. While the old Chinese immigrants tended to settle in Chinatowns in California, Hawaii, and New York, the new Chinese immigrants chose various places as their new home, including not only long-established Chinatowns in coastal cities, but new emerging Chinese communities in Midwest and South as well (see table 5.4).

Conditions for New Immigrants

The new immigrant women had various experiences in the new land, depending on their education, personality, and financial ability. While most working-class immigrant women struggled for survival and hoped for success, many of the female students and professionals enjoyed upward socioeconomical mobility after the initial years of hardship and difficulty.

The working-class immigrants labored long hours under very difficult conditions, had low pay, and experienced feelings of uncertainty and insecurity. The great majority of Chinese working-class immigrants combined several incomes in a household to survive. Most new immigrant women entered garment factories that had primarily employed Chinese women since the 1960s.[58] Many of these garment workers were aged between 25 and 64, with limited education and marketable skills.[59] A garment worker could make $800 in a month at most, while a restaurant helper earned $1,100 a month but worked twelve hours a day, six days a week.[60] Aside from some of the garment and knitwear factories, few operations were unionized. Most working-class immigrant women had few options but to subject to the exploitation of factory owners. The factory owners often cut the pay of their employees in order to balance the loss when they received reduced orders from clothing manufactures.[61] In addition to the low pay, most garment workers worked under unsanitary and hazardous working conditions. Many garment factories located in the old small buildings in Chinatown did not have heating, air-conditioning, ventilation, plumbing, elevators, or fire exits.[62]

In addition to working hard to survive, the new immigrant women coped with other problems such as childcare and unemployment. Many wives of new immigrants stayed at home to take care of their children due to the shortage of day care and the high cost of babysitting. Li Zhiguo, a new Chinese immigrant in Boston, could not find a day care center for his children. Therefore, his wife stayed home to watch their children. With only one income, life for them was quite difficult.[63] Another Chinese couple in Boston, Mr. and Mrs. Huang, both worked in a Chinese restaurant. They had to leave their younger child with an ill and aged grandmother every morning until their eight-year-old daughter returned home from school every afternoon to take over the babysitting.[64] Most new immigrants lived frugally, not being secure in what might happen to their jobs. Mrs. Lou, a Chinese immigrant women in Boston, was not sure how her family would survive if her husband, the only breadwinner for the four-person family, became ill or unemployed.[65]

Some women suffered physical abuse from their husbands. Many of these victims were the wives of well-educated Chinese men. These victims often found that Chinese husbands, who were stressed by work and aware of the gaps between personal expectation and reality, made their families easy targets of their anger and frustration. Community social services in some major Chinese communities made efforts to deal with the problem. The Chinese American Women's Association in New York focused its work on dealing with problems of physical abuse of Chinese women among new immigrant families. The office of the Association received many phone calls from Chinese women, reporting that they had been abused by their husbands. Daoying Chen, the director of the Association, persuaded many of these husbands to go to psychiatrists. Aware of the financial difficulties of most new immigrants, the Association also organized a Family Service Center to provide counseling for the depressed husbands.[66]

This domestic violence resembled that occurred among other Asian immigrant women. Since most women came to America as dependents of their husbands, the economic dependence and vulnerability in legal status made the new immigrant women prone to

Figure 5.3. An elderly Chinese woman in San Francisco, July 1970. Huping Ling Collection.

domestic violence. Jacqueline R. Agtuca's work documented ample cases of domestic violence among the Filipinas in San Francisco. According to her study, 66 percent of the women who were killed in San Francisco in 1990 died as results of domestic violence.[67]

While life was difficult, some new immigrant women maintained a healthy and optimistic attitude. Ms. Wen immigrated to New York from Hong Kong with her husband and two daughters in

Figure 5.4. The kitchen of a Chinese restaurant in Kirksville, Missouri, 1997. Huping Ling Collection.

Figure 5.5. The kitchen of a Chinese restaurant in Kirksville, Missouri, 1997. Huping Ling Collection.

1988. Unable to find cheap housing in Chinatown, Wen and her family found a two bedroom apartment in western Harlem for a monthly rent of $200. She and her husband both worked to support the family. Her husband used to manage a small iron factory in Hong Kong. After their emigration to the United States, he delivered Chinese restaurant ingredients for a company in Chinatown, earning $1,200 a month. Wen had only an elementary education. She first worked in a garment factory. Later she took piece work at home after she had a newborn, making $14 a day for eight hours' work. Even this illegal work, however, could not be found all the time. Though she missed her life in Hong Kong, Wen did not regret their emigration to the United States. "Regretting is to waste my time," she commented, "even though life is difficult here, we both have jobs and we have a nice family. So we are still happy." "I heard some stories of successful Chinese here," she added, "but I understand that most of us are struggling."[68]

The experiences of Chinese female students and professionals, whatever their origin, differed from those of working-class immigrant women. Most students from Taiwan were supported financially by their families or by the savings they had made when they worked in Taiwan before they came America. On the contrary, many students from the mainland were sponsored by the Chinese government and various American groups.[69] Faraway from their families, they studied in American institutions where the systems were unfamiliar to them. The heavy school workload, which was even heavier due to the language difficulty, forced them to study the entire time they were awake. Many female students identified sources of stress in their lives primarily as academic pressure, isolation, and emotional loneliness.[70] Ms. K, whose father owned a large computer company in Taiwan, came to America in 1993 to major in finance at a midwestern university. She expressed her frustration this way:

> We want to find more American friends. But they usually speak English very fast, and if we are in the same group we can not get their meanings. I feel very awful that, if the professor divides us in groups, some people don't want to be with us, because our English is not as good as theirs, and maybe we cannot explain our thinking as well as theirs. . . . So we feel upset because of that.[71]

Ms. X was an English major and taught English for three years in a university in China. After she arrived in the United States in 1985 to pursue a graduate degree in English literature, she still experienced great difficulty with the language, and sensed the isolation caused by the language deficiency:

> I came to West Virginia first. [Then] I really doubted if I knew English at all. I thought I knew English, and I couldn't understand what people were talking about. In so many classes I couldn't quite understand what the classmates were discussing. And at parties some people try to have a conversation with me. Yeah, I was very slow in responding.[72]

The isolation experienced by the highly-educated female students in the past decades, however, was different from that suffered by their counterparts in the nineteenth and early-twentieth century in degree, intensity, and duration. The early Chinese immigrant women, mostly illiterate and from impoverished rural China, viewed by the American public exclusively as prostitutes, suffered legal exclusion from the American government, social discrimination from the general public, and physical isolation from both Americans and their own countrymen as well. The isolation lasted long after they had settled in America.[73] When Mrs. Yip, a Chinese woman in Los Angeles, was interviewed in 1925, she criticized the public discrimination practiced there: "Some of the theaters won't sell you a ticket if you are Chinese.... Most of the theaters will sell you tickets now, but they will give you the worst seats unless you know enough to insist on better ones. And on the street car someone will come along, look you over and then pass on. They won't sit beside you."[74]

Though female students also experienced isolation and discrimination, they entered the United States in a different era. The favorable attitude toward Chinese Americans since World War II, the civil rights movement in the 1960s, the women's liberation movement in the 1970s, the achievements by Chinese middle class in recent decades, and the renewed curiosity about China and the Chinese since President Richard Nixon's China visit in 1972 after a twenty-year period of confrontation, lessened Americans' prejudice toward Chinese in general. Moreover, these well-educated Chinese women learned western culture from books, learned the English language prior to their immigration, and were often better prepared in their academic fields than average American college students. Therefore, they appeared to have a promising future in front of them. They might have had the chance to assimilate into American middle-class society after a period of hard work. The cultural isolation they had felt seemed to be temporary.

If these Chinese female students felt isolated from American society, the wives of Chinese students experienced even greater loneliness in America. Most of them were college-educated and had professional jobs prior to their emigration to the United States. Coming to America to join their husbands, however, meant quitting their own careers and losing their own identities. In Chinese student communities, people often addressed a student's wife by Mrs. so-and-so rather than by her own name. Their visa status prohibited them from finding jobs off campus and their often-limited English comprehension frustrated them in making friends beyond the Chinese student community. Confined to their apartments, they spent their long days cleaning, cooking, reading novels or newspapers in Chinese, making phone calls to other student wives, and looking after children if they had any.

For those wives with children, there was not only the isolation from the outside world but also the threat of financial difficulty. In her article "Dawn Always Comes After Darkness," Wendy Wen-yawn Yen has described the hardship and joy she experienced in the United States as a student wife. She worked in an international hotel in Taiwan and enjoyed a leisurely life there. Since her arrival in America, however, she had begun to taste hardship.

> I arrived in Edmond, Oklahoma on December 20, 1981 in a heavy snow. Then my husband was working on his master in MBA and bachelor in computer. I found I was pregnant and worried about the fact that we could not afford a baby, for my husband was still relying on his parents financially. Facing the fact bravely, my husband found a job in a library as a custodian working from six to ten o'clock in the early morning and another job in a nearby Chinese restaurant washing dishes. Having two jobs plus full-time schooling, he could hardly see me. Watching him walking in the snow in the dawn, I cried behind the blind. As a northerner, my husband preferred noodle to rice. I learned to make dough first and then make the dough into noodle. I thought that was the only thing I could do to help my husband since I could not help him in making money and doing school work. I wanted him to be healthy enough to endure the hard life.
>
> I only stayed a night in hospital after I delivered my daughter because of the limit of our money. On the second day back home, I had fever. Following the folk Chinese prescription, I drank a big bowl of hot ginger soup, took a hot bath, and then covered myself with two big blankets. I was sweating all over my body and the fever was gone.

When summer came, my husband graduated with straight A and two degrees. He was admitted to the Ph.D. program in consulting management at the University of Nebraska. Life was still rough for us. In summer 1985, my husband finally earned his Ph.D. in management and master in computer. He found his first job at Miami University, and the whole family moved to Oxford, Ohio....[75]

To ease the difficulty experienced by Chinese students and their spouses, many organizations both inside and outside of Chinese student communities made great efforts. Chinese Student and Scholar Friendship Associations and Chinese Student Associations had branches at every campus across the country where Chinese students have enrolled, serving Chinese students from the PRC and Taiwan respectively. The major functions of these associations were providing new students with information about the campus and local community, handling problems among Chinese students, and organizing social activities within the student community or between the student community and other organizations or local communities.

In some Chinese student communities, students' spouses formed their own organizations. Wives of Chinese students from Taiwan at Case Western Reserve University in Cleveland, for instance, started the Cleveland Chinese Women's Association on September 1, 1989. It aimed to help student wives adjust to the new environment, exchange knowledge about housekeeping and recreation, and provide information on school applications and childraising. The members met biweekly and held seminars on topics as various as family economy, family affairs, sewing, cooking, papercutting, birth control, makeup techniques, American holidays, and western customs.[76]

Other programs and social services provided by American institutions or local communities also eased the lives of Chinese student wives. Host Family Programs found on almost every campus helped assist international students adjust to both academic and social life during their stay in the United States. Under these programs, each foreign student was provided a voluntary local American family as his or her host family. The responsibilities of these host families ranged from helping the foreign student arrange housing and transportation to providing opportunities to observe American society. The Community Service Program (COSEP) in Oxford, Ohio, for example, was composed of Oxford local residents who were interested in international students. It sought to make the time spent by international students at Miami University more enjoyable by offering them support, friendship, and assistance, easing the adjustments between cultures, and inviting them to be a part of American family and community life. Besides the Host Family Program, COSEP also sponsored the World Wives Program, inviting the spouses of international students to participate in informal weekly or monthly classes and gatherings. These programs were very helpful to international students in general, and to Chinese students in particular.

Like their counterparts decades ago, current Chinese students were concerned with the future of China, urging the Chinese government to carry out democratic politics and economic reform, and supporting the democracy demonstration in China in early 1989. The Tiananmen Incident of 4 June 1989, however, disappointed them. They felt that Chinese intellectuals were powerless under China's Communist system. At the same time, the incident gave them the opportunity to stay in the United States. With the detention and executions of some demonstrators and the harassment and crackdown on intellectuals in China, students in the United States feared being charged as counter-revolutionaries if they were forced to return in the midst of political turmoil. Letters and petitions from Chinese students across the country were sent to members of Congress. Facing the pressure from Congress, President George Bush issued "Administrative Measures for PRC Nationals" on 30 November 1989. The order contained such measures as the waiver of the two-year foreign residence requirement to any Chinese national who was present in the United States on 1 December 1989 and the employment requirement for all Chinese nationals who were in the United States on 5 June 1989.[77] Thus, practically all Chinese students could stay in the United States and be employed upon completion of their academic training.

Taking this opportunity, many Chinese female students decided to stay in the United States and look for employment upon or even before the completion of their education. Although there were not specific statistics on how many Chinese female students entered professions in the United States, individual cases indicated that some Chinese female students became professionals such as professors, lawyers, researchers, and librarians, and that they are making steady progress in their careers.[78] Like their counterparts in the earlier decades, some Chinese female students from the PRC were moving into the Chinese American middle class, and their cultural and socioeconomic importance was gradually noticed.

Similar to World War II that provided a turning point for Chinese immigration and Chinese American society, the civil rights movement and the liberalization of American immigrant policy since the 1960s proved to be another turning point for even more dramatic educational, occupational, economic, political, social, and psychological changes in Chinese American society.

The increase of the Chinese American population since 1965, indeed, was the direct result of the liberalization of American immigration policy. More indirect changes, however, also resulted from the more liberalized immigration regulations. The higher proportion of students and professionals among the new immigrants altered the profile of Chinese immigrants, changed the historical stereotypical "coolie" image of Chinese immigrants, and reinforced the positive features of the lives of middle-class Chinese Americans. The influx of new immigrants enlarged and strengthened the social and economic base for the emerging Chinese American political activists or politicians. The student immigrants, especially, with their better educational and occupational backgrounds, will become a conspicuous force in Chinese American economy and politics in the near future.

Chapter 6

Issues and Concerns

Benefiting from the civil rights movement and the 1965 Immigration Act, Chinese American women made a major stride in advancing their socioeconomic status. This social and economic progress, however, did not protect them from being discriminated against by the reincarnations of the traditional racial and cultural prejudice. Since the 1960s, they became the national focus of a number of issues such as being a "model minority," deriving unfair advantage from affirmative action, and practicing interracial marriage. In addition, they have also faced other problems such as racism, sexism, and ethnic identity.

Model Minority: Myth and Reality

Chinese Americans experienced drastic cultural, political, and emotional changes and achieved remarkable educational, occupational, and political accomplishments since the 1960s. As a result, a popular press image of "model minority" surfaced.[1]

In January 1966, William Peterson published an article in the *New York Times Magazine* to praise Japanese Americans' successful entry to the American mainstream.[2] In December of the same year, *U.S. News and World Report* also featured a story hailing the socioeconomic achievements of Chinese Americans.[3] Promoted by the popular press, the model minority image since then has become a stereotype describing the socioeconomic success achieved by Asian Americans through hard work, respect of traditional values, and accommodation.

Two decades later, the model minority thesis resurfaced in the press. In the 1980s, national television networks and popular magazines vied to report Asian American success.[4] American politicians responded in a timely fashion to the media celebration of model minority. In a speech delivered to a group of Asian Americans in 1984, President Ronald Reagan congratulated Asian Americans' success and recognized its significance.[5]

The model minority image did not emerge from a vacuum. Various statistics proved that Asian Americans made remarkable socioeconomic progress. According to the 1970 census, the median family income of Chinese and Japanese Americans surpassed that of white Americans. The Japanese American median family income was $3,000 higher and Chinese American income was $1,000 higher than the U.S. median family income.[6] The 1980 census also indicated that a higher percentage of Asian Americans had completed a four year college education than did black, Hispanic, and white Americans. The figures were Filipino (21.7), Korean (21.2), Chinese (15.8), Japanese (15.6), Asian Indian (14.1), white (9.4) black (4.9), and Hispanic (3.5).[7]

Although the model minority thesis recognized Asian Americans' socioeconomic achievements since World War II, its appearance in the 1960s served certain political purposes. The Asian American success story of upward mobility relying on hard work and Asian values was used against black and Hispanic civil rights activists who were engaging in militant activities to improve their social conditions. The model minority thesis further underscored the notion that America was still a land of opportunity, and American democracy had continued to guarantee individual success.

Moreover, the model minority thesis, with its rosy picture of Asian American success, overlooked the factors that contradict all success "model" experiences. First, an increasing number of Chinese and other Asian Americans entered the middle-class social stratum, resided in suburban white neighborhoods, and enjoyed mainstream life styles. However, the majority of Chinese Americans, especially the newcomers, were still confined in the inner-city Chinatowns. They struggled with problems of limited job opportunities, unhealthy and hazardous working conditions, crowded and substandard housing, and emotional stress. These problems were overlooked despite being well-documented.[8]

Second, although more Chinese and Asian Americans attained higher education than black, Hispanic, and white Americans, they received lower income than their black, Hispanic, and white counterparts with the same years of education. According to the 1980 census, with the exception of Japanese Americans, all Asian Americans with a college degree had lower annual earnings than black, Hispanic, and white American college graduates.[9]

Third, the typical "model" Chinese and Asian Americans were well-educated professionals: professors and teachers, doctors and nurses, librarians and technicians. Few Asian Americans climbed to the managerial and administrative level due to the glass ceiling that projected Asian Americans as "quiet" and "uncomplaining" and therefore unfit for leadership positions. Only 0.3 percent of the senior male executives in the Fortune 1000 industrial companies and Fortune 500 service industries were Asian Americans.[10]

Fourth, more Chinese and other Asian American women worked full time to supplement family income. In 1970, about 60 percent of all Chinese and Japanese American families had more than one income-earner, while only 51 percent of all American families had more than one earner.[11] In 1989, 56 percent of native-born and 50 percent of foreign-born Chinese American families had two workers, while 41.7 percent of total American families had two workers.[12]

The model minority thesis not only misrepresented the reality of Chinese Americans, but also impeded their socioeconomic progress. For instance, about one-third of San Francisco's poor who qualified for public assistance were Asians, but only six percent of the city's social welfare program funds were granted to help them.[13] The limited political participation of Asian Americans certainly attributed to this unfair distribution of public assistance. Doubtless, the model minority stereotype also affected many decision makers who saw less need to assist a minority group that was believed to have achieved socioeconomic success. Therefore, the model minority thesis in fact worked as a new form of racial and cultural prejudice against Chinese and other Asian Americans.

Debate Over Affirmative Action

The establishment of an affirmative action policy can be traced to President John F. Kennedy's Executive Order 10925 issued in March 1961. This led to establishment of the President's Committee on Equal Employment Opportunity. Intended to end discrimination in employment by the government and its contractors, the order demanded every federal contractor pledge that "the contractor will not discriminate against any employee or applicant for employment because of race, creed, color, or national origin. The contractor will take affirmative action, to ensure that applicants are employed, and that employees are treated during employment, without regard to their race, creed, color, or national origin."[14]

Affirmative action became a legal requirement for any federally funded institution and agency under the Civil Rights Act of 1964. Title VI declared that "no person in the United States shall, on the ground of race, color, or national origin, be excluded from participation in, be denied the benefits of, or be subjected to discrimination under any program or activity receiving federal financial assistance."[15]

In 1965, President Johnson issued Executive Order 11246, declaring that "it is the policy of the Government of the United States to provide equal opportunity in federal employment for all qualified persons, to prohibit discrimination in employment because of race, creed, color or national origin, and to promote the full realization of equal employment opportunity through a positive, continuing program in each department and agency."[16] Johnson further promulgated affirmative action rules and regulations. In December 1971, the Department of Labor issued Revised Order No. 4. It required all contractors to develop "an acceptable affirmative action program" to recruit more women and minority groups including "Negroes, American Indians, Orientals, and Spanish Surnamed Americans."[17]

The Asian American community was divided over affirmative action. While some supported affirmative action, others questioned its usefulness for the educational and occupational advancement of Asian Americans. Asian American affirmative action advocates listed the facts of historical discrimination against Asians in education, employment, and promotion, and asserted the need for affirmative action.[18]

Many Asian Americans strongly opposed affirmative action. A 1993 poll by the California Policy seminar indicated that while a majority of African Americans in California supported affirmative action programs in university admissions and employment, about two-thirds of Asian Americans opposed such policies.[19] Their opposition was based primarily on the following reasons.

First, they believed that affirmative action programs harmed rather than helped Asian Americans in university admission, employment, and promotion. On May 19, 1995, a group of analysts at the University of California presented the Board of Regents with a computer simulation of admission at Berkeley, Santa Cruz, and San Diego based on income levels instead of race as the criterion for affirmative admissions. The analysts concluded that about fifty percent of African American students and five to fifteen percent of Mexican students now at UC would not be there, while the enrollment of Asian American students would jump fifteen to twenty-five percent.[20]

Second, many Asian Americans resented affirmative action and quotas and saw them as representing a paternalistic and condescending attitude toward minorities. Affirmative action and quotas suggested that minorities were incapable of otherwise obtaining university admission, employment, and promotion. Matthew Tsien, Executive Director of Asian Americans For Merit, for example, declared that "we are opposed to it because we don't need this sort of policy," since Asian Americans achieved the higher income and highest test scores of all the ethnic groups.[21]

Third, many Chinese Americans believed that while designed to eliminate discrimination, the affirmative action programs in fact created discrimination against Asian Americans. The best evidence of this claim was the legal battle of the Chinese American Democratic Club (CADC) against the California Board of Education and the San Francisco Unified School District over the quota system practiced at San Francisco's Lowell High School, one of the city's most prestigious public high schools. In 1983, the San Francisco Unified School District, the NAACP, and the California Department of Education reached a settlement after the NAACP and parents of African-American students enrolled in the districts sued local and state school officials to implement the desegregation mandated by *Brown v. Board of Education*. The settlement, known as a consent decree, mandated that each school of the district recruit students from at least four of nine identified racial/ethnic groups and that no groups constitute more than 40–45 percent of the total enrollment.[22] To maintain the racial cap of 40 percent of the student body, Lowell High School set up different standardized test scores to determine admissions for different ethnic groups: 62 (reduced from the earlier 66) for Chinese, 59 for the white, 58 for the other Asians, and 56 for the Hispanic and African Americans.[23] In order to gain admission, Chinese American students had to outperform whites and all other ethnic minority groups. Consequently, the practice of a quota system resulted in racial discrimination against Chinese Americans.

Fourth, some Asian Americans argued that the original goal of affirmative action was perverted. There were cases in which members of minority groups blackmailed the white employers, accusing them of racism if they failed to promote minority employees.[24]

The division among Asian Americans over affirmative action reflected their dilemma: to preserve the rainbow coalition while protecting the interest of Asian Americans, and to preserve affirmative action while fighting discrimination against Asian Americans generated by practices of affirmative action. It was a difficult task for Asian Americans to accomplish the dual goals. In the 1996 election, Leadership Education for Asian Pacifics, Inc. (LEAP), an organization advocating political empowerment of Asian Americans, urged Asian American communities to vote against "California Civil Rights Initiative," publicly referred to as Proposition 209. If passed, this legislation would eliminate all statewide affirmative action programs.[25]

On November 5, 1996, the election day, Proposition 209 was passed by a margin of 54 percent to 46 percent. However, a majority of Asian Americans who voted (61 percent) opposed Proposition 209, along with African Americans (74 percent) and Latino Americans (76 percent), indicating Asian Americans' efforts in maintaining the rainbow coalition.

The legal battle over Proposition 209 started as soon as the election was over. The American Civil Liberties Union (ACLU, many of whose members are Asian Americans) immediately filed a lawsuit against the measure. On December 23, 1996, Federal Judge Thelton Henderson, known to be sympathetic to affirmative action, issued an injunction to block implementation of Proposition 209 until the case goes to trial.[26] The ACLU won the first round of the battle. Supporters of Proposition 209, however, appealed Judge Henderson's preliminary injunction. The three-judge Court of Appeals, consisting of Judges O'Scannlain, Leavy, and Kleinfels (all Republican appointees) was more sympathetic to Proposition 209. It considered the case on February 10, 1997 and put it on an accelerated schedule. On April 8, 1997, the Court of Appeals ruled unanimously that Proposition 209 does not violate the United States Constitution and therefore nullified Judge Henderson's preliminary injunction. If upheld, the ruling would put the Proposition into effect within twenty-one days. As expected, on April 22, 1997, the ACLU filed a motion for an *en bank* rehearing of the April 8 ruling by the Court of Appeals. Disappointed at the April 8 decision, Asian American activists were determined to fight the prolonged legal battle.[27]

Interracial Marriage

As Chinese Americans' socioeconomic conditions improved in the recent decades, interracial marriage seemed to become a trend. In New York City, interracial marriage among Chinese Americans remained 27 percent of the total marriages in the 1970s and 1980s.[28] In California, a substantial minority among Chinese Americans, 35.6 percent, were intermarried in 1980.[29] In the San Francisco bay area, American-born Asians were more likely to marry outside their own ethnic group. In some ethnic groups, the interracial marriage rate was as high as 80 percent.[30] Among the interracially married couples, more Asian women than Asian men married non-Asians, mostly white Americans. A recent sampling of marriage records for San Francisco County showed that four times as many Asian American women as Asian American men married whites.[31] Some high-profile Asian American women's marriages helped to make the phenomenon more noticeable: politicians Elaine Chao and Julia Chang Bloch, writers Bette Bao Lord, Maxine Hong Kingston, and Amy Tan, and newscasters Connie Chung, Wendy Tokuda, and Jan Yanehiro. Interracial dating has been so ubiquitous at West Coast university campuses that such jargons as "Asian-American syndrome" and "Asian-women-aholics" began to spread.[32]

Scholars have analyzed the interracial marriage among Asian Americans since World War II. Milton Gordon's classic work *Assimilation in American Life* has spearheaded the assimilation theory. This theory has praised interracial marriage as a sign of the growing acceptance of a minority group by the majority group.[33] Most studies of assimilation theory have suggested that interracial marriage served as an indicator of the assimilation of Asian Americans into American majority society.

Meanwhile, an alternative theory of hypergamy has emerged. Originally a concept used in studies of marriage patterns in India, hypergamy has examined the intermarriage between higher-caste males and lower-caste females.[34] Challenging the assimilation theory, the hypergamy theory has seen intermarriage as a function of the inequality within a class and racially-stratified society. In India, a high class male could trade his social status for beauty, intelligence, youth, and wealth through an intermarriage. Similarly, interracial marriage in the United States also allowed both partners of the marriage to benefit mutually each other as a minority male with higher socioeconomic status but lower racial status might upgrade his racial position by marrying a female with the opposite characteristics.[35] After a decade or two of unpopularity, hypergamy theory has reemerged in recent scholarship. Drawing upon hypergamy theory, Larry Hajime Shinagawa and Gin Yong Pang have argued that intermarriage was more likely determined by the marital partners' nativity, gender, age, education, and socioeconomic characteristics.[36]

Similar to the hypergamy thesis, Paul R. Spickard in *Mixed Blood* has analyzed intermarriage from various dimensions of social structure, demography, class status, and intermarriage behavior. Spickard has contended that class, generation, and ethnic concentration in the surrounding population have shaped intermarriage patterns. He has further claimed that there was a distinctive hierarchy of intermarriage preferences.[37]

Both theories have provided meaningful interpretations of intermarriage. Yet, each alone could not explain intermarriage completely. Assimilation theory has hailed intermarriage as an indicator of a minority's acceptance by the majority, and asserted that love and attraction were primary motives of such marriage. However, it has failed to explain why minority members (both male and female) with higher socioeconomic status or why native-born minority members were more likely to outmarry. Hypergamy model has viewed intermarriage as a deal in which the white marital partner traded his or her higher racial status for advantages of physical attraction, youth, or higher socioeconomic status brought to the marriage by the partner of racial minority. It has excluded the factors of love and romance in an intermarriage.

In reality, most marital partners of intermarriages (with the exception of picture brides) have claimed that love or attraction were the major reasons to draw them together. Clearly, the role of love and mutual attraction in intermarriage should not be overlooked. However, few individuals fell in love at first sight; love grew gradually during the interaction between the two partners. The interaction often occurred among individuals with similar educational, occupational, and socioeconomic experiences. Therefore, intermarriage should be understood in terms of the marital partners' education, occupation, and socioeconomic conditions. When a minority member moved to the socioeconomic setting (often an institution of higher education or a professional occupation) in which he or she had the possibility to meet a prospective marital partner of the majority group, his or her status was already upgraded regardless of an intermarriage, since the majority group tended to enjoy better socioeconomic conditions. Therefore, a minority member's assimilation into the majority society was more determined by his or her education, occupation, and class status than by an intermarriage.

The oral history interviews conducted by the author have supported the above argument. Ms. C, as discussed in the previous chapters, was born into an intellectual family in Kowloon, Hong Kong in 1938. She came to the United States in 1955 when she was seventeen. She attained her bachelor, master, and doctoral degrees from University of Chicago respectively in 1959, 1960, and 1963. Then she was employed as a research associate at several prestigious universities between 1963 and 1969. She was hired as an assistant professor of chemistry at a midwestern university in 1969. There she met her husband, a colleague from the same department, and they married in 1971. Even in the beginning of their relationship, Ms. C felt that she "had no problem to adjust to a white American man," because she was already "totally Americanized."[38]

Ms. L was born into a privileged family in Beijing, China in 1957. Her mother was a doctor, and her father was a Communist Party veteran and army general. She and her siblings attended the October First School, a special school in Beijing only open to children of the veterans of the Communist Party. After her graduation from college in 1982, she became an instructor at an agricultural engineering university in Beijing. In 1985, she came to America as a government-sponsored graduate student to major in electrical

Figure 6.1. A family of interracial marriage, Columbia, Missouri, 1992. Huping Ling Collection.

engineering at the University of Missouri at Columbia. Two years later, she met her future husband, a professor of German language at a midwestern university, in a Unitarian Church in Columbia. They shared many common interests. She believed in meditation and he was interested in Daoism. She enjoyed reading Russian novels and singing Russian songs due to her early upbringing (the Soviet Union was the only ally of China during the 1950s and early 1960s). He was also familiar with Russian literature and could sing some Russian tunes. They soon got married. After the marriage, Ms. L continued her education. She first finished a master's degree in electrical engineering, then completed another in library science. She later found employment at a midwestern university as a computer consultant in 1995.[39]

Similarly, Ms. X was born in Shanghai in 1958. Both of her parents were physicians. With a college degree in English, she taught English language for three years at a university in Hebei Province, China before she came to America in 1985. She first worked on a master's degree in English literature at West Virginia University, where she team taught a course on Chinese culture and philosophy with her future husband who was a professor of philosophy. He taught the philosophy part of the course and she taught the literature and culture. After that, they became tennis partners and spent a lot of time together. The romance began, and they married in 1988. When Ms. X completed her master's degree, she did not feel satisfied, and she applied to the doctoral program at the University of Pittsburgh. She was accepted with a scholarship and a teaching assistantship. In 1994, she defended her dissertation and was hired by a midwestern university as assistant professor of English and American literature.[40]

Ms. H was born in Xian, Shaanxi Province, China in 1976. Her father was a manager at a government-owned tourist company before his retirement, and her mother was a housewife. After she graduated from high school in 1994, Ms. H worked in Xian Hotel as a salesclerk selling Chinese handicrafts. She met Todd, an American student at Xian University, in the hotel's disco bar. Ms. H was very interested in different cultures, and she did not mind having a foreign friend. Initially, they were just friends, teaching each other one's own language. When Todd expressed the desire to date Ms. H, she declined because she did not want to marry a foreigner, and she was also aware that some foreigners flirted among Chinese women. A few months later, Todd returned to America. During his absence, Ms. H thought about their relationship. She found that she missed Todd. To her surprise, Todd went to China in the following year just to see her. She now realized that Todd really cared for her. They started dating and soon married. After the wedding, they returned to the United States, both studying at the University of Missouri at Columbia.[41]

In the above cases, these Chinese women (with the exception of Ms. H) obtained higher education and had professional jobs prior to their marriages to white American men. They would have assimilated into the majority society without intermarriage; the intermarriage only accelerated and eased the assimilation.

Other Concerns

In addition to the above issues, other problems also concerned Chinese American women. In the 1990s, racism and sexism still plagued Chinese American women at school and the work place. Some Chinese American activists protested that dating between female Chinese American students and Caucasian professors reflected the resurgence of racism on campus due to the unequal power distribution between the two parties.[42] Many Asian American women abhorred those who pursued them because of their ethnic background rather than their own characteristics.[43]

Even highly-educated Chinese women could not escape racism and sexism, and their opportunities for advancement were limited by cultural prejudice. Dr. Jean Jew's case exemplified this problem. As a professor at the University of Iowa medical school, Jew suffered harassment for years. A male colleague spread rumors that she was trading sexual favors for career advancement. Others in the department joked about her Chinese background. In an attempt to block her promotion, someone made specific sex-related graffiti about her on the walls of the men's room in the department. A drunk professor even verbally insulted her when she walked down a hallway in the department, calling her a "slut," a "bitch," and a "whore." Jew complained repeatedly about the harassment, and the university administration did nothing until November 1990. Settling a five-year-old lawsuit, the university issued a humbling public apology and agreed to pay Jew $50,000 in back pay, $126,000 in damages, and $895,000 in fees and expenses to her attorney. "Dr. Jew deserves our apologies and our respect for her stand," concluded Iowa's President Hunter Rawlings III. The settling of the case, however, created sharp divisions in the university community.[44]

How to maintain their cultural and ethnic identity and also be able to enjoy cultural conformity remained a lasting problem for Chinese American women to solve. Many Chinese American women remained culturally marginal, feeling that they did not belong to either culture. Ms. T expressed this marginal feeling in 1987. Growing up in a well-educated Chinese immigrant family, Ms. T inherited many Chinese cultural values. After receiving a graduate degree from a West Coast university, she went to China to learn classical Chinese dance in the early 1980s. She found, however, that she could not assimilate completely into either Western or Chinese culture. In her thirties, she still remained single. She expressed her frustration by saying, "Nobody likes us. Americans don't like us because we are Chinese. Chinese don't like us because we are foreigners."[45] Her individual dilemma symbolized the common problem of many Chinese American women: being Chinese Americans meant that they were different from both Chinese and Americans.

As Chinese and other Asian Americans made socioeconomic progress in the recent decades, they continued to suffer different forms of discrimination and prejudice. The model minority stereotype misrepresented their socioeconomic reality and prevented their further advancement. While designed for the protection of ethnic minorities, affirmative action and its practices in many places produced new restrictions for Asian Americans. Interracial marriage, in which more Chinese and other Asian American women were involved than their male counterparts, indicated these women's socioeconomic progress. However, Chinese American women still subjected to racism and sexism in interracial dating and other aspects of their lives.

Chapter 7

❧

Conclusion

The observation and analysis of Chinese American women's history over the past one-hundred-fifty years indicate that there are commonalities as well as differences between Chinese American women and other ethnic women. Similar to other immigrant groups, Chinese women's motivations for immigration were related to the social and cultural conditions of their home country. Though motivation for immigration varied from group to group, and individual to individual, the economic impulse was predominant among the various motives. As with other immigrant groups, chain immigration proved to be the dominant pattern in one hundred-fifty years of Chinese immigration history. Also, like other immigrant women and American frontier women, Chinese immigrant women experienced changes in their family life and family structure. Many became co-earners of family income and co-decision-makers in family affairs.

The different experiences of Chinese immigrant women resulting from cultural and physical dissimilarities and racial prejudice and discrimination, however, were significant and distinct. First of all, the process of assimilation of Chinese women differed from that of European immigrant women. Generally, European immigrant groups, after one or two generations, assimilated into Anglo-Saxon culture, and became part of the American mainstream society. The majority of Chinese immigrant women, however, remained separated from American mainstream society until today. The Chinatown masses, including both old Chinatown residents and new Chinese immigrants, remained confined in these cultural enclaves due to the lack of fluency in English language and marketable skills required by the outside world as well as the systematic racial prejudice and bias in the larger society. They suffered from long working hours, low pay, crowded and substandard housing, and crime in Chinatowns across the country. Even for the successful middle-class Chinese women, the process of assimilation and acculturation took longer and was more painful and less complete than that for European immigrant women.

Unlike European American women, Chinese American women (and other Asian American women as well) found their occupational opportunities very limited. Working in laundries, restaurants, grocery stores, and garment factories inside Chinatown communities was (and still is) the most likely choice for the majority of them. Although the highly-educated professional Chinese women managed to get employment in the mainstream market without experiencing the humbling feeling of starting at the very bottom of the social ladder, they still received fewer returns from their educational training than did white women, as noted by many scholars in Chinese American history.[1]

Also unlike other ethnic women, especially European American women, interracial marriage was less common among the early Chinese immigrant women. Although the great differences in custom, culture, language, and tradition between Chinese and non-Chinese remained obstacles for interracial marriage, racial prejudice and social and institutional discrimination proved to be the real barrier.

During and after World War II, the image of China and Chinese began to improve in America, and the anti-Chinese discriminatory laws were repealed one after another. As a result, interracial marriage between Chinese and non-Chinese became acceptable to some European Americans. Since the 1960s, the educational and occupational achievements of Chinese Americans became more noticeable. Consequently, Chinese American interracial marriages occurred on a larger scale. While stereotypical images of Chinese women as exotic and submissive wives still prevailed among a large number of non-Chinese men, many European American males chose to date or marry Chinese American women, in large part because of their academic and professional advancement. Therefore, the "Asian-women-Caucasian-men" phenomenon probably served as an indicator of Chinese American women's socioeconomic progress in recent decades.

Still, unlike other ethnic women, Chinese American women were not visible in American mainstream politics until recent decades. Chinese American women, however, were involved in community works within their own ethnic community as early as the 1920s when they began to form various women's organizations and engage in different community activities. They supported China's revolutionary causes and participated in China's war efforts. Since the 1960s, Chinese American women have moved into mainstream politics, serving in local, state, and federal governments. Although Chinese American women became community leaders, mayors, secretaries of state, and even cabinet members, none have been so far elected to the United States Congress to voice the needs of their communities. Many Chinese American political activists today feel the urge of political empowerment of Chinese Americans in general and Chinese American women in particular.

The century-and-a-half history of Chinese American women proved that these women not only survived on their own terms in the United States, but succeeded and contributed to the multicultural and multiethnic society.

Notes

Introduction

1. Loren W. Fessler, *Chinese in America, Stereotyped Past, Changing Present* (New York: Vantage Press, 1983), 6.

2. United States Census Office, *The Ninth Census* (June 1, 1870), 551.

3. Curt Gentry, *The Madams of San Francisco* (Garden City, N.Y.: Doubleday & Co., 1964), 16–23.

4. Lucie Cheng Hirata, "Chinese Immigrant Women in Nineteenth-Century California," in *Asian and Pacific Experiences: Women's Perspectives* ed. Nobuya Tsuchida (Asian/Pacific American Learning Resource Center and General College University of Minnesota, 1982), 40.

5. William L. Tung, *The Chinese in America 1820–1973, A Chronology & Fact Book* (Dobbs Ferry, N.Y.: Oceana Publications Inc., 1974), 70.

6. Ibid., 18.

7. The United States Census Bureau Publications.

8. Laws permitting Chinese women to enter the United States as wives and fiancées are the War Brides Act of December 28, 1945 and the G.I. Fiancées Act of June 29, 1946. During the former's three-year operation, approximately 6,000 Chinese war brides were admitted. Laws allowing Chinese women to come to America included Displaced Persons Act of 1948 and Refugee Relief Act of 1953. Both granted "displaced" Chinese students, visitors, and others who had their temporary status in the United States adjusted to that of permanent resident and allotting visas to Chinese refugees and Chinese whose passports had been endorsed by the Chinese Nationalist Government.

9. U.S. Bureau of the Census, *U.S. Census of Population: 1950*, Vol. IV, *Special Reports, Nonwhite Population by Race*, 3B–19.

183

10. Fessler, 6.

11. *New York Express*, 22 April 1850.

12. Judy Yung, *Chinese Women of America, A Pictorial History* (Seattle: University of Washington Press, 1986), 17.

13. Yung, *Chinese Women of America*, 114–115.

14. Michael Cimino, *Year of Dragon*, film, 1984.

15. Wayne Wang, *Dim Sum*, film, 1985.

16. Henry Chow, *Liru*, film, 1991.

17. Wayne Wang, *Dim Sum Take-Out*, film, 1990.

18. *With Silk Wings, Asian American Women at Work*, a series of four films: *Four Women, On New Ground*, and *Frankly Speaking* produced and directed by Loni Ding, and *Talking History* produced and directed by Spencer Nakasako, 1990.

19. Arthur Dong, Speech at the Seventh National Conference of Association for Asian American Studies (University of California, Santa Barbara, May 18–20, 1990).

20. Arthur Dong, *Forbidden City, U.S.A.*, 56 min., color video, 1989, in *The American Experience*.

21. Arthur Dong, *Sewing Woman*, 14 min., black & white, 1982.

22. L. T. Townsend, *The Chinese Problem* (Boston: Lee and Shepard, Publishers, 1876; reprint, San Francisco: R & E Research Associates, 1970); S. L. Baldwin, *Must the Chinese Go? An Examination of the Chinese Question* (New York: The Press of H. E. Elking, 1890; reprint, San Francisco: R & E Research Associates, 1970).

23. Mary Coolidge, *Chinese Immigration* (New York: Henry Holt & Co., 1909; reprint, New York: Arno Press, 1969).

24. Stuart Creighton Miller, *The Unwelcome Immigrant: The American Image of the Chinese: 1875–1882* (Berkeley: University of California Press, 1979).

25. Gunther Barth, *Bitter Strength: History of the Chinese in the United States 1850–1870* (Cambridge, Mass.: Harvard University Press, 1964).

26. S. W. Kung, *Chinese in American Life, Some Aspects of Their History, Status, Problems, and Contributions* (Seattle: University of Washington Press, 1962).

27. Although Rose Hum Lee completed her dissertation entitled "The Growth and Decline of Chinese Communities in the Rocky Mountain Region" in 1947, it was not published in book form until 1978. See Rose Hum

Lee, *The Growth and Decline of Chinese Communities in the Rocky Mountain Region* (New York: Arno Press, 1978).

28. Stanford M. Lyman, "Marriage and the Family among Chinese Immigrants to America, 1850–1960," *Phylon* 24 (1968): 321–30, and *Chinese Americans* (New York: Random House, 1974).

29. Fessler, *Chinese in America.*

30. Shin-shan Henry Tsai, *The Chinese Experience in America* (Bloomington: Indiana University Press, 1986).

31. Lucie Cheng Hirata, "Free, Indentured, Enslaved: Chinese Prostitutes In Nineteenth-Century America," *Signs* 5 (1979): 3–29.

32. George Anthony Peffer, "Forbidden Families: Emigration Experiences of Chinese Women under the Page Law, 1875–1882," *Journal of American Ethnic History* 6 (1986): 28–64.

33. Sucheng Chan, "The Exclusion of Chinese Women, 1870–1943," in *Entry Denied* ed. Sucheng Chan (Philadelphia: Temple University Press, 1991), 94-146.

34. Benson Tong, *Unsubmissive Women: Chinese Prostitutes in Nineteenth-Century San Francisco* (Norman and London: University of Oklahoma Press, 1994).

35. Stacey G. H. Yap, *Gather Your Strength, Sisters: The Emerging Role of Chinese Women Community Workers* (New York: AMS Press, 1989).

36. Xiaolan Bao, "'Holding Up More Than Half the Sky': A History of Women Garment Workers in New York's Chinatown, 1948–1991" (Ph.D. diss., New York University, 1991).

37. Yung, *Chinese Women of America.*

38. Judy Yung, *Unbound Feet, A Social History of Chinese Women in San Francisco* (Berkeley: University of California Press, 1995).

39. "New ethnicity" is a term that grew out of the civil rights movement in the 1960s. Traditional historians before the 1960s viewed immigrants as "problems" that would presumably be solved by assimilation. Liberals concentrated on ethnic Americans as victims of institutional discrimination and social prejudice. Contrary to most of these traditional historians and liberals, the "new ethnicity" focuses on searching political and socioeconomic justice for ethnic Americans through collective organization and derives pride from ethnic heritages. For more discussion, see Maxine Schwarts Seller ed., *Immigrant Women* (Philadelphia: Temple University Press, 1981), 8.

40. See George A. Peffer, "The Forces Without: The Regulation of Chinese Female Immigration to America, 1852–1882" (Ph.D. diss., Carnegie-Mellon University, 1989).

Chapter 1

1. Maxine Seller, ed., *Immigrant Women* (Philadelphia: Temple University Press, 1981), 15–22; Hasia Diner, *Erin's Daughters in America, Irish Immigrant Women in the Nineteenth Century* (Baltimore: The Johns Hopkins University Press, 1983), 1–29; Linda Schelbitzki Pickle, *Contented among Strangers, Rural German-Speaking Women and Their Families in the Nineteenth-Century Midwest* (Urbana: University of Illinois Press, 1996), 28–40; Susan A. Glenn, *Daughters of the Shtetl: Life and Labor in the Immigrant Generation* (Ithaca: Cornell University Press, 1990), 8–12; and Josef J. Barton, *Peasants and Strangers, Italians, Rumanians, and Slovaks in an American City, 1890–1950* (Cambridge, Mass.: Harvard University Press, 1975), 27. See also Robert Henry Billigmeier, *Americans from Germany* (Belmont, Calif.: Wadsworth Publishing Company, 1974); Jacob R. Marcus, *The American Jewish Women, 1654–1980* (New York: Ktav Publishing House, 1980); and Kathie Friedman-Kasaba, *Memories of Migration: Gender, Ethnicity, and Work in the Lives of Jewish and Italian Women in New York, 1870–1924* (Albany: State University of New York Press, 1996).

2. Shih-shan Henry Tsai, *The Chinese Experience in America*, 2–3; Ronald Takaki, *Strangers from a Different Shore* (Boston: Little, Brown and Company, 1989), 80.

3. Roger Daniels, *Asian America: Chinese and Japanese in the United States Since 1850* (Seattle: University of Washington Press, 1988), 9–12.

4. One myth, for instance, tells the story of a female creator named *Nuwa* who mended the cracked sky and created humans.

5. John King Fairbank, *East Asia, Tradition and Transformation* (Boston: Houghton Mifflin Company, 1973), 142.

6. Ibid., 49.

7. Shi Jun, "Confucius and Chinese Culture," *China Reconstructs* 38 (September 1989):12–15.

8. Olga Lang, *Chinese Family and Society* (New Haven: Yale University Press, 1946), 43.

9. Ibid.

10. Ibid., 42.

11. Philip C. C. Huang, *The Peasant Economy and Social Change in North China* (Stanford: Stanford University Press, 1985), 192; Philip C. C. Huang, *The Peasant Family and Rural Development in the Yangzi Delta, 1350–1988* (Stanford: Stanford University Press, 1990), 13.

12. Fairbank, 142; Xu Xishan, "Sancun JinLian" [Bound Feet], *The World Journal*, 8–10 March 1997.

13. Lang, 45.

14. Fairbank, 143; Xu.

15. Lang, 46.

16. Ai Ra Kim, *Women Struggling for A New Life* (Albany: State University of New York Press, 1996), 6–8.

17. Evelyn Nakano Glenn, *Issei, Nisei, War Bride* (Philadelphia: Temple University Press, 1986), 203.

18. Pickle, 23–24.

19. Diner, 10 and 16.

20. See Ronald Takaki, "They Also Come: The Migration of Chinese and Japanese Women to Hawaii and the Continental United States," *Chinese America: History and Perspectives 1990* (San Francisco: Chinese Historical Society of America, 1990), 3–19.

21. The translation is cited in Robert F. Dernberger, ed. *The Chinese: Adapting the Past, Building the Future* (Ann Arbor: The University of Michigan Center for Chinese Studies, 1986), 259.

22. Entry 132, "Chinese General Correspondence, 1898–1908," RG 85, National Archives, Washington, D.C.

23. Case 3358d, Entry 134, "Customs Case File Related to Chinese Immigration, 1877–1891," RG 85, National Archives, Washington, D.C.

24. Case 3358a, Entry 134, ibid.

25. "Survey of Race Relations," document 245, Hoover Institution on War, Revolution and Peace archives, as quoted in Sucheng Chan, "The Exclusion of Chinese Women, 1870–1943," 96.

26. Case 3358d, Entry 134, ibid.

27. Curt Gentry, *Madames of San Francisco* (New York: Doubleday, 1964), 52.

28. Ibid., 51.

29. Ibid., 52–53.

30. "Story of Wong Ah So," in *Orientals and Their Culture*, Social Science Institute, Fiske University (Nashville: Fiske University, 1946), 31–33.

31. Interview 7.

32. Y. C. Wang, *Chinese Intellectuals and the West, 1872–1949* (Chapel Hill: University of North Carolina Press, 1966), 49.

33. Daniels, 17.

34. It is debatable if early Chinese immigrants came as coolies or free immigrants. While some writers describe Chinese laborers as "coolie," such as S. W. Kung, *Chinese in American Life* (15–18), and Roger Daniels, *Asian America* (10), others challenge the term "coolie" asserting that most early Chinese immigrants came as free agents. The examples of the latter are, Mary Coolidge, *Chinese Immigration* (1909, 49–54), one of the earliest such efforts, Stan Steiner, *Fusang: The Chinese Who Built America* (New York: Harper & Row, 1979, 113), Jack Chen, *The Chinese of America* (San Francisco: Harper & Row, 1980, 25), and Shih-shan Henry Tsai, *China and the Overseas Chinese in the United States, 1868–1911* (Fayetteville: University of Arkansas Press, 1983, 16). The history of early Chinese immigration was complex; the early Chinese immigrants included coolies, contract laborers or indentured laborers, and free laborers.

35. Case 19571/18–5, RG 85, National Archives, Pacific Sierra Region, San Bruno, CA.

36. "Survey of Race Relations," document 251, Hoover Institution on War, Revolution and Peace archives, as cited in Sucheng Chan, *Entry Denied*, 96.

37. Chan, *Asian Americans*, 104.

38. Cases 19571/18–5, 14284/4–4, RG 85, National Archives, Pacific Sierra Region, San Bruno, CA.

39. See Stuart C. Miller, *The Unwelcome Immigrant: The American Image of the Chinese 1785–1882*; Elmer C. Sandmeyer, *The Anti-Chinese Movement in California* (Urbana: University of Illinois Press, 1973); Alexander P. Saxon, *The Indispensable Enemy: Labor and the Anti-Chinese Movement in California* (Berkeley: University of California Press, 1971); and Francis L. K. Hsu, *The Challenge of the American Dream: The Chinese in the United States* (Belmont, Calif.: Wadsworth Publishing Co., Inc., 1971).

40. Vincent Tang, "Chinese Women Immigrants and the Two-Edged Sword of Habeas Corpus," in *The Chinese American Experience: Papers from the Second National Conference on Chinese American Studies*, ed. Genny Lim (Chinese Historical Society of America & the Chinese Cultural Foundation of San Francisco, 1980), 48–56.

41. Peffer, "Forbidden Families."

42. Sucheng Chan, "The Exclusion of Chinese Women."

43. Entry 132, "Chinese General Correspondence, 1898–1908," Entry 134, "Customs Case File No. 3358d Related to Chinese Immigration, 1877–1891," Entry 135, "Chinese Smuggling File, 1914–1921," Entry 136, "Chinese Division File, 1924–1925," Entry 137, "Applications for Duplicate Certificates of Residence, 1893–1920," Record Group 85, National Archives, Washington, D.C.

44. Lin Yutang, *Chinatown Family* (New York: John Day, 1948), 11.

45. Entry 135, "Chinese Smuggling File," RG 85, National Archives, Washington, D.C.

46. Chinese Exclusion Cases Habeas Corpus Petitions, Case File 103, U.S. District Court for the Eastern District of Missouri, St. Louis, RG 21, National Archives-Central Plains Region, Kansas City, Missouri.

47. Betty Lee Sung, *Mountain of Gold* (New York: The MacMillan Company, 1967), 97.

48 Him Mark Lai, Genny Lim, and Judy Yung, *Island, Poetry and History of Chinese Immigrants on Angel Island* (Seattle: University of Washington Press, 1980), 14.

49. U.S. Bureau of the Census.

50. See Leslie Allen, *Ellis Island* (Liberty Island, New York: Evelyn Hill Group, Inc., 1995), 18–21.

51. Lai, *Island*, 14–15.

52. Case 19571/18–5, RG 85, National Archives, Pacific Sierra Region, San Bruno, CA.

53. Case 14284/4–4, RG 85, National Archives, Pacific Sierra Region, San Bruno, CA. In this case, the applicant's name was filed as Wong Shee, but the author used her maiden name Wong Yee Gue in the text in order to distinguish her from previously discussed Wong Shee in case 19571/18–5.

54. *Chung Sai Yat Po* (Chinese Daily), May 30 1903.

55. On November 5, 1940 the immigration station moved from Angel Island to 801 Silver Avenue due to a fire on Angel Island that burned the administration building.

56. Case 41369/11–29, RG 85, National Archives, Pacific Sierra Region, San Bruno, CA.

57. Connie Young Yu, "The World of Our Grandmothers," in *Making Waves: An Anthology of Writings by and about Asian Women*, ed. Asian Women United of California (Boston: Beacon Press, 1989), 36.

58. For other details about Chinese immigrants' experiences on Angel Island, see Lai, *Island, Poetry and History of Chinese Immigrants on Angel Island*.

59. Case 10385/5799, RG 85, National Archives, Pacific Sierra Region, San Bruno, CA.

60. Diner, 10.

61. Ibid., 30–34.

62. Rudolf Glanz's study shows that 24.8 percent of Jewish immigrant population in the nineteenth century were children up to fourteen years of age, way ahead of all the other new immigrant groups. See Rudolf Glanz, *The Jewish Women in America: Two Female Immigrant Generations, 1820– 1929* (New York: Ktav Publishing House, Inc. and National Council of Jewish Women, 1976), 1.

63. Barton, 49–53.

64. Yamato Ichihashi, *Japanese in the United States* (Stanford: Stanford University Press, 1932), 10; and Chan, *Asian Americans*, 107.

65. Eun Sik Yang, "Korean Women in America: 1903–1930," in *Korean Women in Transition, at Home and Abroad*, eds. Eui-Young Yu and Earl H. Phillips (Los Angeles: Center for Korean American and Korean Studies, 1987), 167–181. A good survey on Korean immigrant women in America during the early decades of the century.

66. Sung, *Mountain of Gold*, 11–13.

67. Case 3358d, Entry 134, "Customs Case File No. 3358d Related to Chinese Immigration, 1877–1891," RG 85, National Archives, Washington, D.C.

68. Case 1355, Entry 132, "Chinese General Correspondence, 1898– 1908," RG 85, National Archives, Washington, D.C.

69. Interview 7.

70. Interview 9.

71. Case 1151, Entry 132, RG 85, National Archives, Washington, D.C.

72. Lin Yutang, 196–197.

73. Ibid., 7.

74. Ibid., 10–11.

75. Case 19571/18–5, RG 85, National Archives, Pacific Sierra Region, San Bruno, CA.

76. Yung, *Chinese Women of America*, 18.

77. Victor and Brett de Bary Nee, *Longtime Californ'* (New York: Pantheon Books, 1973), 84.

78. "Life History—'Rose' Slave Girl," William Carlson Smith Documents, A–83, Special Collection, University of Oregon, Eugene, Oregon.

79. For studies on the educational effort of Protestant missionaries for Chinese women, see Huping Ling, "A History of Chinese Female Students in the United States, 1880s–1990s," *The Journal of American Ethnic His-*

tory 16, no. 3 (spring 1997): 81–109; Mary Releigh Anderson, *A Cycle in the Celestial Kingdom* (Mobile, Alabama: Heiter-Starke Printing Co., 1943); and Peggy Pascoe, *Relations of Rescue: The Search for Female Moral Authority in the American West, 1874–1939* (New York: Oxford University Press, 1990).

80. Anderson, 60.

81. Ibid., 88.

82. Ibid., 83.

83. Canton Missionary Conference, "Program of Advance," 27.

84. Anderson, 202.

85. Ibid., 210.

86. Wang, 49.

87. Case 1139, Entry 132 "Chinese General Correspondence, 1898–1908," RG 85, National Archives, Washington, D.C.

88. Case 12994/6–18, RG 85, National Archives, Pacific Sierra Region, San Bruno, CA.

89. Ibid.

90. Cases 10433/2855 A, B, C, and D, RG 85, National Archives, Pacific Sierra Region, San Bruno, CA.

91. Jian Jie and Meng Qi, *Jiang Jieshi He Song Meiling* [Chiang Kai-shek and Soong Mayling] (Changchun: Ji Lin Culture and History Publishing Co., 1991), 53–60.

92. Wang, 73.

93. Ibid. The government scholarship here referred to the Boxer Indemnity Scholarship by Qing government. When the anti-imperialist Boxer Uprising occurred in China in 1900, the Western powers invaded China and forced the Qing government to sign an unequal treaty and to pay an indemnity of 450 million taels. In May 1908, however, the United States Congress passed legislation to return part of the indemnity to China in order to quiet China's then growing anti-imperialist sentiment. The legislation stipulated that the refund should only be used to improve education in China. Beginning in 1909 when the United States began to pay the refund, the Qing government established the so-called Boxer Indemnity Scholarship to send students to America.

94. Ibid., 111. Different from other regular colleges in China at the time, Qinghua College was in fact a preparation school financed by the Boxer Indemnity Scholarship to recruit and prepare promising youth to study in America.

95. Ibid., 112. During the initial years of Qinghua College, the Republican government did not stipulate the number of years allowed to students in America, but the government generally sponsored students abroad for seven years. In 1914, a new government regulation was approved which restricted scholarships abroad to six years. Later, the scholarships were further reduced to five years, and then to four years.

96. Ibid., 113.

97. Ibid., 101.

98. China Institute in America, *A Survey of Chinese Students*, 27.

99. Rosalind Mei-Tsung Li, "The Chinese Revolution and the Chinese Women," *The Chinese Students' Monthly* 8 (June 1922): 675.

100. U.S. Census Bureau Publications.

101. Ibid.

102. For studies on urban Chinese communities, see Chalsa M. Loo, ed., *Chinatown: Most Time, Hard Time* (New York: Praeger, 1992), and Min Zhou, *Chinatown: The Socioeconomic Potential of an Urban Enclave* (Philadelphia: Temple University Press, 1992).

103. The Chinese Six Companies are social organizations of Chinese in America based on ancestry and region of origin. They help Chinese immigrants and maintain the social order of Chinese American society. Kong Chow Company (or Gangzhou Huiguan), Sam Yup Company (or Sanyi Huiguan), Yeoung Wo Company (or Yanghe Huiguan), Yan Wo Company (or Renhe Huiguan), Ning Yung Company (or Ningyang Huiguan), and Hop Wo Company (or Hehe Huiguan), respectively founded between 1851 and 1862, formed Chinese Consolidated Benevolent Association (or Zhonghua Huiguan)in 1882, and was widely known to Americans as the Chinese Six Companies.

104. Entry 132, "Chinese General Correspondence, 1898–1908," RG 85, National Archives, Washington, D.C.

105. See Him Mark Lai, "Historical Development of the Chinese Consolidated Benevolent Association/Huiguan System," in *Chinese America: History and Perspectives, 1987* ed. Chinese Historical Society of America (San Francisco: Chinese Historical Society of America, 1987), 19–20.

106. Since the 1960s, influenced by the Civil Rights movement, various social agencies and civic and political organizations connected to a larger society have reduced Six Companies' authority in Chinese American communities. Responding to the changes, Six Companies, in recent decades, have carried out some reforms. These reforms range from sponsoring programs to improve conditions in Chinatowns, to moving toward greater political involvement in American society, to including women in their

offices. On December 29, 1996, Ye Lili, a journalist emigrated from Taiwan in 1974, was elected by Renhe Huiguan as its representative to the board of governors in the Chinese Consolidated Benevolent Association (CCBA). Ye became one of the fifty-five board members and the first female in the office since the foundation of the CCBA. See *The World Journal*, 5 January 1997.

107. John Kuo Wei Tchen, *Genthe's Photographs of San Francisco's Old Chinatown* (New York: Dover Publications, 1984), 44.

108. Ibid.

109. "Map of Chinese Firms in Chinatowns, San Francisco, 1894," RG 85, National Archives, Pacific Sierra Region, San Bruno, CA.

110. Rose Hum Lee, *The Growth and Decline of Chinese Communities in the Rocky Mountain Region* (New York: Arno Press, 1978), 252.

111. Yu, "The World of Our Grandmothers," 37.

112. Interview 9.

113. Herbert Blumer, "Collective Behavior," in *New Outline of the Principles of Sociology*, ed. Alfred McClung Lee (New York: Barnes & Noble, 1949, 1951), 199.

Chapter 2

1. Nee, 85.

2. Hirata, "Free, Indentured, Enslaved," 23–24.

3. See Mary Coolidge, *Chinese Immigration*; and George Anthony Peffer, "Wife? Prostitute! A Critical Examination of the 1870 and 1880 Census Enumerations of San Francisco's Chinese Community," paper presented at the 13th National Conference of the Association for Asian American Studies, May 29–June 2, 1996, Washington, D.C.

4. Records of Women's Occidental Board of Foreign Missions of the Presbyterian Church, 1873–1920, San Francisco. Carol Green Wilson, *Chinatown Quest* (San Francisco: California Historical Society with Donaldina Cameron House, 1974). Interviews conducted by Victor G. & Brett de Bary Nee in *Longtime Californ'*. For recent scholarly works, see Curt Gentry, *Madames of San Francisco*, (New York: Doubleday, 1964); Marion S. Goldman, *Gold Diggers and Silver Mines: Prostitution and Social Life on the Comstock Lode* (Ann Arbor: University of Michigan Press, 1981); Lucie Cheng Hirata, "Free, Indentured, Enslaved: Chinese Prostitutes in Nineteenth-Century America," and "Chinese Immigrant Women in Nineteenth-Century California"; Mildred Crowl Martin, *Chinatown's Angry*

Angel: The Story of Donaldina Cameron (Palo Alto, Calif.: Pacific Books, Publishers, 1977); Pascoe, *Relations of Rescue*; and Benson Tong, *Unsubmissive Women: Chinese Prostitutes in Nineteenth-Century San Francisco.* See also Ruthanne Lum McCunn, *Thousand Pieces of Gold: A Biographical Novel* (San Francisco: Design Enterprises, 1981).

5. Hirata, "Free, Indentured, Enslaved."

6. Tong, *Unsubmissive Women.*

7. Hirata, "Free, Indentured, Enslaved," 6; Goldman, 96.

8. See Alexander MacLeod, *Pigtails and Gold Dust* (Caldwell, Idaho: Caxton Printers, 1948), 180–81.

9. Hirata, "Chinese Immigrant Women in Nineteenth-Century California," in *Asian and Pacific American Experience*, 38–55.

10. Ibid.

11. Nee, 85.

12. Chinese Mortuary Record of the City and County of San Francisco, National Archives, Pacific Sierra Region, San Bruno, CA.

13. Goldman, 95.

14. Yung, *Chinese Women of America*, 19.

15. Goldman, 96.

16. Ibid., 97.

17. Yung, *Chinese Women of America*, 19.

18. *Idaho Statesman*, 11 December 1875, c. 1–2, p. 2; Li-hua Yu, "Chinese Immigrants in Idaho," Ph.D. diss., Bowling Green State University, 1991, 210.

19. Kingsley Davis, "The Sociology of Prostitution," *American Sociological Review* 2 (October 1937):746–48.

20. Goldman, 73.

21. Goldman, 98.

22. Joan Hori, "Japanese Prostitution in Hawaii During the Immigration Period," in *Asian and Pacific American Experiences: Women's Perspectives*, 56–65.

23. Ibid., 58–59.

24. Ibid., 61.

25. Ibid., 60.

26. Julie Roy Jeffrey, *Frontier Women: The Trans-Mississippi West 1840–1880* (New York: Hill and Wang, 1979): 121.

27. Ruth Rosen, *The Lost Sisterhood, Prostitution in America, 1900–1918* (Baltimore: The Johns Hopkins University Press, 1982), xiv.

28. Hirata, "Chinese Immigrant Women in Nineteenth-Century California."

29. See Pascoe, *Relations of Rescue*, 13–17.

30. Nee, 85–86.

31. Martin, 43–44.

32. Wilson, 31.

33. The Chinese women discussed in this section include a wide range of occupations. While many of them were wives of merchants such as owners of laundries, restaurants, and grocery stores, a large number of them were entrepreneurs themselves, running restaurants and grocery stores. Still many of them were garment workers, either taking work at home or working in garment factory. Since most Chinese women entered the United States between 1882 and 1943 were under the category of wives of merchants, I use the term "merchant wives" in this section for the convenience of discussion.

34. See Tchen, *Genthe's Photographs*, 106.

35. See Lee, *The Growth and Decline of Chinese Communities in the Rocky Mountain Region*, 252.

36. Pascoe, 52.

37. See photographs in Tchen, *Genthe's Photographs*, 99, and 105.

38. Betty Lee Sung, *The Story of the Chinese in America* (New York: Collier Books, 1971), 190.

39. Paul C.P. Siu, *Chinese Laundryman: A Study of Social Isolation* (New York: New York University Press, 1987), 52.

40. Ibid., 58.

41. Kirksville City Directories, 1892–1992, Special Collection, Pickler Memorial Library, Truman State University, Kirksville, Missouri.

42. Maxine Hong Kingston, *The Woman Warrior, Memoirs of a Girlhood among Ghosts* (New York: Alfred A. Knopf, 1977), 104–105.

43. Sung, *The Story of the Chinese in America*, 197–198.

44. Liu Bo-ji, *Meiguo Huaqiao Shi* [History of the Overseas Chinese in the United States] (Taipei: Li Ming Publishing Co., 1981), 297.

45. See Sue Fawn Chung, "Gue Gim Wah: Pioneering Chinese American Woman of Nevada," *History and Humanities* ed. Francis X. Hartigan (Reno: University of Nevada Press, 1987), 45–79.

46. Sung, *The Story of the Chinese in America*, 203.

47. Cases 16135/5–11, 19938/4–11, 12017/36900, 33610/7–1, RG 85, National Archives, Pacific Sierra Region, San Bruno, CA.

48. Case 19938/4–11, ibid.

49. Case 12017/36900, ibid.

50. Case 33610/7–1, ibid.

51. Yu, "The World of Our Grandmothers," 37.

52. Lily Chan, "My Early Influences," 25 October 1926, William Carlson Smith Documents, MK-2.

53. Case 10385/5799, RG 85, National Archives, Pacific Sierra Region, San Bruno, CA.

54. Case 9514/536, RG 85, National Archives, Pacific Sierra Region, San Bruno, CA.

55. Cases 9514/537, 9514/538, and 9509/37, RG 85, National Archives, Pacific Sierra Region, San Bruno, CA.

56. Lee, *The Growth and Decline of Chinese Communities in the Rocky Mountain Region*, 193–94.

57. Interview 7.

58. Case 19938/4–11, RG 85, National Archives, Pacific Sierra Region, San Bruno, CA.

59. Interview 9.

60. See Xiaolan Bao, "Holding up More Than Half the Sky: A History of Women Garment Workers in New York's Chinatown, 1948–1991," 61; Richard Kim et al., "A Preliminary Investigation: Asian Immigrant Women Garment Workers in Los Angeles," *Amerasia Journal* 18: 1 (1992): 71; and Miriam Ching Louie, "Immigrant Asian Women in Bay Area Garment Sweatshops: After Sewing, Laundry, Cleaning and Cooking, I Have No Breath Left to Sing," *Amerasia Journal* 18: 1 (1992): 11.

61. Daniels, 78.

62. Hirata, "Chinese Immigrant Women in Nineteenth-Century California," 46.

63. *Chinese Digest*, July 1937; March 1938; and July 1938.

64. Patricia M. Fong, "The 1938 National Dollar Store Strike," *Asian American Review* 2, no. 1 (1975): 184; John Laslett and Mary Tyler, *The ILGWU in Los Angeles: 1907–1988* (Inglewood, CA: The Star Press, 1989), 31.

65. Entry 155, "H/M 1989 Formal and Informal Unfair Practices and Representation Case Files, 1938–49," RG25, National Archives, Washington, D.C.

66. China Institute in America, *A Survey of Chinese Students*, 34–35; see also Li, "The Chinese Revolution and the Chinese Women," 674.

67. *A Survey of Chinese Students* stated that "the general academic record achieved by the Chinese students in American universities and colleges has always been on high level," 21.

68. Howard L. Boorman, ed., *Biographical Dictionary of the Republic of China* (New York: Columbia University Press, 1970), vol. 3, 147.

69. Li, "The Chinese Revolution and the Chinese Women," 674.

70. Ye Guochao, "Madame Chiang at Wesleyan College," *The World Journal*, 29 April 1990.

71. Jung Chang, *Mme Sun Yat-Sen* (New York: Viking Penguin Inc., 1986), 25–26.

72. China Institute in America, *A Survey of Chinese Students*, 23.

73. Li, "The Chinese Revolution and the Chinese Women," 673–675.

74. Wang, 49.

75. Interview 1.

76. See the author's entry on Mme. Chiang Kai-shek in Franklin Ng, ed., *The Asian American Encyclopedia* (New York: Marshall Cavendish Corp., 1995).

77. Douglas W. Nelson, "The Alien Land Law Movement of the Late Nineteenth Century," *Journal of the West* 9 (1970): 46–59.

78. Ibid., 52–53.

79. Liu Bo-ji, 305–310.

80. Case 18362/3-3, RG 85, National Archives, Pacific Sierra Region, San Bruno, CA.

81. Sucheng Chan, *This Bitter-Sweet Soil: The Chinese in California Agriculture, 1860–1910* (Berkeley: University of California Press, 1986), 397.

82. Yung, *Chinese Women of America*, 36.

83. "Autobiography of a Chinese Student," William Carlson Smith Documents, Ad-55.

84. See Clarence E. Glick, *Sojourners and Settlers: Chinese Migrants in Hawaii* (Honolulu: Hawaii Chinese History Center and the University Press of Hawaii, 1980), 52–54.

85. "Autobiography of a Chinese Student," William Carlson Smith Documents, Ad-55.

86. Sarah R. Mason, "Family Structure and Acculturation in the Chinese Community in Minnesota," in *Asian and Pacific American Experience: Women's Perspectives*, 160–171.

87. Dong, *Forbidden City, U.S.A.*

88. Ibid.

89. See Chung, "Gue Gim Wah: Pioneering Chinese American Woman of Nevada," 45–79.

90. Fern Coble Trull, "The History of the Chinese in Idaho from 1864 to 1910," M.A. Thesis, the University of Oregon, 1946. Trull's study is one of the early research on Polly Bemis. Mary Alfreda Elsensohn, *Idaho Chinese Lore* (Cottonwood, Idaho: Idaho Corporation of Benedictine Sisters, 1971). A most reliable source on Polly Bemis. Ruthanne Lum McCunn, *The Thousand Pieces of Gold: A Biographical Novel* (San Francisco: Design Enterprises of San Francisco, 1981). Though a novel with romanticism, McCunn's book is considered an authentic account of Polly Bemis' personal story.

91. McCunn, 13–50.

92. Elsensohn, 82.

93. McCunn, 182–184, 190–200; Elsensohn, 83.

94. According to Elsensohn, their original marriage certificate is held in St. Gertrude's Museum, Cottonwood, Idaho.

95. Elsensohn, 83–84.

96. Trull, 104.

97. "Story of a Chinese Girl Student," William Carlson Smith Documents, A-56.

98. Glick, 13.

Chapter 3

1. Examples of the former are Coolidge's *Chinese Immigration* and Barth's *Bitter Strength*. For examples of the latter, see Tsai, *The Chinese Experience in America*, Daniels, *Asian America*, and Chan, *This Bitter Sweet Soil*.

2. Evelyn Nakano Glenn, "Split Household, Small Producer and Dual Wage Earner: An Analysis of Chinese-American Family Strategies," *Journal of Marriage and the Family* 45, no. 1 (1983): 35–46. For comparative study, also see Peter S. Li, "Immigration Laws and Family Patterns: Demographic Changes among Chinese Families in Canada, 1885–1971," *Canadian Ethnic Studies* 12 no. 1 (1980): 58–73.

3. Glenn, ibid., 40.

4. Ibid., 35.

5. David Beesley, "From Chinese to Chinese American: Chinese Women and Families in a Sierra Nevada Town," *California History,* Vol. 67 (Sept. 1988): 168–79.

6. Ibid.

7. Yung, *Chinese Women of America,* 44.

8. Kingston, 104.

9. Diner, 46.

10. Jeffrey, 44–45, 60–65.

11. Chung, "Gue Gim Wah," 50; Connie Young Yu, "The World of Our Grandmothers," 37; and Jade Snow Wong, *Fifth Chinese Daughter* (New York: Harper & Row, 1945), 5.

12. "Life History," William Carlson Smith Documents, MK–12.

13. Virginia Yans-McLaughlin, *Family and Community: Italian Immigrants in Buffalo, 1880–1930* (Urbana: University of Illinois Press, 1982), 91, 99, and 223.

14. Pickle, 75.

15. Mary Paik Lee, *Quiet Odyssey* (Seattle: University of Washington Press, 1990).

16. Beesley, 174.

17. Daniels, 96.

18. Ibid.

19. Ibid., 96–97.

20. For works on anti-miscegenation laws, see Sucheng Chan, "Exclusion of Chinese Women," 128–129 and *Asian Americans,* 59–60; Megumi Dick Osumi, "Asians and California's Anti-Miscegenation Laws," in *Asian and Pacific American Experiences: Women's Perspectives* 1–37; Robert J. Sickels, *Race, Marriage, and the Law* (Albuquerque: University of New Mexico Press, 1972), 64; and Betty Lee Sung, *Chinese American Intermarriage* (New York: Center for Migration Studies, 1990), 2.

21. *New York Times*, March 13, 1966, Sec. 4, p. 12; Fowler V. Harper and Jerome H. Skolnick, *Problems of the Family* (New York: Bobbs-Merrill, 1962), 96–105.

22. *California Statutes*, 1880, Code Amendments, Ch. 41, Sec. 1, p. 3.

23. *California Statutes*, 1905, Ch. 481, Sec. 2, p. 554.

24. "Story of a Chinese Girl Student," 1 August 1924, William Carlson Smith Documents, A-56.

25. See Chung, "Gue Gim Wah: Pioneering Chinese American Woman of Nevada," 45–79.

26. "Story of a Chinese Girl Student," 1 August 1924, William Carlson Smith Documents, A-56.

27. Pascoe, 53.

28. Confucius: *Lunyu* [Conversations].

29. Fairbank, 142.

30. Zhonghua Renmin Gongheguo Hunyin Fa [Marriage Law of the PRC] 1980, in Zhongguo falu nianjian bianjibu [Editorial Department of the Law Yearbook of China], *Zhongguo Falu Nianjian 1987* [Law Yearbook of China 1987] (Beijing: Falu Chubanshe, 1987), 168–69.

31. See Ba Jin, *Family* (Garden City, N.Y.: Doubleday & Company, Inc., 1972).

32. Entry 132, Record Group 85, National Archives, Washington, D.C.

33. Martin, 221–23.

34. Lee, *The Growth and Decline of Chinese Communities in The Rocky Mountain Region*, 253.

35. Ibid.

36. Lucy M. Cohen, *Chinese in the Post-Civil War South, A People Without a History* (Baton Rouge: Louisiana State University Press, 1984), 147; James W. Loewen, *The Mississippi Chinese: Between Black and White* (Cambridge, Mass.: Harvard University Press, 1971), 75; Sarah R. Mason, "Family Structure and Acculturation in the Chinese Community in Minnesota," in *Asian and Pacific American Experiences: Women's Perspectives*, 160–171; and John Kuo Wei Tchen, "New York Chinese: The Nineteenth-Century Pre-Chinatown Settlement," *Chinese America: History and Perspectives, 1990* (Chinese Historical Society of America, 1990), 157–192.

37. Tenth Census, 1880, New Orleans, Louisiana, population schedules, as cited in Cohen, 147.

38. Mason, 163.

39. Tchen, "New York Chinese," 176–177.

40. Mason, 168.

41. "Los Angeles Chinatown," Clara Gilbert, 12 June 1924, William Carlson Smith Document, AX 311.

42. Interview 9.

43. Hirata, "Chinese Immigrant Women in Nineteenth-Century California," 48.

44. Interview 7.

45. Interview 9.

46. Lily Chan, "My Early Influences," 25 October 1926, William Carlson Smith Documents, MK-2.

47. Daniels, 69.

48. "Life History," by a Chinese girl at McKinley High School, Honolulu, 20 November 1926, William Carlson Smith Documents, MK-12.

49. Interview 9.

50. "Life History," 20 November 1926, William Carlson Smith Documents, MK-12.

51. Interview 7.

52. Interview 9.

53. "Life History," 20 November 1926, William Carlson Smith Documents, MK-12.

54. "Story of a Chinese College Girl," 1 August 1924, William Carlson Smith Documents, A-54.

55. "Life History," 20 November 1926, William Carlson Smith Documents, MK-12.

56. Tchen, *Genthe's Photographs*, 28 and 98; Case 25103/7–20, RG 85, National Archives, Pacific Sierra Region, San Bruno, CA.

57. "Story of a Chinese Girl Student," San Francisco, 1 August 1924, William Carlson Smith Documents, A-56.

58. "Interview with Mrs. Machida," 2 July 1924, William Carlson Smith Documents; Interview 9.

59. *Forbidden City, U.S.A.*, 12/8/89, videocassette.

60. "Story of a Chinese Girl Student," 1 August 1924, William Carlson Smith Documents, A-56.

61. "Life History," 20 November 1926, William Carlson Smith Documents, MK-12.

62. "A Wedding in Chinese and in American," no date, William Carlson Smith Documents, A-108.

63. Lily Chan, "My Early Influences," 25 October 1926, William Carlson Smith Documents, MK-2.

64. Janie Chii, "The Oriental Girl in the Occident," *Women and Missions* 3, No. 5 (1926): 174–75, as cited in Yung, *Chinese Women of America*, 49.

65. "Life History," 1 August 1924, William Carlson Smith Documents, A-31.

66. Wong, *Fifth Chinese Daughter*, 129.

67. Amy Tan, *The Joy Luck Club* (New York: G.P. Putnam's Sons, 1989), 37.

68. Lee, *The Growth and Decline of Chinese Communities in the Rocky Mountain Region*, 252.

69. Ibid.

70. Tan, 20.

71. "Letter from Young Chinese Girl after Her Return to China," 23 June 1923, William Carlson Smith Documents, A-128.

72. Nee, 86.

73. For examples of works on Christian churches as grassroots organizations that reinforced ethnic identity, see Eun Sik Yang, "Korean Women in America, 1903–1930," in *Korean Women in Transition, at Home and Abroad*, 173–74.

74. Some writers have documented that even in the 1980s, Christian churches among Korean Americans continued to reflect the characteristics of traditional Korea: conservative, hierarchical, and male-dominant, and women were only allowed to provide menial services in church activities. See Eui-Young Yu, "The Activities of Women in Southern California Korean Community Organizations," in *Korean Women in Transition*, 289–90.

75. Ronald Riddle, *Flying Dragons, Flowing Streams: Music in the Life of San Francisco's Chinese* (Westport, CT: Greenwood Press, 1983), 145.

76. Interview 9.

77. Riddle, 179.

78. Mary Field Parton ed., *Autobiography of Mother Jones* (Chicago, 1925; reprint, North Stratford, NH: Ayer Company & Publishing Inc., 1974).

79. Diner, 101–102.

80. Susan A. Glenn, *Daughters of the Shtetl: Life and Labor in the Immigrant Generation* (Ithaca: Cornell University Press, 1990), 167–169.

81. Esther Ngan-Ling Chow, "The Feminist Movement: Where Are All the Asian American Women?" in *Making Waves*, 367–370.

82. Jonathan D. Spence, *The Gate of Heavenly Peace: The Chinese and Their Revolution, 1895–1980* (New York: Penguin Books, 1988), 165.

83. Glenda Riley, *Inventing the American Women* (Arlington Heights, IL: Harlan Davidson, Inc., 1987), 153–177.

84. Judy Yung, "The Social Awakening of Chinese American Women as Reported in *Chung Sai Yat Po*, 1900–1911," *Chinese America: History and Perspectives*, 1988, ed. Chinese Historical Society of America (San Francisco: The Chinese Historical Society of America, 1988), 80–102.

85. *San Francisco Chronicle*, 3 November 1902.

86. "Story of a Chinese Girl Student," 1 August 1924, William Carlson Smith Documents, A-56.

87. "The revolutionary efforts" refer to attempts and activities associated to the overthrow of Manchu monarch and the founding of Republic in China, which actually happened in 1911.

88. *Chung Sai Yat Po*, 26 April 1904.

89. *Chung Sai Yat Po*, 14 February 1905.

90. *San Francisco Call Bulletin*, 13 February 1911, as cited in Yung, *Chinese Women of America*, 60.

91. Liu Bo-ji, 566–73.

92. See the author's entry on Mme. Chiang Kai-shek, *The Asian American Encyclopedia*.

93. *The World Journal*, 2 June 1943.

94. *The Chinese Nationalist Daily* (New York), 24 January 1944.

95. *The Chinese Nationalist Daily*, 20 December 1944.

96. Sung, *Mountain of Gold*, 282.

97. *The Chinese Nationalist Daily*, 10 January 1944.

98. Tsai, 98.

99. Yung, *Chinese Women of America*, 61.

100. Peter Kwong, *Chinatown, New York* (New York: Monthly Review Press, 1979), 99–100.

Chapter 4

1. See Fred W. Riggs, *Pressures on Congress: A Study of the Repeal of Chinese Exclusion* (New York: King's Crown Press, 1950), 43–183.

2. Tung, 79–80.

3. Ibid., 32.

4. Annual Reports, Immigration and Naturalization Services, 1945–1949.

5. Annual Reports, Immigration and Naturalization Services, 1948.

6. Annual Reports, Immigration and Naturalization Services, 1945–1954.

7. Tung, 39.

8. U.S. Department of Commerce, *The U.S. Census of Population, 1960.*

9. Rose Hum Lee, "The Recent Immigrant Chinese Families of the San Francisco-Oakland Area," *Marriage and Family Living* 18 (1956): 14–24. For more detailed and dramatized information on Chinese war brides, see Louis Chu's novel *Eat A Bowl of Tea* (Seattle: University of Washington Press, 1979), and the featured film with the same title adopted from the novel.

10. *The New Encyclopedia*, Vol. 12 (Chicago: Encyclopedia Britannica, Inc., 1985), 776; *The World Journal*, 11 February 1996; Interview 40.

11. Interview 8; see also Huping Ling, "Sze-Kew Dun: A Chinese American Woman in Kirksville," *Missouri Historical Review* XCI, no. 1 (October 1996): 35–51.

12. Interview 1.

13. Chen Yuan-tsung, *The Dragon's Village* (New York: Pantheon Books, 1980), 34–36.

14. Interview 5.

15. Interview 32.

16. Rose Hum Lee, "The Stranded Chinese in the United States," *Phylon*, XIX (summer 1958) No. 2, 181.

17. Bette Bao Lord, *Legacies, A Chinese Mosaic* (New York: Alfred A. Knopf, 1990), 18.

18. For information on postwar Chinese women, see Huping Ling, "A History of Chinese Female Students in the United States, 1880s–1990s."

19. Dong, *Forbidden City, U.S.A.*; Fangzhi Yang, "Forbidden City, the Night Club," *The World Journal*, 8 December 1996.

20. Jim Marshall, "Cathay Hey-Hey," *Colliers* 109 (1942), 53, as cited in Riddle, 178.

21. Dong, *Forbidden City, U.S.A.*

22. *The Chinese Nationalist Daily*, 27 November 1944.

23. Yung, *Chinese Women of America*, 72.

24. Frank Quinn, Fair Employment Practices Commission hearing transcript, December 10, 1970, 38; in Yung, *Chinese Women of America*, 90.

25. Rose Hum Lee, *The Chinese in the United States of America* (Hong Kong University, 1960).

26. *The New Encyclopedia Britannica*, Vol. 12, 776; *The World Journal*, 11 February 1996; Interview 40.

27. China Institute in America, *A Survey of Chinese Students*, 18. The numbers quoted here were derived from different statistics by the China Institute in America and they are different from those in table 4.4. The greater numbers here are probably due to duplication in the process of compilation.

28. Interview 8; Ling, "Sze-Kew Dun."

29. Interview 1.

30. Interview 4.

31. Interview 1.

32. Philip E. Vernon, *The Abilities and Achievements of Orientals in North America* (New York: The Academic Press, 1982), 28.

33. Translation by the author.

34. Interview 8; Ling "Sze-Kew Dun."

35. See Ling-chi Wang, *Chinese Americans: School and Community Problems* (Chicago: Integrated Education Associates, 1972), 12–17.

36. Yung, *Chinese Women of America*, 81.

37. Kingston, 113–160.

38. Lyman, 153.

39. Interview 4.

40. Interview 1.

41. Tan, *The Joy Luck Club.*

42. Ibid., 28.

43. Ibid., 27.

44. Ibid., 38–41.

45. Interview 6.

46. Interview 1.

47. Interview 8; Ling, "Sze-Kew Dun."

48. Yap used a pseudonym "Northville" to imply Boston, Massachusetts.

49. Yap, *Gather Your Strength, Sisters*, 25.

50. Ibid., 45–85.

51. Ibid., 28–29.

52. Ibid., 29.

Chapter Five

1. See, for example, Daniels, *Asian America* 283; and Chan, *Asian Americans*, 121.

2. Tsai, *The Chinese Experience in America*, 152; and Ronald Takaki, *Strangers from a Different Shore, A History of Asian Americans* (Boston: Little, Brown and Company, 1989), 420.

3. Russell Endo and William Wei, "On the Development of Asian American Studies Programs," *Reflections on Shattered Windows*, ed. Gary Okihiro et al. (Pullman: Washington State University Press, 1988), 5–15. This is one of the first articles that describes the evolution of Asian American studies programs on the West Coast. Peter Nien-chu Kiang, "The New Wave: Developing Asian American Studies on the East Coast," *Reflections on Shattered Windows*, 43–50, discusses the development of Asian American studies on the East Coast. Don T. Nakanish and Tina Yamano Nishida eds., *The Asian American Educational Experience, A Source Book for Teachers and Students* (New York: Routledge, 1995) is a collection of articles on educational issues that concerned Asian Americans.

4. Kiang, 43–44.

5. *San Francisco Chronicle*, 1 December 1983.

6. Yung, *Chinese Women of America*, 106.

7. *Central Daily News*, 23 April 1992.

8. *Central Daily News*, 9 December 1994.

9. Charles Gandee, "The Other Side of Maya Lin," *Vogue*, V.185, No.4 (April 1995): 346–403.

10. Ibid., 348.

11. Jere Longman, "Kwan Is Young, Graceful, and an Alternate for Norway," *New York Times* 25 January 1994; E. M. Swift, "Red Hot," *Sports Illustrated*, V. 84 (April 1996): 28–30; *The World Journal*, 24 March 1996.

12. Yung, *Chinese Women of America*, 100.

13. Chan, 173.

14. Ibid.

15. *Overseas Chinese Daily*, 19 September 1988.

16. *People's Daily*, 26 October 1990.

17. *People's Daily*, 12 November 1990.

18. *People's Daily*, 22 April 1989.

19. *The World Journal*, 21 July 1990.

20. Jack Anderson, "Her Life is 'A Massage'," *Parade Magazine*, 3 February 1991.

21. Wayne Wang, *Dim Sum*, 1985.

22. Jade Snow Wong, *No Chinese Stranger* (New York: Harper & Row, 1975), xii.

23. Daniels, 328.

24. Diane Yen-Mei Wong, *Dear Diane: Letters from Our Daughters* (U.S. Department of Education), 39–41.

25. Vernon, 248–61; Susana McBee, "Asian-Americans, Are They Making the Grade?" *U.S. News and World Report*, 2 April 1984, 41–47; Jennie H. Y. Yee, "Parenting Attitudes, Acculturation and Social Competence in the Chinese-American Child" (Ph.D. diss., Boston University, 1983).

26. Marcus Lee Hansen, "The Problem of the Third Generation Immigrant," republication of the 1937 address with introductions by Peter Kivisto and Oscar Handlin (Rock Island: Swenson Swedish Immigration Research Center and the Augustana College Library, 1987), 15.

27. Ibid., 11–19.

28. *Statutes at Large*, Washington, D.C.: U.S. Government Publishing Company, 1965, V. 79, 912–913.

29. David M. Reimers, *Still the Golden Door: The Third World Comes to America*, New York: Columbia University Press, 1985, 75–76.

30. Interview 1.

31. Cheng, *The Dragon's Village*, 134.

32. *The World Journal*, 6 August 1990, p. 3.

33. Interview 13.

34. John T. Ma, "Chinese Americans in the Professions," in *The Economic Condition of Chinese Americans*, ed. Yuan-li Wu (Chicago: Pacific/Asian American Mental Health Research Center, 1980), 67.

35. Jessy Chain Chou, "A Survey of Chinese Students in the United States, 1979–1987" (Ed.D. diss., Columbia University Teachers College, 1989), 1, 87.

36. Thomas B. Gold, *State and Society in the Taiwan Miracle* (Armonk, New York: M. E. Sharpe, Inc., 1986). Some other writers have also associated the study abroad craze in Taiwan since the 1960s with the island's political instability. See Yen-Fen Tseng, "Beyond 'Little Taipei': The Development of Taiwanese Immigrant Business in Los Angeles," *International Migration Review*, Vol. 29, No. 1 (spring 95): 33–58.

37. Interviews 10, 11, 12, 13, 14, 15, and 20.

38. Interview 13.

39. Shiqi Huang, "Contemporary Educational Relations with the Industrial World: A Chinese View," in *China's Education and the Industrialized World*, eds. Ruth Hayhoe and Marianne Bastid (Armonk, N.Y.: M. E. Sharpe, 1987), 226–227.

40. Since the 1980s, it has become a common practice for many universities and colleges in China to promote faculty members who had studied in a foreign institute for a certain period of time, in accordance with the open door policy from the Chinese central government. Among the twenty-seven visiting scholars from the PRC interviewed by the author between 1985 and 1987, most indicated that the major motivation for them to come to America was to be promoted when they return to China after the completion of their training or research projects in America. Interviews 75–101. See also Ling, "A History of Chinese Female Students in the United States, 1880s–1990s."

41. Of the thirty-two interviewees who came to America from the PRC since the 1980s as female students, a majority of them originally intended to return to China after the completion of their education in America and hoped their training in the United States would help their future careers in China. Interviews 2, 17, 18, 19, 22, 23, 24, 25, 26, 27, 28, 29, 30, 34, 59, 62, 63, 64, 65, 66, 67, 68, 69, 70, 71, 72, 73, 74, and 102.

42. Ibid.; interviews 75–101.

43. Interviews 58, 60, and 61.

44. *China Daily*, 15 February 1988.

45. Chou, "A Survey of Chinese Students in the United States, 1979–1987," 61.

46. "Chinese Students Win Waiver," *Congressional Quarterly Weekly Report* 47 (November 25, 1989): 3245.

47. "Bush Veto of Chinese Immigration Relief," *Congressional Quarterly Weekly Report* 47 (December 2, 1989): 3331.

48. The so-called J-1 visa requires its holder to return home for at least two years before seeking an adjustment in immigration status (usually permanent residency in the United States, commonly known as a "Green Card"). Whereas, the F-1 visa has no such restriction. The J-1 visa was designed to alleviate the "brain drain" suffered by other nations when their students attain an education in the United States and then refuse to go home. Normally, the government-sponsored Chinese students or scholars are issued J-1 visas. Therefore, the American immigration restrictions and the public help they received through Chinese government make them legally and emotionally obligated to serve their country upon completion of their education or training in the United States.

49. Interview 2.

50. This percentage comes from the author's analysis of interviews and surveys of female students from the PRC.

51. This slogan was coined by the famous Qing scholar-official Zhang Zhidong during the "Hundred Day" Reform of 1898 in China.

52. According to the author's survey.

53. State Education Commission of the People's Republic of China,"State Education Commission Provisions on Study Abroad," Section V, p.9.

54. Ibid.

55. According to the survey conducted by the author among Chinese student wives at Miami University, ninety-six percent of them expressed their desire to earn a graduate degree in an American university; also interviews 18, 19, 22, 23, 24, 25, 26, 27, 28, and 29.

56. Interviews 18, 19, 22, 23, 26, and 29.

57. According to surveys conducted by the author.

58. Peter Kwong, *The New Chinatown* (New York: Hill and Wang, 1987), 30.

59. Min Zhou, *Chinatown: The Socioeconomic Potential of an Urban Enclave* (Philadelphia: Temple University Press, 1992), 162–165.

60. Zhou Yun-zhi, "Life for Chinese in New York," in *The World Journal Weekly*, 15 July 1990, 4.

61. Kwong, 31.

62. Bao, "Holding Up More Than Half the Sky," 52.

63. *The World Journal*, 24 July 1990, 15.

64. Ibid.

65. Ibid.

66. *Overseas Chinese Daily*, 21 September 1988.

67. Jacqueline R. Agtuca, *A Community Secret For the Filipina in An Abusive Relationship* (Seattle: Seal Press, 1992), 22.

68. Zhou Yun-zhi, ibid.

69. Orleans, 91.

70. Interviews 2, 3, 11, 12, 13, 14, 15, 17, 34, 51, 60, and 64.

71. Interview 51.

72. Interview 34.

73. See examples discussed in chapter 1.

74. Mr. and Mrs. William S. Yip, Los Angeles, California, interview by Catharine Holt, January 13, 1925, William Carlson Smith Documents, #315.

75. Wendy Wen-yawn Yen, "Dawn Always Comes After Darkness," *The World Journal Weekly* 8, 9, and 10 May 1990. Translated by Huping Ling.

76. *The World Journal*, 12 April 1990.

77. According to a cable sent to all INS (the U.S. Immigration and Naturalization Service) field offices on 4 December 1989.

78. Interviews 17, 18, 19, 22, and 30.

Chapter Six

1. For scholarly discussion on model minority, see Bob H. Suzuki, "Educational and the Socialization of Asian Americans: A Revisionist Analysis of the 'Model Minority' Thesis," *Amerisia Journal* 4 (1977): 23–51, one of the earliest critiques of the model minority thesis. Keith Osajima, "Asian Americans as the Model Minority: An Analysis of the Popular Press Image in the 1960s and 1980s," *Reflections on Shattered Windows*, 165–174, is one of the recent scholarly discussions on the topic. Ronald Takaki, *Strangers From A Different Shore*, 474–484, and Sucheng Chan, *Asian Americans* (1991), 167–170, both summarized the debate on model minority.

2. William Peterson, "Success Story, Japanese-American Style," *New York Times Magazine*, 9 January 1966, 20–43.

3. "Success Story of One Minority in the U.S.," *U.S. News and World Report*, December 26, 1966, 73–78.

4. Takaki, ibid., 552, note 3; Osajima, 173, note 9.

5. President Ronald Reagan, speech to a group of Asian and Pacific Americans in the White House, February 23, 1984, reprinted in *Asian Week*, 2 March 1984.

6. U.S. Department of Health, Education, and Welfare, *A Study of Selected Socio-Economic Characteristics of Ethnic Minorities Based on the 1970 Census, Vol. II: Asian Americans* (Washington, D.C.: Department of Health, Education, and Welfare, 1974), 108, 112.

7. Herbert R. Barringer et al., "Education, Occupational Prestige, and Income of Asian Americans," *The Asian American Educational Experience*, ed. Don T. Nakanishi and Tina Yamano Nishida (New York: Routledge, 1995), 150.

8. Kwong, 62–65; Nee, *Longtime Californ'*, 278–319; Bernard Wong, "The Chinese: New Immigrants in New York's Chinatown," *New Immigrants in New York*, ed. Nancy Foner (New York: Columbia University Press, 1987), 243–271; and Zhou, 159–182.

9. Barringer, 152.

10. Korn/Ferry International, U.S. Glass Ceiling Commission, reprinted in Leadership Education For Asian Pacifics, Inc., *Newsletter* (October 1996): 5.

11. Department of Health, Education, and Welfare: *A Study of Selected Socio-Economic Characteristics of Ethnic Minorities Based on the 1970 Census*, 108, 112.

12. "Labor Force Characteristics of Selected Asian and Pacific Islander Groups by Nativity, Citizenship, and Year," *1990 Census of Population: Asians and Pacific Islanders in the United States* (U.S. Department of Commerce, 1993), 111–112; Missouri State Census Data Center, "Basic Demographic Trend Report: United States."

13. "All Things Considered Weekend Edition," National Public Radio, Saturday, 8 March 1997.

14. Steven M. Cahn, ed., *The Affirmative Action Debate* (New York: Routledge, 1995), xi.

15. Civil Rights Act of 1964, Sec. 601, United States, *United States Statute at Large*, Vol. 78 (Washington, D.C.: United States Government Publishing Office, 1964), 252.

16. Executive Order 11246: Equal Employment Opportunity, Federal Register excerpt, September 28, 1965, pp. 87–95.

17. Cahn, xii.

18. Karen K. Narasaki, "Discrimination and the Need for Affirmative Action Legislation," *Common Ground, Perspectives on Affirmative Action*, 5–8.

19. Daniel Choi, "False Front," *A Magazine* (October/ November 1995): 86.

20. *San Francisco Examiner*, 20 May 1995, A4.

21. Nina Chen, "Asian Pacific Americans Speak Out Against Affirmative Action," *Asian Week*, 21 April 1995.

22. The nine groups identified by the consent decree are Spanish-surname, other white, black, Chinese, Japanese, Korean, Filipino, American Indians, and other nonwhite. See Selena Dong, "'Too Many Asians': The Challenge of Fighting Discrimination Against Asian-Americans and Preserving Affirmative Action," *Stanford Law Review*, Vol. 47 (May 1995): 1027–1057. This essay is the best discussion on the case.

23. Richard Low, "Quota or No Quota," *Asian Week*, 20 January 1995.

24. Chen, "Asian Pacific Americans Speak Out Against Affirmative Action."

25. *LEAP Newsletter*, October 1996.

26. G. Pascal Zachary, "Judge's Block on California Prop. 209 Marks First of Prolonged Legal Battles," *The Wall Street Journal*, 29 November 1996.

27. Peter Schmidt, "A Federal Appeals Court Upholds California Measure Barring Racial Preferences" *The Chronicle of Higher Education*, 18 April 1997; Student Against Discrimination and Preferences at UCSD, "Proposition 209 in Federal Court," 1997.

28. Sung, *Chinese American Intermarriage*, 10–11.

29. Larry Hajime Shinagawa and Gin Yong Pang, "Intraethnic, Interethnic, and Interracial Marriages among Asian Americans in California, 1980," *Berkeley Journal of Sociology* 33 (1988): 95–114.

30. Joan Walsh, "Asian Women, Caucasian Men," *Image*, 2 December 1990: 11–16.

31. Ibid., 12.

32. Ibid., 11.

33. Milton Gordon, *Assimilation in American Life* (New York: Oxford University Press, 1964), 80; other works with similar views are: John N. Tinker, "Intermarriage and Assimilation in a Plural Society: Japanese Americans in the U.S.," *Intermarriage in the United States*, eds. Gary A. Cretser and Joseph J. Leon (New York: Hayworth Press, 1982), 61–74; Harry Kitano et al., "Asian American Interracial Marriage," *Journal of Marriage and the Family* 46, No. 1 (February 1984): 179–190; and Sung, *Chinese American Intermarriage*.

34. Kingsley Davis, "Intermarriage in Caste Societies," *American Anthropologist* 43, no. 3 (July–September 1941): 376–395.

35. Davis, 386–390.

36. Shinagawa and Pang, 98.

37. Paul R. Spickard, *Mixed Blood: Intermarriage and Ethnic Identity in Twentieth-Century America* (Madison: The University of Wisconsin Press, 1989), 6–9.

38. Interview 1.

39. Interview 17.

40. Interview 34.

41. Interview 124.

42. Speech of Mari Matsuda, "The Resurgence of Racism on Campus," at the Eighth National Conference of the Association for Asian American Studies, Honolulu, Hawaii, May 29–31, 1991.

43. Deng, *Slaying the Dragon*.

44. Barbara Kantrowitz and Heather Woodin, "Diagnosis: Harassment, A Medical-School Professor Overcomes Sexual Slurs," *Newsweek*, 26 November 1990, 62.

45. Interview 6.

Chapter Seven

1. Sucheng Chan, *Asian Americans*, 169; Tsai, *The Chinese Experience in America*, 160; and Yung, *Chinese Women of America*, 106.

Selected Bibliography

Although some of the sources listed here are not cited in the text, they are significant and have been consulted during the preparation of the book.

Primary Sources

Documents

Center For Immigration Studies. Washington D.C. Four areas of concern include immigration's efforts on national social, economic, demographic, and environmental interests.

Chinese American Cultural Association Library. Chesterland, Ohio. Collection includes Chinese American heritage, and history.

Chinese Culture Foundation. San Francisco Library. Collection contains Chinese American history and culture.

Chinese Institute in America Library. New York City. Collection on Chinese immigration, heritage, and contribution to America.

Civil Rights Issues of Asian and Pacific Americans: Myths and Realities: May 8–9, 1979, Washington, D.C., a consultation. Sponsored by the United States Commission on Civil Rights. Washington, D.C., the Commission 1980.

Immigration and Naturalization Service Records. 1787–1954. 959 cu. ft. and 11,476 microfilm reels. National Archives and Records Service, Washington D.C., contains records of general immigration, Chinese immigration, passenger arrival, Americanization, naturalization, field offices, and alien internment camps.

Immigration and Naturalization Service Records. *(continued)*
National Archives-Pacific Sierra Region, San Bruno, California, holds unique records. Among the subjects covered are Chinese exclusion and immigration, the development of Pearl Harbor and mainland coastal fortifications, gold mining, migrant labor camps, and tribal land claims.

National Archives-Central Plain Region, Kansas City, Missouri. Two records are related to Chinese: Chinese Exclusion Cases Habeas Corpus Petitions: 1857–1965 and Criminal Records, 1871–1918, U.S. District Court for Eastern District of Missouri. The former involves Chinese in Iowa, Kansas, Minnesota, Missouri, Nebraska, North Dakota, and South Dakota. The latter contains cases related to Chinese in Missouri involved in manufacturing, selling, and smoking of opium.

Kubli General Store, Jacksonville, Oregon, Account Books, 1858–1886. 6 Volumes. Special Collections, Main Library, University of Oregon, Eugene. Many of the store's patrons were Chinese miners.

Smith, William Carlson Documents, 1912–1961. Special Collections, Main Library, University of Oregon, Eugene. The documents consist of interviews with and autobiographies of Chinese, Japanese, Mexican and other immigrants and first-generation Americans. Most of the autobiographies were written by school children in California and Hawaii. There are also copies of official letters and published items concerning race relations.

United States District Court: Northern District of California Records. 1851–1951. 4500 cu. ft. and 4 microfilm reels. Federal Archives and Records Center, San Francisco Archives Branch. Contains documents relating to individual cases brought before the Court. Case files on Chinese immigrants, who frequently appeared before the Court on a writ of habeas corpus, include passports with photos, statement of wealth or occupation, and occasionally testimony about previous residency in the U.S. Cases pertaining to Chinese women who were accused of being involved in prostitution may include photos, statements about the personal history and character of the defendant, court testimony, and other legal papers.

Women's Occidental Board of Foreign Missions of the Presbyterian Church, San Francisco. Records. 1873–1920. 4 volumes. The Board promoted mission work in California and aboard from 1873 until 1920. A nearly complete set of annual reports contains handwritten corrections and additions, bylaws, correspondence, notes, history, extracts from missionaries' journals, statistical reports, pamphlets, and other records in various areas, including the Occidental Mission School and Home in San Francisco, which was superintended by [Miss] Donaldina M. Cameron. Cameron oversaw the rescue of young

Chinese women who were thought to be held captive in Chinatown. Collection also contains a report of the house to house visitation committee, which was intended to help overcome the seclusion of women at home in Chinatown.

Newspapers

Chung Sai Yat Po [The Chinese Daily]. San Francisco, CA. Chinese language newspaper. Established by Presbyterian minister Ng Poon Chew in 1900, CSYP was heavily influenced by American republicanism, Christianity, and Western middle-class ideology. Available on microfilm at the Ethnic Studies Library and East Asiatic Library, University of California, Berkeley.

Jin Shan Shyr Pao [Chinese Times]. San Francisco, CA. Established in 1924. Ethnic newspapers printed in Chinese. Contents include news on domestic, foreign, and Chinese group affairs and events.

Mei Jo Jih Pao [The Chinese Journal]. New York, NY. Established in 1926. Daily newspaper printed in Chinese. Includes world and national news, and news from the Chinese ethnic communities in the United States. Available on microfilm at the New York Public Library.

Min Ch'i Jih Pao [The Chinese Nationalist Daily]. New York, NY. Established in 1928? Daily newspaper printed in Chinese. Available on microfilm at the New York Public Library.

Niu-Yuen Hsin Pao [The China Tribune]. New York, NY. Established in 1943? Daily newspaper printed in Chinese. Available on microfilm at the New York Public Library.

Pacific Citizen. Los Angeles, CA. Established in 1929. Japanese American and Asian/Pacific American newspaper.

People's Daily. San Francisco, CA. Current Chinese newspaper.

San Francisco Chronicle. San Francisco, CA. Established in 1865. A general newspaper.

Shao Nien Chung Kuo Ch'en Pao [The Young China Daily]. San Francisco, CA. Established in 1910. Ethnic newspaper printed in Chinese. Covers national, international, and group news.

Tai Ping Young Jow Bao [Chinese Pacific Weekly]. San Francisco, CA. Established in 1946. Ethnic newspaper in Chinese. This newspaper is "devoted to the improvement and progress of the Chinese community" (editor's statement). It contains commentaries and special news as well as feature articles dealing with the ethnic situation, events in China, and national and local affairs.

The Chinese World. San Francisco, CA. Established in 1891. Contains news on Chinese communities in the United States.

The World Journal. New York. Current Chinese newspaper.

Films

Dim Sum, produced and directed by Wayne Wang, 100 min., color video, 1985. Portrait of mother-daughter relationship in a Chinese American family.

Dim Sum Take-Out, produced and directed by Wayne Wang, 12 min., color video, 1990. Five Chinese American women explore issues of ethnicity, independence, and sexuality. National Asian American Telecommunications Association (NAATA), 346 Ninth Street, Second Floor, San Francisco, CA 94103.

Forbidden City, U.S.A., produced and directed by Arthur Dong, 56 min., color/black and white video, 1989. Story of a Chinese nightclub of San Francisco in the 1930s and 1940s. Deep Focus Productions 22D Hollywood Ave., Ho-Ho-Kus, New Jersey 07423.

Liru, produced and directed by Henry Chow, 25 min., color video, 1991. Drama about a Chinese American woman's search for ethnic and personal identity. NAATA.

Sewing Woman, produced and directed by Arthur Dong, 14 min., black and white video, 1982. A Chinese immigrant woman's story from war-torn China to America. NAATA.

Slaying the Dragon, produced and directed by Deborah Gee, 60 min., color video, 1990. Images of Asian American women in the media. NAATA.

With Silk Wings: Asian American Women at Work, a series of four films: *Four Women, On New Ground*, and *Frankly Speaking* produced and directed by Loni Ding, and *Talking History* produced and directed by Spencer Nakasako, 30 min. each, color video, 1990. NAATA.

Articles, Books, Dissertations, and Theses

Asians and Asian Americans in General

Asian Women United of California, eds. *Making Waves: An Anthology of Writings by and about Asian American Women*. Boston: Beacon Press, 1989.

Chan, Sucheng. *Asian Americans: An Interpretive History*. Boston: Twayne Publishers, 1991.

Cheng, Lucie, and Edna Bonacich, eds. *Labor Immigration Under Capitalism: Asian Workers in the United States Before World War II*. Berkeley: University of California Press, 1984.

Chow, Esther Ngan-ling. "The Influence of Sex-Role Identity and Occupational Attainment on the Psychological Well-Being of Asian American-Women." *Psychology of Women Quarterly* 11, no. 1 (1987): 69–81.

Costello, Julia G., et al. *Rice Bowls in the Delta: Artifacts Recovered from the 1915 Asian Community of Walnut Grove, California*. Los Angeles: University of California, Los Angeles, Institute of Archaeology, 1988.

Daniels, Roger. *Asian America: Chinese and Japanese in the United States Since 1850*. Seattle, WA.: University of Washington Press, 1988.

Dong, Selena. "'Too Many Asians': The Challenge of Fighting Discrimination Against Asian-Americans and Preserving Affirmative Action." *Stanford Law Review* 47 (May 1995): 1027–1057.

Endo, Russell, et al., eds. *Asian-Americans: Social and Psychological Perspectives*. Ben Lomond, Calif.: Science & Behavior Books, Inc., 1980.

Fairbank, John King. *East Asian, Tradition and Transformation*. Boston: Houghton Mifflin Company, 1973.

Fawcett, James T., and Benjamin Carino. *Pacific Bridges: The New Immigration from Asian and the Pacific Islands*. Staten Island, N.Y.: Center for Migration Studies, 1987.

Fong, Eva Chow. "Barriers to Educational Leadership Aspirations as Perceived by California Asian Women Administrators." Ph.D. diss., University of the Pacific, 1984.

Fugita, Stephen. *Asian Americans and Their Communities of Cleveland*. Cleveland: Cleveland State University, 1977.

Fukida, Kikimo Ann. "Chinese American and Japanese Women in California Public School Administration." Ph.D. diss., University of Southern California, 1984.

Gardner, Robert W. *Asian Americans: Growth, Change and Diversity*. Washington, D.C.: Population Reference Bureau, Inc., 1985.

Glenn, Evelyn Nakano. "Racial Ethnic Women's Labor: The Intersection of Race, Gender and Class Oppression." *Review of Radical Political Economics* 17, no. 3 (1985): 86–108.

Hing, Bill Ong. *Making and Remaking Asian America Through Immigration Policy 1850–1990*. Stanford: Stanford University Press, 1993.

Hsia, Jayjia. *Asian Americans in Higher Education and at Work*. Hillsdale, N.J.: Lawrence Eribaum Associates, 1987.

Hundley, Norris, ed. *The Asian American: The Historical Experience*. Santa Barbara, Calif.: American Bibliographical Center-Clio Press, 1976.

Hune, Shirley. *Pacific Migration to the United States Microform: Trends and Themes in Historical and Sociological Literature*. Washington, D.C.: Research Institute on Immigration and Ethnic Studies, Smithsonian Institution, 1977.

Jameson, E. "Toward a Multicultural History of Women in the Western United States." *Signs* 13 no. 4 (1988): 761–91.

Kim, Bok-Lim C. *The Asian Americans, Changing Patterns, Changing Needs*. Montclair, N.J.: Association of Korean Christian Scholars in North America, 1978.

Kim, Hyung-Chan, ed. *Dictionary of Asian American History*. New York: Greenwood Press, 1986.

———, ed. *Asian American Studies: An Annotated Bibliography and Research Guide*. New York: Greenwood Press, 1989.

Kim, Richard, et al. "A Preliminary Investigation: Asian Immigrant Women Garment Workers in Los Angeles." *Amerasia Journal* 18: 1 (1992): 69–82.

Kitano, Harry H. L., and Roger Daniels. *Asian Americans: Emerging Minorities*. Englewood Cliffs, N.J.: Prentice Hall, 1995.

Knoll, Tricia. *Becoming Americans: Asian Sojourners, Immigrants and Refugees in the Western United States*. Portland, Oregon: Coast to Coast Books, 1982.

Kumagai, Gloria L. "The Asian Women in America." *Explorations in Ethnic Studies* 1 no. 2 (1978): 27–39.

Lim, Geok-lin, and Amy Ling, eds. *Reading the Literatures of Asian America*. Philadelphia: Temple University Press, 1992.

Lim, Shirley. *The Forbidden Stitch: An Asian-American Women's Anthology*. Corvallis, Oregon: Calyx Books, 1988.

Louie, Miriam Ching. "Immigrant Asian Women in Bay Area Garment Sweatshops: After Sewing, Laundry, Cleaning and Cooking, I Have No Breath Left to Sing." *Amerasia Journal* 18: 1 (1992): 1–26.

Lyman, Stanford M. *The Asian in North America*. Santa Barbara, Calif.: ABC-Clio Books, 1977.

———. *Chinatown and Little Tokyo: Power, Conflict, and Community among Chinese and Japanese Immigrants to America*. Millwood, New York: Associated Faculty Press, 1986.

Mangiafico, Luciano. *Contemporary American Immigrants: Patterns of Filipino, Korean, and Chinese Settlement in the United States*. New York: Praeger, 1988.

Melendy, H. Brett. *Chinese and Japanese Americans*. New York: Hippocrene Books, 1984.

Nakanish, Don T., and Tina Yamano Nishida, eds. *The Asian American Educational Experience: A Source Book for Teachers and Students*. New York: Routledge, 1995.

Nandi, Proshanta K. *The Quality of Life of Asian Americans: An Exploratory Study in a Middle-Size Community*. Chicago: Pacific/Asian American Mental Health Research Center, 1980.

Nelson, Douglas W. "The Alien Land Law Movement of the Late Nineteenth Century." *Journal of The West* 9 (1970): 46–59.

Nomura, Gail M., et al., eds. *Frontiers of Asian American Studies: Writing, Research, and Criticism*. Pullman, Washington: Washington State University Press, 1989.

Okihiro, Gary Y., et al., eds. *Reflections on Shattered Windows: Promises and Prospects for Asian American Studies*. Pullman, Washington: Washington State University Press, 1988.

Osajima, Keith. "Asian Americans as the Model Minority: An Analysis of the Popular Press Image in the 1960s and 1980s." In *Reflections on Shattered Windows: Promises and Prospects for Asian American Studies*, 165–174. Pullman, Washington: Washington State University Press, 1988.

Osumi, Megumi Dick. "Asians and California's Anti-Miscegenation Laws," In *Asian and Pacific American Experiences: Women's Perspectives*, ed. Nobuya Tsuchida, 1–37. Minneapolis: Asian/Pacific American Learning Resource Center and General College, University of Minnesota, 1982.

Schuyler, Robert L. *Archaeological Perspectives on Ethnicity in America: Afro-American and Asian-American Culture History*. Farmingdale, N.Y.: Baywood Pub. Co., 1980.

Shieh, Janejane. "The Assimilation of Asian Americans." Thesis, Ohio State University, 1986.

Sue, Stanley, and James K. Morishima. *The Mental Health of Asian Americans: Contemporary Issues in Identifying and Treating Mental Problems*. San Francisco: Jossey-Bass, Inc., 1982.

Suzuki, Bob H. "Educational and the Socialization of Asian Americans: A Revisionist Analysis of the 'Model Minority' Thesis." *Amerisia Journal* 4 (1977): 23–51.

Takaki, Ronald. *Strangers from a Different Shore: A History of Asian Americans*. Boston: Little, Brown & Company, 1989.

Tsuchida, Nobuya, et al., eds. *Asian and Pacific American Experience: Women's Perspectives*. Minneapolis: Asian/Pacific American Learning Resource Center and General College, University of Minnesota, 1982.

Ueda, Reed. "The Coolie and the Model Minority: Reconstructing Asian-American History." *Journal of Interdisciplinary History* 20 (1989): 117–24.

Vernon, Philip E. *The Abilities and Achievements of Orientals in North America*. New York: The Academic Press, 1982.

Warren, Marian Helen. "Influences Affecting Career/Life Planning Aspiration as Perceived by Intellectually-Gifted, Ethnically-Diverse Adolescent Girls: A Case Study." Ph.D. diss., University of San Diego, 1987.

Watanabe, Sylvia, and Carol Bruchac, eds. *Home to Stay, Asian American Women's Fiction*. Greenfield Center, N.Y.: The Greenfield Review Press, 1990.

Wong, Morrison G. "Labor Force Participation and Socioeconomic Attainment of Asian-American Women." *Sociological Perspectives* 26 no. 4 (1983): 423–446.

Woo, Deborah. "The Socioeconomic Status of Asian American Women in the Labor Force: An Alternative View." *Sociological Perspectives* 28 no. 3 (1985): 307–338.

Wunsch, Marie Ho. "Walls of Jade: Images of Men, Women and Family in Second Generation Asian-American Fiction and Autobiography." Ph.D. diss., University of Hawaii, 1977.

Yamanaka, Keiko. "Labor Force Participation of Asian-American Women: Ethnicity, Work, and the Family." Ph.D. diss., Cornell University, 1987.

Yun, Grace, ed. *A Look Beyond the Model Minority Image: Critical Issues in Asian America*. New York: Minority Rights Group, 1989.

Chinese and Chinese Americans

Aiken, Rebecca B. *Montreal Chinese Property Ownership and Occupational Change, 1881–1981*. New York: AMS, 1988.

Armentrout-Ma, Eve. *Revolutionists, Monarchists and Chinatowns: Chinese Politics in the Americas and the 1911 Revolution*. Hawaii: 1990.

Aubitz, Shawn. *Chinese Immigration to Philadelphia*. Philadelphia, PA: National Archives, Philadelphia Branch, 1988.

Ayscough, Florence. *Chinese Women, Yesterday and Today*. Boston: Honghton Miffin Co., 1937.

Baldwin, S. L. *Must the Chinese Go? An Examination of the Chinese Question*. New York: The Press of H. E. Elking, 1890; reprint, San Francisco: R & E Research Associates, Publishers and Distributors of Ethnic Studies, 1970.

Bao, Xiaolan. "Holding Up More Than Half the Sky: A History of Women Garment Workers in New York's Chinatown, 1948–1991." Ph.D. diss., New York University, 1991.

Barlow, Jeffrey G. *China Doctor of John Day*. Portland, OR: Binford & Mort, 1979.

Barth, Gunther. *Bitter Strength: A History of the Chinese in the United States, 1850–1870*. Cambridge, Mass.: Harvard University Press, 1964.

Basch, Linda G. *The Spirit of Nairobi and the U.N. Decade for Women*. Staten Island, N.Y.: Center for Migration Studies of New York, 1986.

Bee, Fred A. *The Other Side of the Chinese Question*. San Francisco: R & E Research Associates, 1971.

Beesley, David. "From Chinese to Chinese American: Chinese Women and Families in a Sierra Nevada Town." *California History* 67 (September 1988): 168–79.

Book, Susan W. *The Chinese in Butte County, California, 1860–1920*. San Francisco: R & E Research Associates, 1976.

Braun, Jean S. "Attitude toward Women—Comparison of Asian-Born Chinese and American Caucasians." *Psychology of Women Quarterly* 2 no. 3 (1978): 195–201.

Brownstone, David M. *The Chinese-American Heritage*. New York: Facts on File, 1988.

Buck, Pearl S. *Of Men and Women*. New York: John Day Co., 1941.

Buck, Ray. *Tiffany Chin: A Dream on Ice*. Chicago: Children's Press, 1986.

Cather, Helen Virginia. *The History of San Francisco's Chinatown*. San Francisco: R & E Research Associates, 1974.

Chan, Sucheng. *This Bitter-Sweet Soil: The Chinese in California Agriculture, 1860–1910*. Berkeley: University of California, 1986.

———, ed. *Entry Denied: Exclusion and the Chinese in America, 1882–1943*. Philadelphia: Temple University Press, 1991.

Chan, Won-loy. *Burma: The Untold Story*. Novato, CA: Presidio, 1986.

Chang, June. *Mme Sun Yat-Sen*. New York: Viking Penguin Inc., 1986.

Chang, Lydia Liang-Hwa. "Acculturation and Emotional Adjustment of Chinese Women Immigrants." Thesis, Columbia University, 1980.

Chang, Pao-min. *Continuity and Change: A Profile of Chinese Americans*. New York: Vantage Press, 1983.

Chao, Hao-sheng. 趙浩生 *Chung-kuo Hsueh Jen Tsai Mei-kuo* [Chinese Intellectuals in America] (中國學人在美國). Taipei: Biographical Literature Publishing Co., 1969.

Chen, Jack. *The Chinese of America.* San Francisco: Harper and Row, 1982.

Chen, Hsiang-Shui. *Chinatown No More: Taiwan Immigrants in Contemporary New York.* Ithaca: Cornell University Press, 1992.

Chen, Jerome. *China and the West: Society and Culture, 1815–1937.* Bloomington: Indiana University Press, 1979.

Chen, Jui-Ho. "Clothing Attitudes of Chinese and American College Women." Ph.D. diss., University Park: The Pennsylvania State University, 1970.

Chen, Julia I. Hsuan. *The Chinese Community in New York.* San Francisco: R & E Research Associates, 1974.

Chen, Pen-ch'ang. *Mei-kuo Hua Ch'iao Ts'an Kuan Kung Yeh* [Chinese American Restaurants] (美國華僑餐館工業). Taipei: Taiwan Far East Books Co., 1971.

Chen, Yuan-tsung. *The Dragon's Village.* New York: Pantheon Books, 1980.

Cheng, Nien. *Life and Death in Shanghai.* New York: Penguin Books, 1988.

Chin, Art. *Golden Tassels.* Seattle: Chin, 1977.

Chin, Frank. *The Chickencoop Chinaman and the Year of the Dragon.* Seattle: University of Washington Press, 1981.

———. *The Chinaman Pacific and Frisco R. R. Co.: Short Stories.* Minneapolis: Coffee House Press, 1988.

Chin, Ginger. *The History of Chinese Immigrant Women, 1850–1940.* North Bergen, N.J.: G. Chin, 1977.

China Institute in America. *A Survey of Chinese Students in American Colleges and Universities in the Past Hundred Years.* New York, 1954.

Chinese American Restaurant Association of Greater New York, ed. *Chinese American Restaurant Association of Greater New York, Inc.* New York: The Association, 1959.

Chinese Historical Society of America, ed. *Chinese America: History and Perspectives, 1990.* San Francisco: Chinese Historical Society of America, 1990.

Chinn, Thomas W. *Bridging the Pacific: San Francisco Chinatown and Its People.* San Francisco: 1989.

Chiu, Ping. *Chinese Labor in California: An Economic Study*. Madison: University of Wisconsin, 1967.

Chong, Denise. *The Concubine's Children: The Story of a Chinese Family Living on Two Sides of the Globe*. Penguin Books, 1994.

Chong, Key Ray. *Americans and Chinese Reform and Revolution, 1898–1922*. Lanham, MD: University Press of America, 1984.

Chou, Jesse Chain. "A Survey of Chinese Students in the United States, 1979–1987." Ph.D. diss., Columbia, 1989.

Christy, Lai-Chu-Tsui. "Culture and Control Orientation: A Study of Internal-External Locus-of-Control in Chinese and American Chinese Women." Ph.D. diss., University of California, Berkeley, 1977.

Chu, Daniel. *Passage to the Golden Gate*. Garden City, N.Y.: Doubleday, 1967.

Chu, Louis. *Eat A Bowl of Tea*. Seattle: University of Washington Press, 1979.

Chua, Cheng Lok. "Golden Mountain: Chinese Versions of the American Dream in Lin Yutang, Louis Chu, and Maxine Hong Kingston." *Ethnic Groups* 4, no. 1–2 (1982): 33–59.

Chuan, Sau-Wah Wong. "Perceived Usefulness of Higher Education-Major Choices and Life Goal Values among Chinese-American Students (Asian, Women, Sex-Roles)." Ph.D. diss., California School of Professional Psychology, 1985.

Chun, James H. *The Early Chinese in Punaluu*. Punaluu, Honolulu, Hawaii: Yin Sit Sha, 1983.

Chung, Sue Fawn. "Gue Gim Wah: Pioneering Chinese American Women of Nevada." *History and Humanities*, ed. Francis X. Hartigan. Reno: University of Nevada Press, 1989, 45–79.

———. "The Chinese Experience in Nevada: Success Despite Discrimination." *Nevada Public Affairs Review* No. 2 (1987), special issue on Ethnicity and Race in Nevada, eds. Elmer Rusco and Sue Fawn Chung, 43–51.

Cohen, Lucy M. *Chinese in the Post-Civil War South: A People Without a History*. Baton Rouge: Louisiana State University Press, 1984.

Colman, Elizabeth. *Chinatown U.S.A.* New York: The John Day Co., 1946.

Coolidge, Mary R. *Chinese Immigration*. New York: Henry Holt & Co., 1909; reprint, New York: Arno Press, 1969.

Daley, William. *The Chinese Americans*. New York: Chelsea House, 1987.

Dicker, Laverne Mau. *The Chinese in San Francisco: A Political History*. New York: Dover Publications, 1979.

Dillon, Richard H. *Images of Chinatown*. San Francisco: Book Club of California, 1976.

Edson, Christopher Howard. *The Chinese in Eastern Oregon, 1860–1890*. San Francisco: R & E Research Associates, 1974.

Ellenwood, James Lee. *One Generation After Another*. New York: Charles Scribner & Sons, 1953.

Elsensohn, M. Alfred. *Idaho Chinese Lore*. Cottonwood, Idaho Corp. of Benediction Sisters, 1970.

Fessler, Loren W., ed. *Chinese in America, Stereotyped Past, Changing Present*. New York: Vantage Press, 1983.

Fong, Timothy P. *The First Suburban Chinatown: The Remaking of Monterey Park, California*. Philadelphia: Temple University Press, 1994.

Gentry, Curt. *Madames of San Francisco: An Irreverent History of the City by the Golden Gate*. New York: Doubleday, 1964.

Gibson, O(tis). *The Chinese in America*. New York: Arno Press, A New York Times Co., 1978.

Gillenkirk, Jeff. *Bitter Melon*. Seattle: University of Washington Press, 1987.

Glenn, Evelyn Nakano. "Split Household, Small Producer and Dual Wage Earner—An Analysis of Chinese-American Family Strategies." *Journal of Marriage and the Family* 45 no. 1 (1983): 35–46.

Glick, Clarence Elmer. *Sojourners and Settlers: Chinese Migrants in Hawaii*. Honolulu: University Press of Hawaii, 1980.

Godley, Michael R. "The Sojourners: Returned Overseas Chinese in the PRC." *Pacific Affairs* no. 62 (fall 1989): 330–352.

Guthrie, Grace Pung. *A School Divided: An Ethnography of Bilingual Education in a Chinese Community*. Hillsdale, NJ: Erlbaum, 1985.

Harper, Fowler V., and Jerome H. Skolnick. *Problems of the Family*. New York: Bobbs-Merrill, 1962.

Hayhoe, Ruth, and Marianne Bastid, eds. *China's Education and the Industrialized World: Studies in Cultural Transfer*. Armonk, N.Y.: M. E. Sharpe, 1987.

Heyer, Virginia. "Patterns of Social Organization in New York City's Chinatown." Ph.D. diss., Columbia University, 1953.

Hirata, Lucie Cheng. "Free, Indentured, Enslaved: Chinese Prostitutes in 19th Century America." *Signs* 5 (1979): 3–29.

Ho, Chi-Kwan. "Gender Role Perception: A Study of Two Generations of Chinese American Women." Ph.D. diss., College Park: University of Maryland, 1993.

Ho, Samuel P.S. *Economic Development of Taiwan, 1860–1970*. New Haven: Yale University Press,1978.

Hsu, Francis L. K. *The Challenge of the American Dream: The Chinese in the United States*. Belmont, Calif.: Wadsworth Publishing Co., Inc., 1971.

Huang, Philip C. C. *The Peasant Economy and Social Change in North China*. Stanford: Stanford University Press, 1985.

———. *The Peasant Family and Rural Development in the Yangzi Delta, 1350–1988*. Stanford: Stanford University Press, 1990.

Huang, Tsen-ming. *The Legal Status of Chinese Abroad*. Taipei: China Central Service, 1954.

Hune, Shirley. "Politics of Chinese Exclusion: Legislative Executive Conflict, 1876–1882." *American Journal* 9 (1982): 5–27.

Iu, Carol Rita. "Ethnic and Economic Correlates of Marital Satisfaction and Attitude towards Divorce of Chinese American Women." Ph.D. diss., University of California, Los Angeles, 1982.

Jue, Jenniffer J. "Chinese American Women's Development of Voice and Cultural Identity: A Participatory Research Study Via Feminist Oral History." Ed.D. diss., University of San Francisco, 1993.

Kingston, Maxine Hong. *The Woman Warrior, Memoirs of a Girlhood among Ghosts*. New York: Alfred A. Knopf, 1977.

———. *China Men*. New York: Alfred A. Knopf, 1980.

Kung, S. W. *Chinese in American Life: Some Aspects of Their History, Status, Problems, and Contributions*. Seattle: University of Washington Press, 1962.

Kuo, Chia-ling. *Social and Political Change in New York's Chinatown: The Role of Voluntary Associations*. New York: Praeger, 1977.

Kuo, W. H., and Nan Lin. "Assimilation of Chinese Americans in Washington, D.C." *Sociological Quarterly* 18 (1977): 340–52.

Kwong, Peter. *Chinatown, New York: Labor and Politics, 1930–1950*. New York: Monthly Review Press, 1981.

———. *The New Chinatown*. New York: Hill and Wang, 1987.

Lai, H. Mark, and Philip P. Choy. *Outlines: History of the Chinese in America*. San Francisco: H. M. Lai and P. P. Choy, 1971.

Lai, H. Mark, Genny Lim, and Judy Yung. *Island, Poetry and History of Chinese Immigrants on Angel Island*. San Francisco: Hoc Doi: distributed by San Francisco Study Center, 1980.

————. *A History Reclaimed: An Annotated Bibliography of Chinese Language Materials on the Chinese in America*. Los Angeles: Resource Development and Publications, Asian American Studies Center, University of California, Los Angeles, 1986.

————. "Historical Development of the Chinese Consolidated Benevolent Association/Huiguan System." In *Chinese America: History and Perspectives, 1987*, by Chinese Historical Society of America, 13–51. San Francisco: Chinese Historical Society of America, 1987.

Lan, Dean. *Prestige with Limitations: Realities of the Chinese-American Elite*. San Francisco: R & E Research Associates, 1976.

Lang, Olga. *Chinese Family and Society*. New Haven: Yale University Press, 1946.

Lee, Christina Chau-Ping. "Acculturation and Value Change: Chinese Immigrant Women." Ph.D. diss., University of British Columbia, 1984.

Lee, Rose Hum. "The Recent Immigrant Chinese Families of the San Francisco-Oakland Area." *Marriage and Family Living* 18, no. 1 (1956): 14–24.

————. "The Stranded Chinese in the United States." *Phylon* 19, no. 2 (summer 1958): 180–194.

————. *The Chinese in the United States of America*. Hong Kong: Hong Kong University, 1960.

————. *The Growth and Decline of Chinese Communities in the Rocky Mountain Region*. New York: Arno Press, 1978.

Leung, Edwin P. "The First Chinese College Graduate in America: Yung Wing." *Asian Profile* 16 no. 5 (1988): 453–458.

Liestman, Daniel. "The Chinese in the Black Hills, 1876–1932." *Journal of the West* 27 no. 1 (1988): 74–83.

Lim, Genny, ed. *The Chinese American Experiences: Paper from the Second National Conference on Chinese American Studies* (1980). San Francisco: The Chinese Historical Society of America and the Chinese Culture Foundation of San Francisco, 1980.

Lin, Alice P. *Grandmother Had No Name*. San Francisco: China Books, 1988.

Lin, Mao-Chu. "Identity and Chinese-American Experience: A Study of Chinatown American Literature Since World War II." Ph.D. diss., University of Minnesota, 1987.

Lin, Yutang. *Chinatown Family*. New York: John Day, 1948.

Ling, Amy. *Between Worlds: Women Writers of Chinese Ancestry*. New York: Pergammon, 1990.

———. *Immigrating America: Stories from the Promised Land*. New York: Persea Press, 1991.

Ling, Huping. "Surviving on the Gold Mountain: A Review of Sources about Chinese American Women." *The History Teacher* 26, no. 4 (August 1993): 459–470.

———. "Chinese Merchant Wives in the United States, 1840–1945." In *Origins and Destinations: 41 Essays on Chinese America*, ed. Chinese Historical Society of Southern California and UCLA Asian American Studies Center, 79–92. Los Angeles: Chinese Historical Society of Southern California, Inc. and UCLA Asian American Studies Center, 1994.

———. "Sze-Kew Dun: A Chinese American Woman in Kirksville." *Missouri Historical Review* XCI, no. 1 (October 1996): 35–51.

———. "A History of Chinese Female Students in the United States, 1880s–1990s." *The Journal of American Ethnic History* 16, no. 3 (Spring 1997): 81–109.

———. "A History and Historiography of Chinese American Women." *American Studies* 1, no. 1 (1997): 127–146.

Liu, Bo-ji. *Meiguo Huaqiao Shi*, [History of the Overseas Chinese in the United States] (美國華僑史). Taipei: Li Ming Publishing Co., 1981.

Liu, Haidong. "Lives of Chinese Students' Wives in an American University Setting." Ph.D. diss., Pennsylvania State University, 1992.

Loewen, James W. *The Mississippi Chinese: Between Black and White*. Cambridge, Mass.: Harvard University Press, 1971.

Loo, Chalsa M., ed. *Chinatown: Most Time, Hard Time*. New York: Praeger, 1992.

Lord, Bette. *Legacies: A Chinese Mosaic*. New York: Alfred A. Knopf, 1990.

Lou, Raymond. "The Chinese American Community of Los Angeles, 1870–1900: A Case of Resistance, Organization, and Participation." Ph.D. diss., University of California, 1982.

Louie, Constance. "Breaking Down the Walls of Jade: A Study of Acculturation and Second-Generation Chinese-American Women." Ph.D. diss., California School of Professional Psychology, 1994.

Low, Victor. *The Impressible Race: A Century of Educational Struggle by the Chinese in San Francisco*. San Francisco: East/West Publishing Co., 1982.

Ludwig, Edward W., and Jack Loo. *Gumshan: The Chinese American Saga*. Los Gatos, Calif.: Polaris Press, 1982.

Lum, Arlene, ed. *Sailing for the Sun: The Chinese in Hawaii, 1789–1989*. Honolulu, Hawaii: Three Heroes, 1988.

Lydon, Sandy. *Chinese Gold: The Chinese in the Monterey Bay Region*. Capitola, Calif.: Capitola Book Co., 1985.

Lyman, Stanford M. *Chinese Americans*. New York: Random House, Inc., 1974.

———. "Marriage and the Family Among Chinese Immigrants to America, 1850–1960." *Phylon* 24 (1968): 321–330, and *Chinese Americans* (New York: Random House, 1974), 86–105.

McClellan, Robert. *The Heathen Chinee, A Study of American Attitudes toward China, 1890–1905*. Columbus: Ohio State University Press, 1971.

McCunn, Ruthanne Lum. *Thousand Pieces of Gold: A Biographical Novel*. San Francisco: Design Enterprises of San Francisco, 1981.

———. *Chinese American Portraits: Personal Histories 1828–1988*. San Francisco: Chronicle Books, 1988.

Martin, Mildred Crowl. *Chinatown's Angry Angel: The Story of Donaldina Cameron*. Palo Alto, Calif.: Pacific Books, 1977.

Mason, Sarah R. "Family Structure and Acculturation in the Chinese Community in Minnesota." In *Asian and Pacific American Experiences: Women's Perspectives,* ed. Nobuya Tsuchida, 160–171. Minneapolis: Asian/Pacific American Learning Resource Center and General College, University of Minnesota, 1982.

Meng, Chih. *Chinese American Understanding, A Sixty-Year Search*. New York: China Institute in America, 1981.

Miller, Stuart Creighton. *The Unwelcome Immigrant: The American Image of Chinese, 1785–1882*. Berkeley: University of California Press, 1979.

Minnick, Sylvia Sun. *Samfow = Chin-shan San-pu: The San Joaquin Chinese Legacy*. Fresno, Calif.: Panorama West Pub., 1988.

Nee, Victor G., and Brett de Bary Nee. *Longtime Californ': A Documentary Study of an American Chinatown*. New York: Pantheon Books, 1973.

Nordyke, Eleanor, and Richard K.C. Lee. "The Chinese in Hawai: Historical and Demographic Perspective." *Hawaiian Journal of History* 23 (1989): 196–216.

Orleans, Leo A. *Chinese Students in America: Policies, Issues, and Numbers*. Washington, D.C.: National Academy Press, 1988.

Pan, Lynn. *Sons of the Yellow Emperor: A History of the Chinese Diaspora*. Boston: 1990.

Peffer, George Anthony. "Forbidden Families: Emigration Experiences of Chinese Women under the Page Law, 1875–1882." *Journal of American Ethnic History* 6 no.1 (1986): 28–46.

———. "The Forces Without: The Regulation of Chinese Female Immigration, 1852–1882." Ph.D. diss., Carnegie-Mellon, 1989.

Perrin, Linda. *Coming to America: Immigrants from the Far East*. New York: Delacorte Press, 1980.

Pozzetta, George E. "The Chinese Encounter with Florida, 1865–1920." In *Chinese America: History and Perspectives, 1989*, by Chinese Historical Society of America, 43–57. San Francisco: Chinese Historical Society of America, 1989.

Riddle, Ronald. *Flying Dragons, Flying Streams: Music in the Life of San Francisco's Chinese*. Westport, CT: Greenwood Press, 1983.

Riggs, Fred Warren. *Pressures on Congress: A Study of the Repeal of Chinese Exclusion*. New York: King's Crown Press, 1950.

Sandmeyer, Elmer C. *The Anti-Chinese Movement*. Urbana: University of Illinois Press, 1973.

Saxton, Alexander. *The Indispensable Enemy: Labor and the Anti-Chinese Movement in California*. Berkeley: University of California Press, 1971.

Schwendinger, Robert J. *Ocean of Bitter Dreams: Maritime Relations Between China and the United States, 1850–1915*. Tucson, AZ: Westernlore Press, 1988.

Seward, George F. *Chinese Immigration: Its Social and Economical Aspects*. New York: C. Scribner's Sons, 1881; reprint, New York: Arno Press, 1970.

Siu, Paul C. P. *The Chinese Laundryman: A Study of Social Isolation*. New York: New York University Press, 1987.

Steiner, Stan. *Fusang, The Chinese Who Built America*. New York: Harper & Row, Publishers, 1979.

Stockard, Janice. *Daughters of the Canton Delta: Marriage Patterns and Economic Strategies in South China, 1860–1930*. Stanford, Calif.: Stanford University Press, 1989.

Sui, Sin Far. "The Chinese Women in America." *Land of Sunshine* 6 (January 1897): 62.

Sung, Betty Lee. *Mountain of Gold: The Story of the Chinese in America.* New York: The Macmillan Co., 1967.

———. *The Chinese in America.* New York: The Macmillan Co., 1972.

———. *A Survey of Chinese-American Manpower and Employment.* New York: Praeger, 1976.

———. *Gangs in New York's Chinatown.* New York: Office of Child Development, Dept. of Health, Education and Welfare, 1977.

———. *Statistical Profile of the Chinese in the United States 1970 Census.* New York: A New York Times Co., 1978.

———. *The Adjustment Experience of Chinese Immigrant Children in New York City.* New York: Center for Migration Studies, 1987.

Takaki, Ronald. "They Also Came: The Migration of Chinese and Japanese Women to Hawaii and the Continental United States." In *Chinese America: History and Perspectives 1990*, by Chinese Historical Society of America, 3–19. San Francisco: Chinese Historical society of America, 1990.

Tan, Amy. *The Joy Luck Club.* New York: G. P. Putnam's Sons, 1989.

Tan, Mely G. *The Chinese in the United States: Social Mobility and Assimilation.* Taipei: Orient Cultural Service, 1971.

Tan, Thomas Tsu-wee. *Your Chinese Roots: The Overseas Chinese Story.* Singapore: Times Books International, 1986.

Tang, Vincent. "Chinese Women Immigrants and the Two-Edged Sword of Habeas Corpus." In *The Chinese American Experiences: Paper from the Second National Conference on Chinese American Studies*, ed. Genny Lim, 48–56. San Francisco: The Chinese Historical Society of America and the Chinese Culture Foundation of San Francisco, 1980.

Tchen, John Kuo Wei. *Genthe's Photographs of San Francisco's Old Chinatown.* New York: Dover Publications, 1984.

———. "New York Chinese: The Nineteenth-Century Pre-Chinatown Settlement." In *Chinese America: History and Perspectives, 1990*, by Chinese Historical Society of America, 157–192. San Francisco: Chinese Historical Society of America, 1990.

Thompson, Richard H. *Toronto's Chinatown: The Changing Social Organization of an Ethnic Community.* New York: AMS, 1987.

Tong, Benson. *Unsubmissive Women: Chinese Prostitutes in Nineteenth-Century San Francisco.* Norman: University of Oklahoma Press, 1994.

Townsend, L. T. *The Chinese Problem.* Boston: Lee and Shepard, Publishers, 1876; reprint, San Francisco: R & E Research Associates, 1970.

Trull, Fern Coble. "The History of Chinese in Idaho from 1864 to 1910." M.A. Thesis, The University of Oregon, 1946.

Tsai, Shih-shan Henry. *China and the Overseas Chinese in the United States, 1868–1911*. Fayetteville: University of Arkansas Press, 1983.

———. *The Chinese Experience in America*. Bloomington: Indiana University Press, 1986.

Tung, William L. *The Chinese in America 1820–1973, A Chronology & Fact Book*. Dobbs Ferry, N.Y.: Oceana Publications Inc., 1974.

Wallace, Ian. *Chin Chiang and the Dragon's Dance*. New York: Atheneum, 1984.

Wang, Ling-Chi, et al. *Chinese Americans: School and Community Problems*. Chicago: Integrated Education Associates, 1972.

Wang, Quihui. "The Role of Attitudes in Social Change: A Comparative Study of Mobilization Versus Administrative and Legal Reforms and Implications for the Status of Women in the People's Republic of China and the United States." Ph.D. diss., Boston University, 1985.

Wang, Y. C. *Chinese Intellectuals and the West, 1872–1949*. Chapel Hill: University of North Carolina Press, 1966.

Wei, Katherine. *Second Daughter: Growing Up in China, 1930–1949*. Boston: Little Brown, 1984.

Williams, Stephen. *The Chinese in the California Mines, 1848–1860*. San Francisco: R & E Research Associates, 1971.

Wilson, Carol Green. *Chinatown Quest: One Hundred Years of Donaldina Cameron House 1874–1974*. San Francisco: California Historical Society, 1974.

Wong, Bernard P. *A Chinese American Community: Ethnicity and Survival Strategies*. Singapore: Chopmen Enterprises, 1979.

———. *Chinatown, Economic Adaptation and Ethnic Identity of the Chinese*. New York: Holt, Rinehart and Winston, 1982.

———. *Patronage, Brokerage, Entrepreneurship and the Chinese Community of New York*. New York: AMS Press, 1988.

Wong, Diane Yen-Mei. *Dear Diane: Questions and Answers for Asian American Women*. San Francisco: San Francisco Study Center, 1983.

———. *Dear Diane: Letters from Our Daughters*. San Francisco: San Francisco Study Center, 1983.

Wong, Jade Snow. *Fifth Chinese Daughter*. New York: Harper & Row, 1950.

———. *No Chinese Stranger*. New York: Harper & Row, 1975.

Wong, James I. *Aspirations and Frustrations of the Chinese Youth in the San Francisco Bay Area: Aspersions upon the Societal Scheme.* San Francisco: R & E Research Associates, 1977.

————. *A Selected Bibliography on the Asians in America.* Palo Alto, Calif.: R & E Research Association, 1981.

————. *Selected Topics in Chinese-American History.* Stockton, Calif.: Koinonia Productions, 1984.

Wong, J. Y. "Three Visionaries in Exile: Yung Wing, Kang Yu-wei and Sun Yat-sen, 1894–1911." *Journal of Asian Studies* 20 (1986): 1–32.

Wong, Kay-Sun. "Chinese-American Women: A Phenomenological Study of Self-Concept." Ph.D. diss., The Wright Institute, 1983.

Wong, Sandra M. J. "For the Sake of Kinship: The Overseas Chinese Family." Ph.D. diss., Stanford University, 1987.

Wu, Cheng-Tsu, ed. *"Chink!" A Documentary History of Anti-Chinese Prejudice in America.* New York: World Pub., 1972.

Wu, William F. *The Yellow Peril: Chinese Americans in American Fiction.* Hamden, CT.: Archon Books, 1982.

Wu, Yuan-li, ed. *The Economic Condition of Chinese Americans.* Chicago: Pacific/Asian American Mental Health Research Center, 1980.

————. "The Economic Progress of Chinese-Americans Since World War II." *Sino-American Relations* 8–9 (summer 1982): 45–60.

Yap, Stacey G. H. *Gather Your Strength, Sisters: The Emerging Role of Chinese Women Community Workers.* New York: AMS Press, 1989.

Ye, Guochao. "Madame Chiang at Wesleyan College." *The World Journal.* 29 April 1990.

Yee, Jennie H. Y. "Parenting Attitudes, Acculturation and Social Competence in the Chinese-American Child." Ph.D. diss., Boston University, 1983.

Yin, Xiao-huang. "The Population Pattern and Occupational Structure of Boston's Chinese Community in 1940." *Maryland Historian* 20 (1989): 59–69.

Young, Nancy Foon. *The Chinese in Hawaii: An Annotated Bibliography.* Honolulu: University of Hawaii, 1973.

Yu, Li-hua. "Chinese Immigrants in Idaho." Ph.D. diss., Bowling Green State University, 1991.

Yu, Renqiu. *To Save China, To Save Ourselves: The Chinese Hand Laundry Alliance of New York.* Philadelphia: Temple University Press, 1992.

Yung, Judy. *Chinese Women of America, A Pictorial History*. Seattle: University of Washington Press, 1986.

——. *Unbound Feet: A Social History of Chinese Women in San Francisco*. Berkeley: University of California Press, 1995.

Yung, Wing. *My Life in China and America*. New York: Henry Holt & Company, 1909.

Zhou, Min. *Chinatown: the Socioeconomic Potential of an Urban Enclave*. Philadelphia: Temple University Press, 1992.

Other Asian Americans

Afkhami, Mahnaz. *Women in Exile*. Charlottesville, Virginia: University Press of Virginia, 1994.

Agtuca, Jacqueline. *A Community Secret for the Filipina in an Abusive Relationship*. Seattle: Seal Press, 1992.

Chan, Sucheng, ed. *Hmong Means Free: Life in Laos and America*. Philadelphia: Temple University Press, 1994.

Espiritu, Yen Le. *Filipino American Lives*. Philadelphia: Temple University Press, 1995.

Glenn, Evelyn Nakano. *Issei, Nisei, War Bride: Three Generations of Japanese American Women in Domestic Service*. Philadelphia: Temple University Press, 1986.

Kim, Ai Ra. *Women Struggling for a New Life*. Albany: State University of New York Press, 1995.

Kim, Elaine H., and Eui-Young Yu, eds. *East to America: Korean American Life*. New York: New Press, 1996.

Lee, Mary Paik. *Quiet Odyssey: A Pioneer Korean Woman in America*. Seattle: University of Washington, 1990.

Melendy, H. Brett. *Asians in America: Filipinos, Koreans, and East Indians*. Boston: Twayne Publishers, 1977.

Muir, Karen L. S. *The Strongest Part of the Family: A Study of Lao Refugee Women in Columbus, Ohio*. New York: AMS Press, 1988.

Nakano, Mei. *Japanese American Women: Three Generations, 1890–1990*. Berkeley: Mina Press Publishing, 1990.

Peterson, William. "Success Story, Japanese-American Style." *New York Times Magazine*. 9 January 1966, 20–43.

Shan, Nita. *The Ethnic Strife: A Study of Asian Indian Women in the United States.* New York: Pinkerton and Thomas Publications, 1993.

Yanagisako, Sylvia. *Transforming the Past: Tradition and Kinship among Japanese Americans.* Stanford: Stanford University Press, 1985.

Yu, Diana. *Winds of Change: Korean Women in America.* Silver Spring, Maryland: The Women's Institute Press, 1991.

Yu, Eui-Young, and Earl H. Phillips, eds. *Korean Women in Transition: At Home and Abroad.* Los Angeles: Center for Korean-American and Korean Studies, California State University, 1987.

African and Mexican Americans

Anderson, Karen. *Changing Women: A History of Racial Ethnic Women in Modern America.* New York: Oxford University Press, 1996.

Blackwelder, Julia Kirk. *Women of the Depression: Caste and Culture in San Antonio, 1929–1939.* College Station: Texas A&M University Press, 1984.

Blea, Irene I. *Toward a Chicano Social Science.* New York: Praeger, 1988.

———. *La Chicana and the Intersection of Race, Class, and Gender.* New York: Praeger, 1992.

Clark-Lewis, Elizabeth. *Living in, Living Out: African American Domestics in Washington, D.C., 1910–1940.* Washington and London: Smithsonian Institution Press, 1994.

Frankel, Noralee, and Nancy S. Dye, eds. *Gender, Class, Race, and Reform in the Progressive Era.* Lexington: The University Press of Kentucky, 1991.

Lemke-Santangelo, Gretchen. *Abiding Courage: African American Migrant Women and the East Bay Community.* Chapel Hill: The University of North Carolina Press, 1996.

Malson, Micheline, et al., eds. *Black Women in America: Social Science Perspectives.* Chicago: The University of Chicago Press, 1990.

National Association for Chicana Studies. *Chicana Voices: Intersections of Class, Race, and Gender.* Albuquerque: University of New Mexico Press, 1993.

Rooks, Noliwe M. *Hair Raising: Beauty, Culture, and African American Women.* New Brunswick, N.J.: Rutgers University Press, 1996.

Ruiz, Vicki L., and Susan Tiano, eds. *Women on the U.S.-Mexico Border.* Boston: Allen & Unwin, 1987.

Schlissel, Lillian, Vicki L. Ruiz, and Janice Monk, eds. *Western Women: Their Land, Their Lives*. Albuquerque: University of New Mexico Press, 1988 (chapter 4 deals with Mexican American women).

Staples, Robert. *The Black Women in America: Sex, Marriage, and the Family*. Chicago: Nelson Hall Publishers, 1973.

Wallace, Phyllis A. *Black Women in the Labor Force*. Cambridge: The MIT Press, 1980.

European Americans

Barton, Josef J. *Peasants and Strangers, Italians, Rumanians, and Slovaks in an American City, 1890–1950*. Cambridge, Mass.: Harvard University Press, 1975.

Billigmeier, Robert Henry. *Americans from Germany*. Belmont, Calif.: Wadsworth Publishing Co., 1974.

Cohen, Miriam. *Workshop to Office: Two Generations of Italian Women in New York City 1900–1950*. Ithaca: Cornell University Press, 1992.

Diner, Hasia R. *Erin's Daughters in America: Irish Immigrant Women in the Nineteenth Century*. Baltimore: The Johns Hopkins University Press, 1983.

Ewen, Elizabeth. *Immigrant Women in the Land of Dollars: Life and Culture on the Lower Side, 1890–1925*. New York: Monthly Review Press, 1985.

Friedman-Kasaba, Kathie. *Memories of Migration: Gender, Ethnicity, and Work in the Lives of Jewish and Italian Women in New York, 1870–1924*. Albany: State University of New York Press, 1996.

Gabaccia, Donna. *From Sicily to Elizabeth Street: Housing and Social Change among Italian Immigrants 1880–1930*. Albany: State University of New York Press, 1984.

———. *Militants and Migrants*. New Brunswick: Rutgers University Press, 1988.

Glanz, Rudolf. *The Jewish Women in America: Two Female Immigrant Generations 1820–1929*. New York: Ktav Publishing House, Inc., 1976.

Glenn, Susan A. *Daughters of the Shtetl: Life and Labor in the Immigrant Generation*. Ithaca: Cornell University Press, 1990.

Jeffrey, Julie Roy. *Frontier Women: The Trans-Mississippi West, 1840–1880*. New York: Hill and Wang, 1979.

Kramer, Sydelle, and Jenny Masur, eds. *Jewish Grand-Mothers*. Boston: Beacon Press, 1976.

Lamphere, Louise. *From Working Daughters to Working Mothers: Immigrant Women in a New England Industrial Community*. Ithaca: Cornell University Press, 1987.

Marcus, Jacob R. *The American Jewish Women, 1654–1980*. New York: Ktav Publishing House, 1980.

Pickle, Linda Schelbitzki. *Contented among Strangers: Rural German-Speaking Women and Their Families in the Nineteenth-Century Midwest*. Urbana: University of Illinois Press, 1996.

Yans-McLaughlin, Virginia. *Family and Community: Italian Immigrants in Buffalo 1880–1930*. Urbana: University of Illinois Press, 1982.

Immigration and Ethnicity

Allen, Leslie. *Ellis Island*. Liberty Island, New York: Evelyn Hill Group, Inc., 1995.

Bodnar, John. *The Transplanted: A History of Immigrants in Urban America*. Bloomington: Indiana University Press, 1985.

Daniels, Roger. *Coming to America: A History of Immigration and Ethnicity in American Life*. New York: Harper Collins Publishers, 1990.

Dinnerstein, Leonard, and David M. Reimers. *Ethnic Americans: A History of Immigration and Assimilation*. New York, N.Y.: Harper & Row, 1982.

Foner, Nancy, ed. *New Immigrants in New York*. New York: Columbia University Press, 1987.

Gabaccia, Donna, ed. *Seeking Common Ground: Multidisciplinary Studies of Immigrant Women in the United States*. Westport, CT: Greenwood Press, 1992.

———. *From the Other Side: Women, Gender, and Immigrant Life in the U.S., 1820–1990*. Bloomington: Indiana University Press, 1994.

Glazer, Nathan, and Daniel P. Moynihan, eds. *Beyond the Melting Pot*. Cambridge, Mass.: The MIT Press, 1970.

Hansen, Marcus Lee. *The Problem of the Third Generation Immigrant*. Augustana College Library, 1987.

Kivisto, Peter, and Dag Blanck, eds. *American Immigrants and Their Generations: Studies and Commentaries on the Hansen Thesis after Fifty Years*. Urbana & Chicago: University of Illinois Press, 1990.

Lerda, Valeria, ed. *From "Melting Pot" to Multiculturalism*. Roma: Bulzoni Editore, 1990.

Reimers, David M. *Still the Golden Door: The Third World Comes to America*. New York: Columbia University Press, 1985.

Seller, Maxine S. *Immigrant Women*. Philadelphia: Temple University Press, 1981.

Takaki, Ronald, ed. *From Different Shores: Perspectives on Race and Ethnicity in America*. New York: Oxford University Press, 1987.

Yans-McLaughlin, Virginia. *Immigration Reconsidered: History, Sociology, and Politics*. New York: Oxford University Press, 1990.

Interracial Marriage

Cerronilong, E. L. "Marring Out—Social-Cultural and Psychological Implications of Intermarriage." *Journal of Comparative Family Studies* 16 no.1 (1985): 25–46.

Connor, John W. *A Study of the Marital Stability of Japanese War Brides*. San Francisco: R & E Research Associates, 1976.

Crester, Gary A., and Joseph J. Leon, eds. *Intermarriage in the United States*. New York: Hayworth Press, 1982.

Davis, Kingsley. "Intermarriage in Caste Societies." *American Anthropologist* 43, no. 3 (July–September 1941): 376–395.

Gordon, Albert. *Intermarriage: Interfaith, Interracial, Interethnic*. Westport, CT: Greenwood Press, Publishers, 1980.

Gorton, Milton. *Assimilation in American Life*. New York: Oxford University Press, 1964.

Kitano, Harry, et al. "Asian American Interracial Marriage." *Journal of Marriage and the Family* 46, no. 1 (February 1984): 179–190.

Shinagawa, Larry Hajime, and Gin Yong Pang. "Intraethnic, Interethnic, and Interracial Marriages among Asian Americans in California, 1980." *Berkeley Journal of Sociology* 33 (1988): 95–114.

Sickeles, Robert J. *Race, Marriage, and the Law*. Albuquerque: University of New Mexico Press, 1972.

Spickard, Paul R. *Mixed Blood: Intermarriage and Ethnic Identity in Twentieth-Century*. Madison: The University of Wisconsin Press, 1989.

Stuard, Irving R., ed. *Interracial Marriage: Expectations and Realities*. New York: Grossman Publishers, 1973.

Sung, Betty Lee. *Chinese American Intermarriage*. New York: Center for Migration Studies, 1990.

Walsh, Joan. "Asian Women, Caucasian Men." *Image* 2 December 1990: 11–16.

Wong, Morrison G. "A Look at Intermarriage among Chinese in the United States in 1980." *Sociological Perspectives* 32 no.1 (1989): 87–107.

Women's History

Berkin, Carol Ruth, and Mary Beth Norton, eds. *Women of America: A History*. Boston: Houghton Mifflin, 1979.

Burnet, Jean, ed. *Looking into My Sister's Eyes: An Exploration in Women's History*. Toronto: The Multicultural History Society of Ontario, 1986.

Goldman, Marion S. *Gold Diggers and Silver Miners: Prostitution and Social Life on the Comstock Lode*. Ann Arbor: University of Michigan Press, 1981.

Pascoe, Peggy. *Relations of Rescue: The Search for Female Moral Authority in the American West, 1874–1939*. New York: Oxford University Press, 1990.

Riley, Glenda. *Inventing the American Women*. Arlington Heights, IL.: Harlan Davidson, Inc., 1987.

Rosen, Ruth. *The Lost Sisterhood: Prostitution in America, 1900–1918*. Baltimore: The Johns Hopkins University Press, 1982.

Timberlake, Andrea. *Women of Color and Southern Women: A Bibliography of Social Science Research, 1975 to 1988*. Memphis, Tenn.: Center for Research on Women, Memphis State University, 1988.

Index